greetings & Suzanne, whom Rich wants to welcome into the Gestalt community!

Beyond Individualism

Gordon Wheeler

TOWARD A NEW UNDERSTANDING OF SELF, RELATIONSHIP, & EXPERIENCE

Gordon Wheeler

selected titles from *gicpress* --

ORGANIZATIONAL CONSULTING: A GESTALT APPROACH
Edwin C. Nevis

GESTALT RECONSIDERED: A NEW APPROACH TO CONTACT AND RESISTANCE
Gordon Wheeler

GESTALT THERAPY: PERSPECTIVES AND APPLICATIONS
edited by Edwin C. Nevis

BODY PROCESS: WORKING WITH THE BODY IN PSYCHOTHERAPY
James I. Kepner

THE VOICE OF SHAME: SILENCE AND CONNECTION IN PSYCHOTHERAPY
edited by Robert G. Lee & Gordon Wheeler

COMMUNITY & CONFLUENCE: UNDOING THE CLINCH OF OPPRESSION
Philip Lichtenberg

THE COLLECTIVE SILENCE: GERMAN FAMILIES & THE LEGACY OF SHAME
Barbara Heimannsberg & Christopher J. Schmidt
edited and translated by Cynthia Oudejans Harris & Gordon Wheeler

BACK TO THE BEANSTALK: ENCHANTMENT AND REALITY FOR COUPLES
Judith R. Brown

ON INTIMATE GROUND: A GESTALT APPROACH TO WORKING WITH COUPLES
edited by Gordon Wheeler & Stephanie Backman

THE DREAMER AND THE DREAM: ESSAYS AND REFLECTIONS ON GESTALT THERAPY
Rainette Fantz; edited by Arthur Roberts

BECOMING A STEPFAMILY
Patricia Papernow

THE NEUROTIC BEHAVIOR OF ORGANIZATIONS
Uri Merry & George I. Brown

CRAZY HOPE AND FINITE EXPERIENCE
Paul Goodman; edited by Taylor Stoehr

THE GENDERED FIELD: GESTALT PERSPECTIVES & READINGS
edited by Deborah Ullman & Gordon Wheeler

HERE NOW NEXT: PAUL GOODMAN AND THE ORIGINS OF GESTALT THERAPY
Taylor Stoehr

IN SEARCH OF GOOD FORM: GESTALT THERAPY WITH COUPLES & FAMILIES
Joseph C. Zinker

INTENTIONAL REVOLUTIONS: A 7-POINT STRATEGY FOR TRANSFORMING ORGANIZATIONS
Edwin C. Nevis, Jean Lancourt, & Helen G. Vassallo

THE HEART OF DEVELOPMENT: GESTALT APPROACHES TO WORKING WITH CHILDREN, ADOLESCENTS & THEIR WORLDS -- Volumes I & II
edited by Mark McConville & Gordon Wheeler

ENCOUNTERING BIGOTRY: BEFRIENDING PROJECTING PERSONS IN EVERY-DAY LIFE
Philip Lichtenberg, Janneke van Beusekom & Dorothy Gibbons

THE UNFOLDING SELF: GESTALT ESSAYS OF JEAN-MARIE ROBINE
Jean-Marie Robine; edited and translated by Gordon Wheeler

A WELL-LIVED LIFE: ESSAYS IN GESTALT THERAPY
Sylvia Fleming Crocker

GETTING BEYOND SOBRIETY: CLINICAL APPROACHES TO LONG-TERM RECOVERY
Michael Craig Clemmens

LOVE & PLAY: GESTALT IN THE LIVING FIELD
Gordon Wheeler

FROM THE RADICAL CENTER: THE HEART OF GESTALT THERAPY
Erving & Miriam Polster

Beyond Individualism

TOWARD A NEW UNDERSTANDING OF SELF, RELATIONSHIP, & EXPERIENCE

Gordon Wheeler

A GICPRESS BOOK

THE ANALYTIC PRESS

HILLSDALE, NJ, distributors

66 Orchard Street, Cambridge MA 02140
email gicpress@aol.com

Distributed by: **THE ANALYTIC PRESS, INC.**
101 West Street
Hillsdale, NJ 07642

Library of Congress Cataloging-in-Publishing Data

Beyond Individualism: Toward a New Understanding of Self, Relationship & Experience / Gordon Wheeler, author

includes bibliographical references and index
ISBN 0-88163-334-8
1. Self. 2. Individualism. 3. Wheeler, Gordon, 2000
394pp.

jacket photo by Joyce Lyke

for Nancy, with love

and with hopes of a better world
for our children and our children's children

"...Grow old with me, the best is yet to be --
the last of life, for which the first was made"

other Gestalt titles by Gordon Wheeler

Gestalt Reconsidered: A New Approach to Contact and Resistance
Gardner Press, 1991

The Collective Silence: German Families and the Legacy of Shame
edited and translated from the German with Cynthia O. Harris
Jossey-Bass Publishers, 1992

On Intimate Ground: Gestalt Approaches to Working with Couples
edited with Stephanie Backman
Jossey-Bass Publishers, 1994

Love, Work, and Play: Gestalt Essays on Childhood
GICPress Monograph Series, 1995

The Voice of Shame: Silence and Connection in Psychotherapy
edited with Robert G. Lee
Jossey-Bass Publishers, 1996

The Gendered Field: Gestalt Perspectives and Readings
edited with Deborah Ullman
GICPress, 1998

The Heart of Development: Gestalt Approaches
to Children, Adolescents, & their Worlds
Volume One: Early and Middle Childhood
Volume Two: Adolescence
edited with Mark McConville
GICPress / Analytic, 2000

Beyond Individualism: Toward a New Understanding
of Self, Relationship, and Experience
GICPress / Analytic, 2000

Love and Play: Gestalt in the Living Field
GICPress / Analytic (in press)

The Unfolding Self: Gestalt Essays of Jean-Marie Robine
edited and translated from the French
GICPress (in press)

Table of Contents

Acknowledgements and Note on Usage

It would be strange indeed if a book with the title "Beyond Individualism" were presented or conceived as the product of one person's thinking. This book represents the best synthesis I can make at this time out of a lifetime of troubled reflection on individualism and related concerns, and some ten years of conscious dialogue on these issues -- with friends, teachers, students, family, patients and clients, as well as workshop participants too numerous to mention, together with my interaction with the written material of other authors, in particular the fertile and challenging work of Paul Goodman, whose radical ideas on self and society were far ahead of their time, and perhaps only now ready to bear their full fruit. For animating and thought-provoking partnership in this dialogue over the years, including new ideas, creativity, commentary, challenge and debate and essential new directions of thinking, I particularly want to thank Anne Alonso, Chris Bentley, Mari Bentley, Michael Borack, Nicole de Schrevel, Eric Erickson, Jay Ferraro, Iris Fodor, Judith Hemming, Lynne Jacobs, Dan Jones, Jim Kepner, Mary Ann Kraus, Bob Lee, Mark McConville, Joe Melnick, Edwin Nevis, Sonia Nevis, Malcolm Parlett, Gabe Phillips, Jean-Marie Robine, Paul Shane, Allan Singer, and Taylor Stoehr; and most especially Arch Roberts and Deborah Ullman, my colleagues and learning partners at GICPress, who read and commented on this manuscript at every stage, and provided the crucial intellectual and emotional support to complete the project when I was overwhelmed with it.

For all this plus limitless encouragement, criticism, support and forebearance all through this writing, I also want to thank my children, Mariam, Benjamin, Rebekah, Sarah and Alexander, and Rolf; and especially my wife and partner, Nancy Lunney

Wheeler. Thanks are also due to the staff and community of Esalen Institute, who graciously provided a nourishing environment for me to concentrate on finishing this book, which represents a pulling together of the diverse strands of the evolution of my teaching and learning over the past decade, since my last treatment of these and related themes in book-length form. As everyone who spends time there knows, Esalen continues to offer, a generation after some of the pathbreaking Gestalt work there of Fritz Perls (which I have both built on and critiqued in my own writing), a rare and inspired holding environment for transitions and transformations in people's thinking and experience, and in their lives and work.

As always in my own work and in my life, I owe a special and ongoing debt of gratitute to the faculty, staff, and students of the Gestalt Institute of Cleveland, which has long provided me with a primary learning community and a second home, as well as to all the members of the New England Gestalt Study Group and the annual GISC Writers' Conference, which for ten years have nurtured my own work as well as that of scores of other clinicians and writers struggling with the challenges and isolation of the writing process.

Both of these last institutions are under the generous and gracious sponsorship and direction of Edwin C. Nevis and Sonia March Nevis, to whom I owe special thanks for direct stimulation and support over the years, not only of me but of an entire extended community of at least two generations of students and practitioners of the Gestalt model -- a community which grounds and informs much of my own thinking and work. I know I speak not just for myself but for this entire community, including a number of the names above and many, many others, in extending this gratitude. Both Sonia and Edwin stand as inspired and inspiring examples of that creative mentoring which is so much sought after and so much missed in our culture today, and to which they each bring remarkable qualities of intelligence, generosity, boundless energy, and that rarest of all hallmarks of mature generativity: the gift for nurturing many offspring and then setting them free.

and a note on usage

Among the many signs of paradigm transition these days is the continuing lack of any good fit between language categories and the realities of gendered experience. In this book both the feminine and masculine pronoun forms will be used, alternately, interchangeably, and/or in combination. This is probably the best we can do at the moment, but it is well to recognize it as only a temporary compensation, pending the emergence of a new language informed by a new paradigm of gender, a large goal which will hopefully be advanced in some way by this book.

Preface: Paradigm and Practice

We live in deconstructive times, somewhere between a past that no longer sustains us and a future we can't yet discern. All around us long-held certainties, familiar categories and assumptions are abandoned or collapse of their own weight every day, in areas ranging from empire and economic systems to gender politics to intimacy and family life, or the biochemistry of our own psyches. Many of the old approaches pass away unlamented, but still oftentimes they leave a hole, without anything very clear or reliable to put in their place. On a global level, few doubt today that the Western-based culture which is expanding now with so little restraint over much of the earth, for all its strengths, has certain flaws at the core, a certain way of being that menaces or even threatens to destroy the world that is so rapidly embracing it. And yet no one seems able to put clear, experiential language on that flaw, in a way that we can take hold of and use in our lives and our work. This leaves us with both an explosion of new knowledge and activity, and at the same time a nagging mood of uncertainty, which sparks talk of decline and the growth of nostalgia movements in every field, from family relations to public policy. Actually, very few of us really want those old days back, and even those few are deceiving themselves about the supposedly more wholesome nature of those times, which were often characterized by levels of inequity and abuse that would be intolerable to us today. Meanwhile, a prevailing sense of disorientation and lack of confidence in our own values and direction make us hesitate at times to make urgently needed interventions in the world around us and in our own work and lives, for fear of doing harm or just wasting our efforts.

Nowhere is this picture more true than in the broad fields

of psychology and psychotherapy -- which is distressing, since these are the domains we've long been accustomed to looking to and relying on, in this psychological century that lies just behind us in the West, for orientation and insight into all our other problems, from the most intimately personal to the most broadly political or deeply spiritual. But today the field of psychology itself seems far too fragmented to respond with any clarity or authority to demands of this kind, or indeed to speak with any coherent voice at all to questions having to do with who we are as human beings, what our basic nature is, or what it means to be a *source or agent of subjective experience, in a world of other subjective beings* -- and therefore what practical methods and models and policies we should be following, in our own lives and work.

Why is this? Why is it that psychology, which has been commenting with such self-assurance -- some would say arrogance -- on matters from the boardroom to the bedroom for the past century, suddenly seems so tongue-tied now when it comes to the most important social and political issues of the day? "One hundred years of psychotherapy," says Jungian psychologist and critic James Hillman, "and the world is getting worse" (1990). This is arguably true, but can the fault be laid at psychotherapy's door? Or are the world and psychology alike in the confused state they are in, as we will be arguing in this book, for some larger, deeper reason? And then what is that reason, and even more importantly, what can we do about it?

It's certainly not as if there were nothing going on in the field. On the contrary, every day seems to bring us an outpouring of new research, from frontiers as exciting and important as infant and child development, cognitive/affective process and brain/mind models, neurology and biochemistry. And yet these strides don't seem to add up to anything like a new integrated-field model of behavior and experience, something that would relate one branch of the field to another, connecting this new data and theory to the ways we actually live and work. In place of this integration what we get is a flood of new and supposedly new methods and packages and *recipes*, amounting to an ever-rising torrent of offerings and propositions -- in the media, in the morning mail, in professional journals and meetings and conferences, -- some of them serious, others just plain gimmicks, and all of them offering new or recycled ways for dealing with seemingly ever-growing numbers of "disorders," each one promising to manage or solve something that hasn't been managed or solved before, and to do it faster, better, and of course at lower cost. The discrediting in one way and another of the great psychological systems of the past, as orienting worldviews -- the Freudian synthesis, behaviorism and learning theory, even the so-called "Third Wave" of humanistic and "human potential" movements of a generation ago -- seems to have left a vacuum in the marketplace, which is now filled with this cacophony of new and dissonant voices, each one trumpeting some new approach with a flourish, and most of them forgotten again by next week, to be replaced by still newer wares, newer "discoveries," and more new answers which may or may not be in response to any really clear question.

Not that all these methods and packages are without any value. On the contrary, many of them may be very useful and productive, at least in their own local area of application, with certain populations or subpopulations, under certain conditions. But then that's just it: in the absence of some coherent wider picture, some overarching frame, how do we know which one to apply where, and when to do this and not that, and with whom? This is what theory is supposed to be *for*, after all: to provide a *context and a map* so we can organize our responses, match the intervention to the situation and person, and thus raise the necessary eclecticism of our work to the level of targeted and coherent choice. Why do the theories we have now seem so unable to serve this purpose, so incomplete? Worse, why do we experience them so often as divorced from the applications they are meant to ground and support, or from any wider picture of human functioning and experience -- as if theory were one thing, and practical reality something else entirely (in which case why bother with theory)? Again, why is there no *unified field theory of psychology and human nature*, hardly even the quest for one any longer -- an integrated picture of *who we are and what we need*, that would join self to the world of other selves, behavior to experience, and context and purpose to meaningful, effective action in the domain of real living?

Finally, what about the questions that lie behind these questions, and are left hanging by the disorganization of the field, and by the general deconstruction of values and assumptions in the culture at large? Who are we -- not just in some academic/ philosophical sense, but in terms our own nature as sentient, experiencing beings in a world of other experiencing beings like ourselves? What is the nature of this self we seem to have or be, which is seemingly the author or at any rate the agent of our behavior and experiences? What does it mean to be in relationship with other selves, other subjective beings like us -- where do we stop, and they begin, or vice versa? How do we take up contact with them, in anything more than the "subject-object," exploitative sense of the classical Freudian model, or indeed of the Western scientific tradition, which seems so far from most of our felt and lived experience? How are we going to have anything like a unified field theory in psychology without addressing and answering questions like these -- and then how do we explore these questions themselves, and know what directions to take up in research and practice themselves, without such an integrated picture of who we are and where we are going, by our nature?

A New Focus on Old Questions

This makes a lot of questions, and all of them touching in some way on the same two basic themes: first, what has happened to psychology and psychotherapy, how is it that the field has both exploded and in a sense imploded on itself at the same time around us, leaving us with fragments of an overarching metatheory, puzzle pieces without an overall picture to fit them into? Why are our theories so incomplete, and so often unrelated to each other or to felt experience and practice? And then secondly, what does it mean to be a human self? What is the nature of these selves we are studying, whose behavior and experience are the subject matter of psychology and psychotherapy alike? And why is it that questions on this level have become somehow difficult to address, in the chaotic and disorganized field that is psychology today?

These are complex and challenging issues; and yet our argument in this book will be that all of them are considerably clarified, at least, by a single answer, one which comes from another level beneath or behind that of research or even theory itself. That answer may seem surprisingly simple, and yet understanding it in anything like its full implications will take up all the rest of this book. In the process, we will need to understand something about the role of *paradigm* in scientific thinking and ideology alike, and then to follow out the implications of that understanding, through areas ranging from cultural history and the philosophy of science, to the concretely-felt and pragmatic concerns of our own moment-to-moment processes of self-organization, relationship, and experience at the practical level of our own lives and work.

Our first pass at this answer, which will be explored in some theoretical detail in Part One and then elaborated in a more practical way all through the rest of the book, is as follows: all these things, everything we see around us in the field of psychology and the wider culture today, including our current confusion about our own nature and experience, *are the signs and symptoms of a fundamental cultural paradigm, the deep and orienting worldview of a great cultural tradition, in a state of active deconstruction and decline.* That is, all this upheaval -- the confusion and cacophony in the fields of the human sciences, the decline and debunking of "theory" (and the accompanying elevation of every local method, every recipe, to the status of "new theory" if not "new paradigm" itself), the mushrooming and conflating of exciting new methodology and outright quackery, the acute sense of *ill fit* between received wisdom and lived experience, the disheartening sensation that we have lost the way and that neither psychology nor the philosophy of human nature can help us -- all these things and more are the effects of something deeper, something which clarifies and organizes this confusing picture around us. That something is the *discrediting of an old and fundamental belief system or story, about who we are and what it means to be a person*, without our yet having any coherent new story to put in its place. The shift is seismic, with effects on every area of life, from the most intimately personal to the most broadly and directly political and ecological; and at the same time the outlines and boundaries of that shift -- where we are coming from and where we need to go -- are far from clear. Beginning at least to organize all these things, and relate them to each other and to our own work and experience in a way that we can feel and use, is the overall idea and purpose of this book.

Human Nature in the Western Tradition

That deep and underlying worldview is what we will be calling here the *paradigm of individualism*, a set of basic assumptions, most of them outside awareness and just taken for granted in the culture and the language, about *human nature and the human self.* This paradigm, or fundamental assumptive set, has a 3000-year pedigree in the West, from the pre-Socratics and the early Hebrew mythmakers right down in a largely unbroken line to the present day -- all of which will be the particular focus of Part One of this book. Today, in a world which is dying, perhaps literally, from the excesses of rampant capitalism and the individualist ethos, many of the particular terms of that paradigm are under heavy suspicion and deconstructive critique -- most often in a partial or fragmented way that fails to see how these various terms fit together in a single coherent worldview, how that worldview has long underlain and informed the diverse strands of the entire Western tradition, and how it continues to inform and in some ways deform our lives and our thinking today. How this happens, and then how we can go about thinking about and even experiencing these same questions in a different, more all-inclusive way, will be taken up in Part One, and then elaborated and developed recursively (and experientially) all through the chapters ahead. But to make sense of that discussion, we first need to be clear about what we mean by this trendy term *paradigm* itself, which is suddenly all around us, the catchword of the day, in a wide and fluid use which seems to cover anything and everything from change on the political or macroeconomic level to new parenting roles to a new wrinkle in your tennis swing (a kind of boundary diffusion in the word itself which may be one more sign of paradigm collapse in the culture). What is a *paradigm*, and how does it operate dynamically to set the stage and the terms of theory and method alike, in our work and in our lives?

The Role of Paradigm

As we use the term paradigm here, we mean it in the particular sense given to it by philosopher Thomas Kuhn (1961), in his analysis of how great human systems of knowledge evolve and change. That is to say, paradigm here means all that complex and interrelated set of underlying beliefs, attitudes, assumptions, and *stories* -- many or most of them out of our awareness most or all of the time -- which lie behind both data and theory itself, and largely determine the available range of theories we can think up, in a given culture and time, and thus of data we can find and integrate meaningfully. Thus by paradigm we mean something deeper than the particular view of the world you are taking or constructing at the moment, whether theoretical or directly pragmatic -- something more like the *point of view*, the *place you stand* in order to take up an observer position in the first place and begin to organize and understand what you see. Your paradigm, in other words, is the story behind the story: not the landscape itself you look out on, so much as the lens you use to look through, and the ground you stand on to hold up that lens, in order to be able to see anything at all. In Kuhn's analysis, we can argue data and method and even theory, but we can't really argue paradigms -- first because they aren't really decided on rational evidentiary grounds, and then too because without some deeper ground of unspoken agreement about basic terms and assumptions, which contains and links the points under debate, no argument is really possible in the first place (basic paradigms finally do change, Kuhn tells us, when and as the adherents of the old view die out).

In the classic example, the gulf between the Copernicans and the older geocentric astronomers in the 16th and 17th Centuries was paradigmatic, because it wasn't really about data at all, but went to the heart of deep questions about our position in the universe, who we are as human beings, and what our relationship is to the cosmos. Thus it wasn't going to be decided finally on "pure science" criteria at all, but rather on the grounds of which worldview people could relate to in their own lives. (In the end it was actually many decades before the predictive data from the new Copernican system were anything like as good as the old Ptolemaic map of the heavens, with its baroque curliques and curious reversals in planetary paths -- reversals which we can still hear echoes of today in astrological circles, where people speak of planets as being "retrograde," meaning going backwards, which they do at times from a stable geocentric point of view. Apparently the problem was that Copernicus -- for unaware, theological reasons -- just presumed that the planetary orbits had to be perfect circles. It was the astrologer Kepler who finally hit upon the more complex formula for elliptical orbits which made the Copernican tables work, after many decades of trial-and-error calculations. Thus the dominance of unexamined assumptions even in matters of "pure science" -- and including of course psychology).

These were not small matters, and in the end many millions died in wars and persecutions which were carried on under the banner, at least, of these different worldviews (Germany alone lost a third of its entire population in the religious wars of the 17th Century). At the same time, however, even fierce antagonists like the cosmologists of those bloody times were in basic agreement on many paradigmatic questions at even deeper levels than these, which provide the common ground from which we can talk meaningfully about their differences now: things like the stability and order of the physical universe, the objectivity of measurement and data, and the detached position of the observer -- all of which are propositions very much under deconstructive scrutiny today. Faced with, say, a strict Vedantist, who maintained that the physical world as well as our individual distinctness in that world is all *maya* or illusion emanating arbitrarily from our own minds, then debate about the laws governing the behavior of the solar system becomes meaningless. The difference of worldview is just too deeply paradigmatic for any meaningful exchange to take place, at least on that topic. That is to say, even beyond Kuhn's scientific paradigms there are deeper cultural paradigms and out-of-awareness assumptions, and levels and hierarchies of paradigm contextualizing disputes at other levels, that frame and ground those discussions in turn.

The Paradigm of Individualism

Perhaps the most basic paradigmatic layer of all is made up of those unexamined beliefs and stories having to do with *who we are when we talk about these things, and what our relationship is to the world we are talking about, and the people we are talking about it with* -- a relationship that is implied and characterized in a particular way by particular notions of "knowledge" itself (notions which vary considerably from one thinker and one period to another, as we will see ahead). In other words, the deepest level of assumptions is all those questions we are raising and laying the ground for addressing in this book, and which are up for grabs in psychology and the wider world of Western culture today, with profound and direct implications for how we live our lives and practice our trades, which after all always involve living and working with other people.

At this deepest level, a level that cuts across historical eras and societal boundaries, great cross-cultural paradigms obviously don't change that easily or that often. When they do change, it is only in response to changes in technology so fundamental as to transform every other area of life, from the productive/economic to the political, the military, and then society and religion themselves. Indeed, the philosopher Ken Wilber (1996) identifies only four or five such tectonic shifts in the whole sweep of human history and prehistory, the last but one dating from the passage from rudimentary cultivation and animal husbandry to large-field and herd agriculture some four or five thousand years ago, a change which made food surplus possible for the first time in human life, permitting the emergence of cities and towns, social and gender stratification at a new level, the arts, priestly and other castes -- and large land armies. The next after that was of course the industrial/scientific revolution, dating from the last five hundred years or so at most, and still in the process of transforming the more remote parts of the globe (remote, that is, relative to the revolution's epicenter in Western Europe). Today, the next seismic upheaval, the revolution in information and communications technology we are in the midst of now in the West, is destructuring and transforming our lives and our categories of thinking and feeling once again, here in the post-industrialized world.

Through all these shifts, at least from the time of field

agriculture itself, the most basic paradigm of human nature in the West has remained remarkably stable and definitive, even through cultural upheaval as deep and transformative as the industrial revolution itself. This is the basic assumptive set we've already referred to here as the *paradigm of individualism*, which probably took root in Western culture with the militarized spread of agriculture (and large-scale warfare) westward and northward from its earlier centers in the mass societies of Egypt and Mesopotamia in the third and fourth millenia BCE. Today, on the cusp of transition to a world transformed by the ongoing revolutions in communications and information processing (and in a world still threatened by ecological degradation and mass destruction), many of the separate terms and components of that paradigm are under critical reexamination -- again, as we have said, mostly without clear realization of how those terms work together as a whole, or how that whole works to constrict and constrain that reexamination itself. This critique is very much the subject matter of this book -- and yet that in itself poses problems for us here, as we try to take up the questions of self and self-experience in the chapters ahead.

Examining our own Paradigm

Those problems come down to this: if we want to talk about paradigm at this most fundamental level, the level that we are saying dictates the terms and categories of our own thinking and feeling about ourselves and our world, then just how are we going to do that, without being hobbled and blinkered from the start by those very terms and categories? What language can we find or construct to talk about the hidden structure of language itself, the vocabulary of self and relationship we inherit from our own tradition? We have said we have to have some lens and some stable point of view, to talk about anything at all: what lens shall we use, and where shall we stand exactly, to take up perspective on the ground we are standing on now? To put it in the metaphor of the dialogic philosopher Mikhail Bakhtin (1986), how are we going to go about seeing the back of our own head?

Our answer to that problem, in terms of the plan of this book, is twofold. First of all is to *begin with our felt experience*, to find, heighten and then capitalize on that *sense of discomfort*, the "poor fit" we were talking about above, between inherited assumptions and lived action and feeling, before we try to analyze the categories of language itself, all on the way to deriving or describing something new. We say this not because we imagine that there is any such thing as "pure experience," completely prior to cultural categories and inherited assumptions (one of those many implications of the old individualist paradigm that no longer strike us as useful or valid), but rather because we see cultural expectation and lived experience as being in a dynamic, interdependent relationship with each other, shaping and informing each other in mutual interplay, each of them meaningless without the other. There is no experience that is felt and constructed outside a particular cultural context, nor any culture that exists outside people's felt experience; they are constructed in and out of each other, within the context of certain given environmental conditions (including the conditions of our neurology and biochemical process), as part of an evolutionary process. We don't just "have" a cultural tradition, or the paradigmatic assumptions that underlie it; rather, we *inhabit* these things, and they inhabit us. Thus we can never stand completely outside our own assumptive inheritance, in the "purely objective" way implied by the old model.

Still, in times of deep paradigm shift, as we can already begin to see, there will be a sort of wiggle-room that opens up, a space between the poles of this dynamic interlock, deriving from that sense of malaise and missed connection we were talking about above. It is in that wiggle-room, that "play" in the system, that we want to pitch our exploration and our discussion of these issues here. To this end each of the chapters ahead, after the beginning discussion of individualism in Part One, opens with or includes an exercise, which the reader is invited either to read along with or actually to stop and participate in, always with the idea of heightening the *feeling pole* of this interaction, this dynamic synthesis of figure and ground, assumption and experience, before we get completely caught up in language that grows out of that old ground itself, and thus may be a poor tool, taken alone, for plowing that same field in a new way.

An Alternative Approach

This is a start, but still we need some frame, some experimental standpoint at least, in order to talk clearly about self and the premises and implications of the old model at all. This new ground we will find in the terms and metaphors of the *Gestalt field model of self and self process*, a dynamic/*ecological* perspective growing out of the premises of the Gestalt cognitive model in psychology, as articulated in particular by the social philosopher and Freudian critic Paul Goodman a half century ago (1951). The Gestalt cognitive/perceptual model completely revolutionized the general field of cognitive psychology, and then psychology in general, beginning in the early years of this past century with the work of Wertheimer, Koffka, Kohler and their associates. So pervasive was this revolution that Gestalt psychology itself hardly exists as a separate school anymore at all, since it has been almost completely absorbed into the field as a whole, to the point where there really is no cognitive psychology today which is not deeply Gestalt in nature (for discussion of this point, see for example Wheeler, 1991). At the same time the radical implications of the model for affect theory and the new cognitive/affective models, self and self-organization theory, and our understanding of the crucial current topics of self, development, intimacy, intersubjectivity, and relationship in general -- as well as its potential as a base for integrating phenomenology with behavioral and biochemical perspectives -- have all been much less widely appreciated and applied. Here we hope to exploit and develop further the promise Gestalt offers for generating and anchoring such an integrative view.

As we go through the book, the order of the chapters itself is meant to be developmental, with each one building on the ones before -- and at the same time flexible and recursive, with enough restatement of the developing picture in each chapter so that they can be read meaningfully in any order. The idea is first of all for the reader who has a particular interest in one or another of the topics -- shame, say, or intimacy and relationship -- to be able to pick up the book at that point, and be led forward or backward from there without missing the basic argument. At the same time, since paradigm is something we don't just talk about but also live, breathe, and inhabit, this recursiveness is meant to give us the chance to *spend some time* with a new view, grounding it in felt experience, so as to support a gradual shift in language itself, without which we will surely just slip right back into the old ways of talking, and then thinking, and then feeling and organizing our experience. Paradigmatic debates, remember, aren't ultimately decided on purely rational grounds; and our argument here will be in the end that this new way of looking at self and relationship offers a *better self-story with a better fit* with our experience and our lives, -- a better ground, in Gestalt terms, for the figures we actually know and want to feel, but may have difficulty getting into focus with the old lens.

The Plan of this Book

That developmental order, after the opening two chapters on individualism itself, is 3) *the relational self*, how we take up contact and negotiate the world of other selves; 4) *self-organization and creative adjustment*, the dynamics of self-process; 5) *support* and the field conditions of self-process and development; 6) *shame* and its inhibiting effect on self-experience; 7) *intimacy and intersubjectivity*, the restoration of self and the conditions of growth. Chapter Eight then offers a new perspective on *narrative and culture*, including considerations of the crucial field dynamic of gender, while the epilogue outlines conclusions, implications for a *field perspective on health, ethics, and politics*, and directions for next steps -- all grounded in the new approach to the question of self developed here, and based on *field integration, relationship, meaning, experiment, emotion, value, and story*. With these new perspectives on self and healthy process in hand, we'll then be in a better position to move, in the words of the title, beyond individualism in living and working with people.

Thus in Chapter Three of Part II we begin with the the question of the *relational self*: how do we take up connection and relatedness in the world of people? What's involved in this essential process, which is key to our evolutionary and personal survival; how do we know *what to do?* Here as in the chapters ahead the discussion opens with a simple exercise, this one of a familiar type often used in training programs for counselors, therapists, managers, and others working with people. Generally this particular exercise is used as a way of getting a feel for the difference between subjectivity or "projection," and objectivity or "pure description" (a clear and fairly rigid distinction, as we shall see, under the old individualist self-paradigm). Here we'll use it slightly differently, questioning in the process whether those two constructive mental activities, imagination and description, can ever really be distinguished so sharply or usefully. The idea here will be to get a feel, out of our own experience and exchange, for how our *integrative self process* actually plays out *in vivo*, with the task that is developmentally the first and then the most ongoingly pervasive of all our life tasks: namely, orienting and connecting and maintaining relationships in the social field.

Chapter Four then takes up the question of self more generally. What do we mean by "integrative self-process?"

Where in the field of our experience do we look for it -- on the "inside," the "outside" -- or both? Where do we find that sense of *cohesion and continuity* that Kohut (1977) and other writers have emphasized as crucial to healthy self-process in any system, and neglected in most? Here it's important to note too that this whole topic may seem at first to be out of logical order, in relation to the chapter before. Shouldn't we first define what the thing is we're talking about, *before* looking at the specific application of it as we were doing back in Chapter Three? After all, Aristotelian logic, which is the bedrock for analysis of any process of examination in our cultural tradition, tells us always to begin a definition with the general, and then move from there to the particular case, in good deductive fashion. So shouldn't we have defined exactly what the self is, before discussing in Chapter Three how we use it in relationship? Our answer here is just that if we do that in that order, we'll have an even more difficult time breaking the set of all the received assumptions and preexisting vocabulary of our culture that we were discussing above, about our own nature and process. Prominent among those assumptions, after all, is the conviction that *self precedes relationship*, which if you think about it can hardly be true developmentally (remember Winnicott's classic dictum in child development, that there is "no such thing as a baby;" because there can only be a *baby plus a mother*, or else no baby at all; see Khan, 1989). By beginning with what it *feels like* to orient in a social field, and what we're up against in real life when we try to do that, as we constantly must from birth on, we hope to get a different kind of purchase on that slippery term "self" itself, closer to developmental experience, and one that holds the whole question more lightly, hopefully not immediately trimming and stretching it to fit the procrustean bed of our inherited culture before we've even started.

Here as in Chapter Three we begin with an exercise, this time of a paper-and-pencil (or keyboard) type that the reader is invited to participate in directly, again with the idea of getting more of a feel for "self," before we unwittingly impose prior boundaries and inherited categories on it. The experience and results of this small exercise are surprising to many of the training program and workshop participants who have tried it, so here in particular it may be worth your while to stop and actually take a few moments to think about it and journal it, before you compare your own responses and reactions to those of others. Key to the whole argument of this book is the idea that "self" is not to be found at all where the individualist models would have us look for it, but in another "place" entirely, which is the locus of the process Goodman called "creative adjustment" (in contradistinction to Freud's emphasis on "adjustment" and social conformism alone, which were thought to be necessary compromises, but antithetical to the true nature of the self). By looking to that new place, we mean to find the ground we need for taking up a new and different perspective on everything else.

With this preliminary discussion of self as a base, we can move in Part III to articulating the *field conditions* of that self-process, which is to say the conditions of *contact*, in the language we will be developing and drawing on here. This brings us in Chapters Five and Six to the twin questions of *support and shame* -- two dynamic field processes and experiences which are fundamental to development and self-integration, and which were almost impossible to explore and articulate usefully, under the old paradigm of self. In a sense Part III, and Chapter Five in particular, is the conceptual linchpin of the argument of this book, because it is here that we see field dynamics in action, in felt experience, as the self develops, integrates that field under those given conditions, and grows. The creative revisioning of the dynamic role and meaning of support in self-process is both the single most practical implication of the model we will be articulating here, and the experiential key to everything else we will be saying in the chapters to follow, about self, field, relationship, and healthy development. Thus the relationship of this chapter to all the others (and for that matter of each chapter to all the others) is meant to be one of figure/ground, not merely linear, logical sequentiality -- though it is hopefully that as well.

In the course of Chapter Five, what we will find is that "support" is another one of those familiar terms, like self, projection, perception and imagination, "adjustment," shame, and so forth that are radically reframed and clarified by the new context of our overall exploration here. In this new perspective support emerges as *the key dynamic field process of contact and self-experience, the polar counterpart to shame*, and as such, the essential precondition for contact or self-process at all. Where in the old model we might ask whether a person "needed support" or could "do it alone," here we will try to demonstrate that the very notion of doing anything "by yourself" contradicts the basic premises of both a field model and real, lived experience and process. In this new model the question is only and always *what kinds of support* are dynamically required, for a certain figure of contact to be realized -- and then where in the experiential field we need to look to find or add those needed supports. The analysis of self and self-experience, we will argue, is always an analysis of *field conditions of support (and shame)* -- a perspective which offers us a bridge between the "intrapsychic" and the "interpersonal," or "self" and "other" as traditionally conceived, in our experience and in our work.

Both here and in Chapter Seven the exercise material which we will use to ground the discussion in felt experience will build on the basic developmental and self-process exercise of Chapter Four. Thus readers who begin the book at this point may want to flip back and participate in that earlier exercise from Chapter Four for a few moments, or at least read it through, along with the discussion which follows it, so as to get up to speed for the material in these two chapters.

This in turn brings us in Chapter Six of Part III to the issue of interruption and inhibition of self-process, leading to a new and clarifying perspective on the experience and dynamics of *shame*. Shame, long a neglected topic in psychotherapy and self-theory, is today the focus of intense popular and theoretical attention. But much or most of that new discourse is uncritically grounded in the assumptions of the old individualistic paradigm. As a result, much of the therapeutic work with people in this area, both popular and more formally clinical, is reduced to not much more than exhortations, affirmations, and a misguided attempt to "talk people out of" their shame experiences -- which can itself be reshaming (first I'm overwhelmed by feelings of shame, and then I feel more shame about feeling something I'm supposed to have gotten over). This work, we will argue here, while well-intentioned and sometimes self-affirming, is inherently limited by the assumptive terms of the underlying self-paradigm. Only a radically new paradigm of self and self-experience can clarify these muddy matters, and lead us toward a fresh and more promising approach.

In our inherited model, after all, shame was first and foremost the affect and sign of *individual deficiency*, the immature form of a feeling whose mature expression would be guilt, or internalized personal responsibility. Thus *shame itself was always shame-tinged* in the old model, the sign of both personal inadequacy and arrested development, generally indicative of *too much connectedness* in the social field, under a model which prized autonomy as the highest pinnacle of development. Here we find rather that shame takes up a role analogous to that of anxiety in the old model: that is, where anxiety in the psychodynamic system was the signal to the individual to restrain or repress his or her drive energy (but more particularly "his," because the classical model was deeply gender-coded), in this new perspective it is shame which is seen as the key signal of *insufficient field connection and support*, for the self-integration (and experiential field-integration) in process. Thus understood from this new perspective, *shame modulates contact and regulates the self.* Once more, with a brief reflective exercise the reader is invited to take a look at these challenging issues in her/his own life, and/or in the experiential material of others.

Discussion of the twin issues of support and shame then prepares us, with Chapter Seven, to talk about the restoration of self and the conditions of growth. This part of our exploration begins with the issue of how we recover from shame and self-inhibition, which then leads us to a deepened perspective on support, development, and growth of self in general in this new sense. These issues involve us in the interrelated themes of *intimacy and intersubjectivity*, two terms which are often "added on" to contemporary discussions of self under older models, but which here emerge as crucial dynamic field processes underlying self-development and the expansion of self-experience. By way of an exercise we'll return once more to the experential material of Chapters Four and Five, again adding a new step to what we've built up before, both experientially and in discussion.

Finally, with Part IV we can talk more generally about what self-experience and development themselves mean, in the kind of whole-field model of self and self-process that we're proposing, exploring together, and constructing here. This will bring us with Chapter Eight to the central *organizing schema* for support, shame, and contact itself in the social/developmental field, which is *narrative and the self story* in this new sense. Narrative, in an older view, belonged to the domain of "content," and thus had no direct place in a "process" model like the one we are building up in these chapters. Here by contrast we understand narrative as the basic structuring dynamic of self-process and self-experience. Again we will use an exercise to get more of a feel for how this organizing dynamic works in our own lives and experience.

Pulling back, we will then be in a position to integrate much of the material of these eight chapters with a discussion of what healthy self-process looks like and means in the kind of dynamic field model of self and experience we are developing through this book. Not surprisingly, we're going to find that once we move beyond an individualistic self-model, it no longer makes any sense to try to talk about individual health, outside of a field context of *other healthy selves*. Like so many of the ideas in this book, this is something we already know, both instinctively and experientially -- but which is unsupported or flat out contradicted by the terms of our inherited and dominant cultural paradigm of self and human nature. What we want to add here, as all through these chapters, is the kind of conceptual and theoretical framework in which that experiential knowing is grounded and related to other concepts and dynamics, rather than floating somewhere apart from our basic language and cultural assumptions, or actually flying in the face of those assumptions. Knowledge and processes of knowing that are deracinated from their context, in the way that theory and experience are separated in our individualistic heritage and framework, cannot empower us or serve as the basis for coherent, grounded interventions in our work, our lives, and our own self-experience.

With a new field definition of health and healthy self-process, we will then be able to close with implications of all these related threads for a *field view of ethics*, deriving from the field view of health outlined above. Since the time of the Enlightenment and the decline of traditional religion in the West, the two branches of inquiry known classically as "natural philosophy" and "moral philosophy" -- what is and what ought to be -- have diverged steadily, despite a number of attempts, from Kant to Nietzsche, to reconcile somehow these apparently opposed domains. So sharp has this dichotomy become in the 20th Century that Bertrand Russell, looking back on nearly a century of life and groundbreaking philosophical and political activity, concluded that his original life's dream, of reunifying the analytic and the ethical, the scientific/theoretical with the pragmatic/ political dimensions of life and thought, was a only romantic chimera, a dream which was contradicted by the basic nature of those two kinds of inquiry (1968). And indeed it is -- under the individualist paradigm of thought. With this new framework, we find the basis at least for a new approach to ethics. Again, this new approach is not really new, and has often been proposed and discussed in recent social approaches to ethical questions, out of various philosophical frameworks. The difference here is that by grounding this kind of thinking in a revised view of human nature, we have the prospect of reunifying these two domains, which we have to live (with or without the new empowerment of this integration) in a single, integrated field of experience and action in the world.

As we have already said, our world today is dying, perhaps literally, for want of a new model for understanding ourselves and our place in things, one that can honor and do justice *both* to our individuality *and* to our unity and connectedness, grounding itself in felt relationships in a way that restores meaning and wholeness to ourselves and our experiential world, transforming our actions and our experience alike. The larger aim of all these chapters is to be a stepping stone along the road to that necessary dream.

To set the stage for all this, we begin in Part I with the old model itself, which we are saying is in a period of crisis and active deconstruction now, at the painful and perilous birthing of something new. This model, which we are calling the *paradigm of individualism*, a set of deep assumptions and beliefs which have animated Western culture for some three thousand years now, is today both seemingly triumphant and everywhere besieged at one and the same time. Here too the reader is meant to have a choice: for an overview of these larger issues in their broad cultural sweep, begin the book with Part I and then continue with the more experiential material ahead in the sections ahead. To start right in with more of a hands-on feel of the ideas, attitudes, and emotions that are our real topics here -- attitudes, we are arguing, which orient and partly determine our experience of ourselves and others, -- begin with Part II, and then use Part I afterwards to look back over where we've come from and where we may now go with it all now. Moreover, the chapters that then follow in Parts II to IV are meant as we said above to be readable in any order. The order they are given in -- relationship, contact, support, shame, intimacy, and narrative -- is intended to provide a developmental frame, with each topic building on the ones before, and each one taking up a problem raised or left by the previous material. At the same time, each one is a crucial piece of the overall discussion of self, and an important developmental topic in its own right. In each case, the idea is to give enough context and reference to make each chapter make sense on its own or ahead of the others -- hopefully in a usefully recursive, not just repetitive way, -- so that the reader who is particularly drawn to one or another of them can begin there and then follow her or his own interest on through, or else skip around and still not sacrifice the gist of the argument.

We don't have an exercise for opening the examination of the old paradigm -- and perhaps we don't need one, since our very lives and our culture are that exercise itself, and that experiment. But experience doesn't become experiment in the full sense until it is held up for deconstruction and dialogue, which is the kind of discourse we will try to initiate in the following section, and then all through this book. That is, if experience is *constructive* (the fundamental Gestalt insight, developed ahead), then experiment is deconstruction, the lifting up of that constructive process itself for focus and analysis in context. In that sense this entire book is meant as a *contact experiment*, an invitation to join in an ongoing discourse and exploration which is very much a work in progress, and an utterly dialogic work by its deepest nature. Some past partners in this dialogue are mentioned in the acknowledgements above; now the reader is invited to join this conversation in progress -- in her/his head, in the margins of the book, or in written form (I can be reached through the publisher, GICPress, 66 Orchard Street, Cambridge MA 02140, or by internet at gicpress@ mindspring.com).

It is not necessary to say again here that our common goal, and my goal with this book, is in the largest sense to have some small part in changing the world. That world is already changing around us and in us, while our goal and our task are rather to join that ongoing change, clarify it as much as possible, and thus influence the outcome of it where we can, in whatever ways we can, in the directions of life, growth, and the fullest human potential. Welcome to the conversation.

Part I -- The Problem of Self: In Search of a New Paradigm

Chapter One: The Legacy of Individualism -- the Paradigm in Practice

What is the self? What do we mean exactly when we use this familiar yet elusive term, at once as near to us as our own skin and still somehow as vanishing as a mirage, always seeming to recede as fast as we try to approach it and pin it down? Is it a thing, a process, or just a feeling? Something we have, or something we do -- or should we be thinking of it rather as something we somehow just are? Is it the little person inside who runs the show -- and then who runs her or him (or should we say "it" -- does self have gender?). Noun, verb -- or more a kind of adjective, something we use for emphasis, as in "I did it my*self*" -- in which case who or what is that adjective supposed to emphasize or describe? Or should we think of self more as a kind of *place*, a point of view in some literal or figurative sense, maybe that domain we refer to when we talk about where somebody is "coming from?" And then where do we find that place: inside us or outside, or somehow both at the same time? (But then here we have to be careful, because this common way of talking about it, "inside" and "outside," seems to leave us with two unclear terms now to work with, where a moment ago we only had one.

First there was "self," and now there's a "me" for that self to be "inside of" or otherwise -- plus possibly the person who is standing off looking at the relationship of those two terms, which may or may not be the same as the person who is talking to you now about standing off and looking in that way, and so on and so on with no obvious stopping point in sight!)

This is what philosophers call an "infinite regress," the kind of backward-spiraling answer which gives us an uncomfortable feeling there was something wrong with the question in the first place. But what? I do feel somehow that I am "myself," and you are "yourself:" why should it be hard for us to talk about that? How is it we seem to get so quickly into difficulties of this kind, the minute we try to stake out a space for dialogue on these slippery slopes, and talk meaningfully about questions like *who we are exactly*, and *what it means to be that person*, or to be a person at all, in relation to ourselves and to other selves in the world. We know ourselves, don't we? -- or don't we? Why is it so difficult to say who or what that self is, that we think we know?

All of these are the riddles that once were answered -- or begged -- in a single swift stroke by the evocation of a Creator: we are who we are, says the Creationist perspective, whatever kind of being or state that is, because Somebody out there made us that way, period, end of story. Of course, that didn't really answer the question of self at all, but it did offer the soothing promise of closing off the discussion. Nowadays, in the absence of that easy answer, the discussion somehow seems to want to chase its own tail, as if language itself were not really very well equipped to deal with our own felt experience on these matters. Which is odd when you think about it, because where else would words and concepts have come from, if not from some underpinning of felt reality and lived experience?

If we keep thinking stubbornly on past this point we may begin to get to a kind of curious split in our own self-experience, that eerie self-mirroring sensation the romantic poets called the "double," and the Existentialists discussed a century or so later on as "alienation," the uncomfortable gnawing sense that I am somehow *not at home in the world I was born into*, perhaps not even in this body itself, which seems to be both me and not me at the same time. And yet our most firmly-held modern creation stories have us evolving straight out of that natural world, which we then surely must belong to and be a direct part of, in some deeply integral way. Thus it is that we arrive at a sudden impasse in our reflections about our selves and our own nature, which may seem to be the validation of what the Existentialists maintained: namely that we are in some sense shipwrecked here on the shores of existence -- "thrown here," as Heidegger put it, an image which has the effect of making us strangers in a strange land indeed: born to live and die essentially homeless, with no naturally given connections or meanings. An impasse of this kind can be finally a kind of wordless place, since language itself seems to be leading us to more and more disconnection, in place of the natural belonging and meaning we were yearning for, leaving us in the end to stare at each other in silence across that Existentialist divide, each of us isolated and lonely, fastened to a dying animal (in Yeats's vivid phrase), imprisoned with some self or being who gives us no comfort, and which we are apparently helpless even to name or define.

But why should this be? Why is it that our reflections on our own nature and being seem to lead us repeatedly up this kind of blind alley? Is this the irreducible absurdity of selfhood and being, an intrinsic part of just existing in the world at all, as some of the Existentialists maintained ("Dasein" or "being there" -- again a coinage of Heidegger's, by which he seemed to mean "pure existence," prior to or isolated from any particular desires and feelings, an imaginary state parodied in the blackly comic Jerzy Koszinski novel and Peter Sellers movie of the same title)?

Or is this impasse, as we will argue here, more the result of a *category of language*, a deep *cultural* structure which shapes how we understand and then actually experience the world and ourselves -- and thus how we take up relationship, and live and work with other people? Other cultures after all have thought and felt differently from us about who we are and how we get that way. Where do our own assumptions about self and experience come from, and then how do those assumptions operate dynamically to influence and predetermine that experience, perhaps even our "inner experience" -- because we know enough by this time about other cultures and other ages to be suspicious, at least, about the idea that there is any such thing as "pure experience" completely free of the developmental influences of culture, subculture, and family and personal history? We know that language prestructures feelings and thought, and even "nature" itself, as post-modern physics tells us, is a *social construction of mind*, a way of looking at things with deep roots in hidden cultural assumptions about what is given and real, which then provide the lens through which we see the world. Where do we get our deepest assumptions about human nature and the self, and then how do they function to predetermine what we assume to be "natural" and irreducible, just "the way things are?" To use the language we were developing in the Preface, what is our *paradigm of selfhood*? Where does it come from, and how does that legacy operate today, to color not just how we think and analyze theoretically, but how we actually feel, and experience, and relate to ourselves and other people?

The Legacy of Western Culture

In our Western tradition, once we begin to speak of origins and sources, usually it isn't very long before we make a move which is so habituated in the cultural stream as to be virtually automatic. This is to *turn to the Greeks*, who are assumed in this tradition to represent a sort of bedrock or zero point for the beginning of almost any discussion, and particularly one about terms and language -- not just what things mean, but even more than that, how we should set about to find that out in some clear and reliable way. The ancients after all lived in far simpler times -- or at any rate so we like to imagine, because imagining this supports our faith that the classic age promises us something solid we can rely on, free of the noise and confusion of modern life, with its relentless overload of "information," all too often a river of data without context, which only seem to cloud the issues we are trying to clarify.[1]

"Man," says Protagoras, a contemporary and sometime adversary of Socrates and Plato, "is the measure of all things" -- the kind of dictum which sums up the age, and gives our tradition of "Western humanism" its focus and its name. Leaving aside for the moment the gendering of that proposition (a topic we will return to, especially in Chapter Eight), who or what is this "man" the ancients have in mind, and how does their perspective inform ours today -- helpfully or otherwise -- in our own search for self? All subsequent philosophy in the West, remarks Bertrand Russell (1972), quoting Whitehead to express this same cultural faith, is *footnote or commentary to Plato* -- by which he meant not that every question had necessarily been answered, 2500 or so years ago, but rather that Plato and his own commentator Aristotle had laid down for us all the *terms and parameters of discussion*, as well as the methods by which questions and answers could rationally and reliably be explored and critiqued, including Plato's own

[1] Indeed, the very word "Western," if we unpack it a bit, contains and implies the legacy of Greek thought. If we think about it, for the term to make any sense at all as a categorization of cultures, we have to imagine ourselves as standing somewhere at the eastern end of the Mediterranean, say a bit west of Istanbul, facing north, and looking to our left ("the West") or right ("the East") respectively -- while resolutely not looking too far over either shoulder or directly behind us, which would be the South, which is by definition "primitive" or unevolved. All of this is a fairly rigid and complex maneuver which is embedded and obscured, again in the way of paradigmatic principles, in the term "Western" itself. We have been sensitized at last to the embedded Eurocentrism in the word "Oriental" -- which means "rising (sun)," or east, again only in relation to that same eastern Mediterranean vantage point (from Japan, obviously, America lies immediately to the east, not the west). Deconstructing our own cultural self-references is more difficult.

proposed answers to basic issues like who we are, what it means to be that person, and thus how we should live with ourselves and each other in our shared world. That these methods and terms themselves might limit or even blind us to other possible ways of seeing and experiencing does not seem to occur to Russell, or his mentor Whitehead -- though it will become a major preoccupation of the next, most recent wave of Western philosophy, the movement that today is called "postmodern," from Russell's own protegé Wittgenstein and on through Foucault and the deconstructionists of our own times (very much including a number of feminist philosophers and psychologists, who have taken leading roles in critiquing assumptions about self and relationship that derive from Freud in particular, -- but are inherited, as we will be tracing here, from Plato and his world, pretty much intact). Many of this group will eventually conclude that the whole Platonic/analytic tradition was a dead end in philosophy -- without always appreciating, we will be arguing, how much they continue to inhabit the Platonic self-paradigm themselves, and how much our view of self, in clinical models and philosophy alike, is still in thrall to Plato's thinking and Greek assumptions about human nature in general.

To understand this, and then to do something about it together, we first have to take a look at those terms and assumptions and that Greek world itself -- again, not just in the abstract, as Plato's own philosophical tradition would seem to suggest, but more *phenomenologically,* meaning in terms of our own felt concerns and experience of self and relationship, looking for the fit and misfit between and among that experience, our inherited tradition of language and thinking, and then the interplay of the form and the content of those two domains. What was Plato's own view of the self and self-experience? What concerns in his world did that view grow naturally and creatively out of? And then how does the legacy of that view inform and influence our approach and our own experience in our lives and work with people today?

The Origins of the Paradigm -- the Self in Greek Perspective

The answer to this question is a curious one, and leads us into another one of those logical circles or experiential dead ends that we're coming almost to expect, as soon as we try to explore self in the language of the individualist tradition. Briefly, that answer is simply that the classical philosophers, who were our first psychologists in the West, would very likely have been puzzled by the issues and questions we are raising here, if not totally nonplussed -- at least in the forms and language we are raising and posing them in now, which all have to do with our felt experience of selfhood in a world of other selves. The problem is not so much that the ancients had no positions on matters like these, of what it means to be a self, with self-experience, in a world of other experiencing selves with realities and points of view of their own. They certainly did have their own answers to all this, implicitly at least if not explicitly -- positions which took a certain view of human nature for granted, and along with it a certain natural social order deriving from that view. That view and that social order included the institution of slavery; the denial of full citizenship to women (though to give him credit, Plato's repressive ideal state, the Republic [1993], does allow for the idea of political participation for women of the elite class, at least -- a notion from which Aristotle [1984] will recoil in horror); the normalization of war; and the relegation of almost all other cultures to the status of "barbarians" (from the onomatopoetic Greek root based on the mocking sound "ba-ba-ba," meaning that foreigners speak tongues which are no more than primitive babble). All those are just a few of the social arrangements and positions that both underlie and derive from the Platonic view of self and the relationships of selves, to each other and to the world.

But that's just it -- all this is taken for granted, based on a view of self that is presumed, not discussed, in the way paradigmatic principles and assumptions generally are, in our own culture or any other. To be a "self," to Plato and his world, meaning a fully human being with a mind and a valid inner process of some kind, yielding a legitimate voice and point of view, is just assumed to mean being adult, male, emancipated, probably propertied, something they would call "rational" -- *and also Greek.* These things are not just specific attributes of particular persons or selves, but are the qualifications for belonging to the class of selves itself, membership in the group we take as fully human, treat as full human voices, and are talking about when we start to spin theories about human nature, the self, and the natural ordering of things. If the criteria themselves aren't generally discussed, that's just because they simply seem too obvious to the Greeks of the classical age and beyond to be in need of any articulation.

By contrast, when Plato and Aristotle do want to talk about human nature and experience, their interest is not at all in our modern preoccupations of identity and self-experience, our human condition as individual selves in relation somehow to other selves. Rather, what concerns Plato in particular is the issue of how those selves, once here, may achieve *reliable knowledge.* Not what it means to be a self, but what it means for that preexistent self to *know the world.* What is knowledge, and how do we come by it? What kinds of knowledge are certain and reliable, and which ones are just opinion or ephemera? How do we know the difference? Specifically, Plato is preoccupied with the question of how we arrive at knowledge that is *solid enough to organize our lives and social systems around, including our moral and political judgments,* in the midst of a physical and perceptual world that is characterized by accident, chance, error, misperception, and (worst of all) constant change.

To Plato as to his contempories this question is urgent, because of their project of deriving *ethics and social policy from human reason alone* -- without the traditional recourse to the guidance of priests and soothsayers or the dictates of tyrants to tell us what to do and how to live. Our lived experience seems such a jumble of fleeting impressions and misimpressions, contingency and hearsay; worst of all, our very selves seem subject to constant change, at least on the level of our physical beings, moods, and sensations. In the face of all this flux, what part of our own experiential process is reliable, and then what should be the rules of discourse and argument, so we can know when we're proceeding on the basis of the reliable parts of what we seem to know, and not just on accident and opinion? The fact that the individual selves who are doing this knowing and deciding are *already there*, fully formed by some prior act of creation, separate and distinct from each other and from the world to be known -- in other words, the individualist paradigm itself -- is a constant in this exploration, just assumed as a given fact, and not itself a subject of inquiry or debate.

Not that Plato would have used the word "self," which likely would have puzzled him mightily, as a substantive noun, as would the questions themselves that we are raising about it here. To Plato the natural word for referring to what is essential about a person would be "soul" -- as it was for that matter to Freud (1939), at the other end of the same tradition.[2] *Self* as a free-standing noun doesn't actually emerge in common usage in the West until some two thousand years after Plato, around the time of Locke and the writers of the British Enlightenment, who were looking for a way of talking about personhood without recourse to the old religiously-derived vocabulary. From there the word eventually works its way back into German from English in the 18th Century (Drosdowski et al, 1963). Freud, who like most

2 That is, to Freud in the original German. It was Strachey, translating Freud and thus establishing the Freudian lexicon in English, who gave us the more "scientific" Latin terms ego and id, in place of Freud's more homely "I" and "it" ("ich" and "es" in the original) -- as well as cumbersome locutions like "mental apparatus" and "psychic mechanism" where Freud said "Psyche" or "Seele," "soul," to refer to the whole essential person. No doubt Strachey feared, probably with good reason, that the oriiginal terms would have a suspiciously Continental or "soft" ring at the time to the empirical English ear.

educated Germans of his day was steeped in Shakespeare and the Renaissance, was not particularly conversant with Locke and the British Enlightenment/empiricist philosophers, with whom he nonetheless shared many assumptions about self and the world (Gay, 1988).

But whether self or soul, the problem of what judgments, what kinds of perception or intuition we can rely on about ourselves and our world remains perplexing, in the absence of absolute kingly or priestly authority -- particularly when we consider that the thinking, perceiving person himself (sic) is also undergoing constant change, on a physical level and also in terms of mood, interest, information, and so on. How can our knowing of anything be anywhere near reliable enough to replace sheer authority as a standard, under these unstable conditions? Plato's solution was ingenious, and enormously influential -- not so much for its explicit terms, which have provoked many critiques but little agreement down through the centuries, as for the implicit assumptions and social/psychological implications of his argument, which carried over into the culture and continue to mark discussion and analysis of self and relationship today.

The answer to the problem of reliable knowledge for the individual self, Plato argued, can only be that this apparent world, this world of accident, approximation, and change, *is not the real world at all.* If it were, there would be no way for us to know anything at all with any certainty, amid all this flux and error. Rather, there must be another world somewhere, more stable and real than this life of ephemeral appearances, which underlies this one, and from which this one takes its real shape and meaning. The proof of this is that we do know anything at all, which would be impossible if the world of sense impressions were all we had to go on -- in which case we wouldn't even know how to recognize ourselves or each other, as we change from moment to moment and day to day. In that other, ideal realm, of which this world of sense impressions is only a pale copy, everything is clear, distinct, absolute, *and eternally unchanging* -- and thus reliable. These are the originals, or archetypes, which the particular things and classes and ideas of this world only roughly reflect -- as shadows on a wall only imperfectly resemble the real things that cast those shadows, in Plato's famous image. Without that other world of reality to underlie the mere "phenomena" of this one, this world of shadows and echoes wouldn't exist at all, and certainly wouldn't be accessible to being known in any way.

Thus there is somewhere an ideal form of, say, "dog," which all the various canines of this experiential world partake of or somehow draw their form and nature from, in their imperfect way. That's what makes them "dogs" -- both as individual cases and as members of the class "dog" -- even though some of them are small, some large, some mean, some dead, some puppies, some imaginary, and so on. And then here comes the interesting part, for our exploration of self and human nature here: we *know* dogs -- both the individuals, as dogs, and the class as a category -- by making mental reference in some way to that archetype, that ideal form, which is *already imprinted* by creation into our brain. That is, when we see a particular, individual, and variable dog, who is different from all other dogs and also looks different in different lights, at different ages, in different doggy moods, and so on, we still know it's a dog, because it always draws its nature from the Ideal Form of dog, *and* we have that Ideal Form stored, so to speak, in our inborn memory -- programmed in, as we might say today, to the hardwiring that is part of our created nature. Thus Plato solves the problem of "reality" -- how the world gets to be organized the way it is, in things and species and classes and categories and events -- *and* the problem of how we can *know* this world, which is separate from ourselves yet plainly known by us, in a single creative stroke. This is probably the tidiest solution ever offered to the problem of how we can know things, without actually being a part of them. To be sure, it's also far-fetched, abstract, arbitrary, and flies in the face of much of our lived experience, in ways that are reminiscent of the theories of classical psychoanalysis, written a couple of thousand years later by an author steeped in German classical gymnasium education, which rested on Plato and the Greeks. Both models insist on the reality of a world of unseen forces, quite contradictory to the world of our experience as we think we know it, and both insist on the "real" existence of certain ideas or forms (such as Justice or the Oedipal Complex), which give shape to particular experience. But for sheer neatness, meaning simplicity and completeness, Plato's model hasn't been surpassed.

What's true of dogs, Plato goes on, is then also true of more collective categories like classes of citizens or political systems, or discrete events like war or civic life -- and even of abstract ideas like beauty, truth, justice, or for that matter individual self/souls or "selfhood" itself, the idea of human individuals, each one rational and distinct. For every notion that we can entertain, every type or unique soul that exists, there already has to be an Ideal Form of that notion or thing, pre-existing in that other, ideal realm. Now as commentators from Aristotle to Russell have suggested, there's another one of those pesky infinite regresses buried in all this, because if you're going to explain how the Ideal Form in your mind helps you to recognize the particular instance of dog, or human self, or justice, then you're going to have to call on the idea of reference or recognition itself. So there must be an Ideal Form for that idea of recognition as well, because otherwise we wouldn't recognize recognition either when we encounter it, and thus wouldn't know when and how to make the connection between the perfect ideal form and the imperfect concrete case in front of us. But this kind of practical application of general to particular, this use and knowing of recognition itself, is then a kind of correspondence at another level of generality, so there has to be an Ideal Form for *that* kind of activity, and so on and so on forever. For every possible kind of thought, there has to be one (or more) Ideal Form -- including the Ideal Form for infinite regress itself. As Plato's own student Aristotle himself pointed out, this other world of Ideal Forms, which was supposed to be such a serene and orderly place, soon comes to be at least as chaotic and crowded as the world of sense and experience it was supposed to explain and simplify, with new Forms logging on, so to speak, thick and fast -- as fast as or faster than we have new kinds of ideas (for which the Ideal Form had to already be there, or we couldn't have had the idea in the first place).

In today's terms, this is what we call an "algorhythm," or set of explanatory steps, that's just as long and complex as the thing it was supposed to explain -- a map, in other words, as large and unwieldy as the territory you're mapping. At the same time, what critics and commentators from Aristotle to our own times haven't been able to notice so clearly is that there is something about the initial hidden assumption itself, that *the perceiving, experiencing self is completely separate by nature from the world experienced and perceived*, that creates this kind of logical complication and self-contradiction in the first place, as the philosopher/psychologist scrambles to reestablish the necessary link between self and the world, or self and other selves, that was just assumed to be broken in the first place by the given nature of the self. In other words, the individualist paradigm itself is somehow creating or contributing to the problem, of how such an isolated self can ever be in meaningful or useful relationship with other selves and the world, that philosophers and psychologists have been trying to solve in West ever since Plato's time -- and trying to solve it *without going outside the terms and assumptions of the paradigm itself*. Small wonder then if we find that arguments and explanations of this kind tend to go in circles -- and will keep on doing that, as we shall see below, right up to the present day, in the history of psychology and current self-theory alike -- and thus in our clinical and related work, and even in our own relationships and conceptions and experience of ourselves.

That's the philosophical quagmire, in everyday terms -- an insoluble conundrum that has continued to plague Western philosophy as well right on up at least through Descartes and Spinoza (who nearly lost his life for trying to solve this same problem by even suggesting that self and the world might in some profound way be one and the same by nature -- an assertion that clearly threatened the dominant cultural worldview and religious/political institutions to an intolerable degree, for reasons which we will be looking at in more detail later on in this discussion). At the same time, the enduring psychological consequences of this whole approach for our methods and models, which are embedded in the paradigm and still with us today, have also been less appreciated. Or rather, these consequences -- the ecological and social irresponsibility that have tended to accompany the triumph of the West -- have themselves been widely critiqued and much lamented at times, but generally without appreciating how those consequences themselves flow directly and inevitably from Plato's individualist/dualist assumptions about self and relationship. Let us take a look at some of these implications and consequences, before going on to trace more briefly the rest of the history of individualism as a worldview in the remainder of this chapter.

The Platonic Legacy Today

1) First of all, there's the profound isolation of the individual self -- a position the Existentialists espoused and presented as a new insight over the past century, but one which actually has always been embedded at the heart of the paradigm of individualism itself (to be sure, it stood out more bleakly once the softening presence of a Creator deity was removed). In Plato's model this isolation follows from the theory of Ideal Forms itself, which was supposed to help us distinguish reliable from unreliable knowledge and judgment in the first place. If each individual soul is an archetype, separate, unique, and eternally preexistent before birth -- and then in some way *added on* or *injected into* the natural physical body, -- then each one is a world unto itself, timeless, unchanging, uninfluenced by contact or relationship with the world or other selves in any real way. Today

we mostly reject Plato's idea that this physical world is just an illusion and isn't the "real world." In place of his somewhat fanciful assertion of another realm to explain this one, we are more likely to rely on an equally deep, perhaps equally unexamined faith in "science," as an answer to the same problem he was struggling with, of how to determine what *kind* of knowing is solid and reliable enough to build on. Where Plato would invoke "pure reason," his claim of a proof by pure logic that the other realm must exist, we appeal rather to "hard facts" -- generally ignoring or denying in the process that these "facts" are never really given "things," but are themselves always perceptions and conclusions in a context, *interpretations of experience*, which are socially agreed on and culturally conditioned, just as his ideas of Truth and Justice were.

At the same time, it is a mistake to think that because the culture is mostly materialist today, that means that Plato's influence, this idea of Ideal Essences that lie behind everyday reality, is gone. It lives on in the dominant paradigmatic notion of an *essential individual self*, which lives before and apart from this world of experience and contact. The later Existentialists set out to criticize this notion of an "essence" that would define the significance of our lives before our own creative determination of our own meaning; but they failed to see that the individual self they imagined as making that creative act was *already given* in essentialist, ideal terms that came down directly from Plato and the Greeks and completely color their own mentors Kierkegaard and Nietzsche -- terms that isolate each self from each other self, and from the world in general. Thus for Sartre, as we shall see below, the degree of "authenticity" (literally, "self-determination") of an experience, *is the same as* its degree of independence from outside influence, by the world or by relationship with other selves.

2) But this in turn means that relationships are never real -- or at least not in the same ultimate way that individual selves are

real. The only relationship that can possibly be real, in Plato's model, would be the one between each imperfect thing or example in this world (including the individual selves we are and meet here) and the Ideal Form of that thing or event or idea in the other world. Again, as long as we believe in a personal God, watching over each of us individually the way the shepherd watches a flock, this softens the harsh isolation and loneliness of this universe somewhat. Still, at best our connection with *other selves* is remote and indirect, stemming only from the fact that each of us participates in some unique but parallel way in that divine realm -- whether a Creator God or Plato's world of Ideal Forms, -- and each of us has those Ideal Forms imprinted in some way in our minds. This too is an idea which persisted powerfully in the Western tradition -- for example in Christianity, where we will find each soul pursuing its own unique path, completely independently of any other soul, yet connected indirectly somehow in the Mind of God, and by virtue of being artifacts, so to speak, of the same creative Hand.

To Kierkegaard, for example, the self is a purely inward, private essence, whose relational aspect exists only in relation to God. Relatedness to the world of other people is thus opposed to self and self-realization, because the world takes us away from God. Increasing self-complexity or growth then equals increasing inwardness, as well as increasing autonomy from the social world around. To Nietzsche, for whom this one real relationship (with the deity) is also ruptured and unreal, the given self, our basic human nature and existence, is then nothing more or less than the isolated Will to Power, utterly alone in a meaningless universe, with nothing more to do than repeat isolated acts of dominance or submission forever.

3) Corollary to this is the fundamental proposition that experience itself -- at least most of our experience, the part that has to do with people and things "outside ourselves," -- isn't real either, and doesn't really mean anything. Experience after all is a

matter of ephemeral and shifting sense impressions, the world of sensations and memories, which always include misperception and chance. For the isolated self, cut off by definition from other isolated selves, there is no way to correct the inevitable error and accident that characterize the world of sense impression and everyday experience, so that we can know what to do and not to do, unless we have recourse to some standard or other of authority. For Plato this authority is "pure reason," our intuitive faculty for eternal verities like logic and number, or Reason itself and the Good, which are all Ideal Forms and thus dependable.

We find this devaluing of experience still with us today, for example, in the works of the classical Freudians and the classical Behaviorists -- both of which schools would agree that the experience you think you're having is not really significant or determinant of anything, but just a self-soothing fiction (classic psychoanalytic drive theory), or a self-explanatory after-effect (classic conditioning theory, both Pavlovian and Skinnerian) -- while what's really going on is the hidden dynamics of unseen principles and invisible forces at work. In other words, to Freud experience is only a symptom, while to Skinner, as to Plato, it is even less than that, a meaningless illusion or by-product of "reality," which is seen as an observable pattern of stimulus/ response conditioning.

The same thing is then true for the increasingly dominant current movement toward an ever-more exclusive reliance on psychopharmacology to treat a wide range of behavioral and mood problems: here too the experience you think you're having is just an artifact of the real world (in this case neurology and biochemistry), and at most, as in Freud, a kind of barometer of the need for expert intervention and adjustment to the biological organism from the outside. Even contemporary physical science no longer looks to empirical experience, but refers everything to unseen fields and imaginary particles that underlie the deceptive apparent world of sense perception and appearances. In all these cases, Plato's assertion that this world is merely appearance, while our felt world of experience is not a reliable place to look for any real, usable knowledge, still lives.

For all that our culture prides itself on its "hard empiricism," each of these systems of thought, including "empirical science" itself, actually relies on an appeal to what Plato would have called "reason" -- which itself rests on a deeper level of unquestioned assumptions, assertions, and intuitions about self and the world -- including of course the unquestioned "intuition" of the separateness and autonomy of the individual self.

4) If experience in general is suspect, then most deceptive and unreliable of all is the whole realm of *emotional* experience, including especially *interpersonal feelings and relational attachments.* After all, nothing seems to change more rapidly than our feelings, moods, affections and aversions, and emotional reactions with and toward other people. Since by definition we are not really connected with these other people in any direct way, and since "ordinary" experience in general is not real anyway, it follows that the illusion we have of relational feeling and personal connection is just that -- an illusion, at most the fleeting reflection of the Ideal Form of, say, love or altruism or even hatred and aversion. Thus it seems perfectly workable to Plato, in his utopian society, to separate children from their parents at birth, and to deny the importance of attachment and relational needs, for infants, children, and adults alike. This too we find directly echoed in Freud's theory, which reduces the intersubjective bonding of infant and parent, for example, to "libidinal cathexis," the predatory expression of individual self-energy, by a self which already exists before the relationship starts, and not a real relational field which connects, shapes, and ultimately cocreates both selves. (The importance of the early mother-child bond, much stressed by later writers in the Freudian tradition such as Erikson [1951], Bowlby [1969] and Ainsworth [1979], is not actually in Freud's own work, which if anything stresses the

importance of the father in infancy [1999]).

Perhaps most of all, we find this presumption of absolute, isolated individualism, and the denial of the reality of relational needs, in all those arenas of modern life that are concerned with male gender roles and the socialization of male children in Western culture. Again, this is a topic we will return to, particularly in Chapter Eight.

5) By the same token, if there is no experience, and no interpersonal or other influence on the real self, then it follows that there is no such thing as learning or development in any real sense. Knowledge, to Plato, is never a matter of learning something new -- because the new is by definition not eternal, and therefore not really true. Rather, knowing is always and only a process of *recognizing* something, which was already present in us as an archetype, and only needed to be brought out, at most with the help of a stimulation to pure rational process such as that Socrates provides to his imaginary interlocutors in Plato's dialogues (a few probing questions on Socrates's part always bring the pliant adversary right around to admitting the intuitive rightness of Socrates's position).

This too we find in modern psychological theories and models, such as current developmental models of the "acorn to oak" type, which outline predetermined, ideal stages that are somehow already contained in the created individual at birth, and only undergo a kind of ideal unfolding toward a predetermined adult state, rather than a real process of open-ended developmental influence and exchange. Thus for example in classical Freudian theory, the self-essence, which would have to be the same as the libidinal and aggressive drives themselves, doesn't undergo development in any real sense, of an accumulating integrated change in its nature. The *focus* of the energy drive, which in a tension-reduction model is more or less the same as the particular itch looking to be scratched, does move from place to place in the body (oral to anal to phallic); but its nature and character don't change. If anything it is the ego -- the system of compromises with an inhospitable world -- that undergoes development. But the ego is not the self, not at the center of a person's essence. This is why we have much discussion of the ego in Freud and the Freudian tradition, and little discussion of the self: because that tradition itself belongs to a larger cultural tradition, going back to Plato, which assumes that the self doesn't change. Again, each self is its own self-contained world and reality -- a Platonic idea we will see elaborated to its highest expression in the work of the Enlightenment philosopher Leibniz, who hands it on to us today (for further discussion, see for example Wheeler, 1998).

6) All of which makes the Platonic tradition and its powerful legacy today *profoundly and inherently conservative*, in a political sense. If each person, each self/soul represents a unique, created archetype, then differences among them are not due to environmental effects and developmental conditions, but are just inherently there, and there's nothing you can do about it. Change or reform in social conditions and economic arrangements won't really change anything real, since the unchanging self is already given before birth. This then makes a powerful argument for leaving the existing arrangements of social privilege or economic inequity the way they are, which is always the essence of conservative political thought, even as the particular strategies for preserving privilege change from one setting to another (more government, less government, free trade, protectionism, greater civil liberty, less civil liberty, and so on). At times the static quality of conservative politics will be eased, as in Plato's system, by a degree of meritocracy, which in practice amounts to the recognition that privilege is best preseved in the long run by admitting some of the most aggressive and talented outsiders into the privileged classes. But the idea that a larger pool of talent is being depressed and marginalized, to the detriment of everybody, by oppressive developmental conditions -- let alone that a redistribution of privilege would relieve human

suffering and foster a general flourishing of creativity, again to the benefit of all -- just doesn't come up, because individual differences are given by creation, and development and learning aren't real anyway.

7) But we can go even further. At a deeper level, behind the appeal to "human reason," Plato's worldview is what we may call a "revealed truth" system; and like all systems of revelation, it is ultimately authoritarian. This is the effect of combining extreme rationalism (the appeal to reason over experience) with an equally extreme individualism (the belief in the absolute, ultimate separation of selves). Take for example Plato's theme of justice: how do we know justice, and then how do we live justly? If the only way to know anything is by comparing it to the Ideal Form of that thing, then any actual political or personal arguments about justice have to be settled by invoking that archetype, and then deciding which particular policy or judgment has more of the Ideal Form of justice in it. But who decides this question, which is ultimately intuitive/evaluative and subjective, not purely objective and rational as Plato and Socrates would seem to imply? In the end, the judgment will be made not by "pure reason" but by the authority of some one person or institution. In Plato's utopia this role is preformed by the "philosopher kings," who will all quite remarkably agree with each other. To be sure, these authorities will then offer the most logical justification they can for their positions -- something which non-utopian judges and kings and priests are generally in the habit of doing in any case.

And authority means power. Unless we submit our own reasoning processes, and the differences between and among them, to some kind of vote or other collective decision by the community -- something Plato emphatically does not intend, -- then the claim of "pure reason" masks arbitrary authority, backed by power, much like the old systems of judgment Plato wants to replace. It is in this sense that the contemporary deconstructionist Michel Foucault, proposed that "knowledge is a regime" [1980], meaning that a system of what counts as "real knowledge" and what doesn't, always rests on power and interest).

We find the same process, and the same masking, down through the centuries since Plato and in our world today, not only in the "rationalist" or "objective science" tradition, but in "fundamentalist" or "revealed truth" movements that draw their authority from biblical or other texts -- two worldviews that have more resemblance than the adherents of either one would generally want to admit. In both cases, what is denied is that any interpretation at all of "objective truth" is going on -- a denial which effectively removes any particular interpretation from debate. In the case of "objective science," the claim is that "the data speak for themselves;" while in "revealed truth" systems such as all the various religious fundamentalisms, the parallel proposition is that "the text speaks for itself."

But data and texts do not speak for themselves; someone has to take them up, construct a particular interpretive meaning, and then argue for that interpretation, at times obscuring or overlooking other, equally plausible interpretations that may follow from different assumptions, different values, different paradigms. (A prominent current example is the use of "IQ" tests to measure something called "intelligence," so as to predict future performance in some area. Once "IQ" is measured, then it is automatically assumed to exist, on the basis of the circular argument that it must exist, since it has just been measured. What is obscured of course is that the tests measure *performance on selected tasks*, not ability or potential, which are themselves interpretive inferences, based on evaluation and selection on the part of the test constructors -- and the constructors of the "entity," "intelligence" itself. Many such instruments have then been "corrected" for culturally biased *content.* The deeper problem, that performance is sensitive to attitudinal and cultural factors such as chronic individual or group affirmation or shaming, is left unaddressed, with the effect that existing cultural structures of inclusion and exclusion are preserved).

With "revealed truth" or "fundamentalist" positions, the same basic pattern applies. The data in question are generally some particular texts, presumably inspired or dictated by absolute divine authority. But whatever its presumed source, the text we *have* is in words, and someone reading it must arrive at a conclusion as to what it means. To take one obvious example, what about the commandment of the Judeo-Christian Bible, forbidding killing. What kind of killing should we take this as applying to? Capital punishment? War? The entire animal kingdom? The unborn? What about the stifling of full human potential, in particular individual or members of disadvantaged groups? Is that covered by the prohibition? And when what if one part of the text seems to contradict another? That same Bible is full of killing sanctioned directly by the Deity.

Likewise, In one book of that text, it is declared an "abomination" for a man to love another man "as with womankind" (Leviticus XVIII:22). Yet some six books later we find that Jonathan's love for David "was wonderful to (David), passing the love of women" (II Samuels I:26). Obviously some interpretive act on the reader's part has to be made here, to resolve contradictions and implications like these. Not surprisingly, we then find a great number of "fundamentalist" groups inferring utterly different meanings, widely varying "revealed truths," from this same text. Again, a "revealed truth" system, be it "fundamentalist," "objective data," or "ideal reason," is ultimately an authority-based system, and the *necessary but denied act of constructive interpretation involved rests on denied power*, the privileging of one person's or one group's interpretation over others.

Behind this mask lies the fundamental and inevitable problem of the Platonic paradigm: namely, that given the essential isolation of the individual self, there is no criterion for knowledge or judgment, which is to say for *interpretation of experience and data*, other than isolated, individual intuition, backed up if possible by authority. And this remains true, whether whether that authority is cloaked with a mantle of "pure reason," pure "data," or some other form of absolute, uninterpreted knowledge and truth.

These then are some of the ways the Platonic legacy, of absolute ideal essences that are prior to experience and context, still lives in our culture and in our thinking today. And all of them are organized and underlain by the *fundamental assumption of the utterly separate self*, created and given prior to relationship, perception, meaning-making, and development -- all of which are relegated to some secondary status, held as less real than the preexistent, individual self. This basic assumption has then permeated and organized the dominant stream of Western culture down to the present day, marking the philosophical systems of "human nature" which were our first psychological models, and still persisting in psychological theory and practice today -- and in many of our relational assumptions and choices in our personal lives as well. To see how this is true -- and again, what we can do about it, -- let us turn more briefly to that development, before beginning to develop an alternative model, growing from the seeds at least of a countertradition, in the next chapter.

The Individualist Paradigm

All this is the expression of what we have already begun calling here the *paradigm of individualism*, a complex and interlocking set of underlying assumptions and hidden presuppostions that has a 3000-year pedigree in the West, running straight back to the Greeks and then forward in a largely unbroken line down through the Hellenized Hebrews, the Christian synthesis and its medieval flowering, the Renaissance with its rediscovery of humanism, the Enlightenment, the 19th-

Century age of scientific materialism, and right on down to our own post-modern times. In the process this paradigm serves to unite thinkers and movements as otherwise diverse as Plato and the Hebrew Prophets, Galileo and the Church, Freud and the Behaviorists, or Carl Jung and Karl Marx, all of whom may disagree vehemently and sometimes violently with each other about the dynamics and determinants of human behavior, the direction of history, the motivation and purpose of life, and so on -- but all of whom are united at this deeper level by underlying assumptions, taken for granted but seldom articulated, about the *nature of the individual self,* which is to say, *who those individual human beings are* who are living that life, and having or creating or submitting to those experiences.

The fundamental propositions of that paradigm, as we have already seen and as we lift them out now for examination, are: 1) that *the individual is prior to relationship, and exists in some essential way apart from relational context and connection,* and 2) that *relationships themselves are therefore secondary, and in some sense less real than the individuals who enter into them,* who after all were already there, fully formed, and can come and go from one relationship to another as their own needs and circumstances dictate, presumably without altering their own essential nature. To Plato, as we have said, these propositions must have seemed incontrovertible and probably too obvious to bear mention -- as indeed they may seem to us, on some purely logical level anyway, even if we do feel some nagging discomfort with them when they're presented in this bald way -- a hesitation growing perhaps out of living or working with infants and children, out of spiritual concerns or experiences we may have had, from intimate relationship and deep commitments, or just from our everyday experiences of living with and caring for other people. The fundamental separation of one individual's *experience* from that of another, which follows directly from these assumptions, would likewise have seemed obvious to Plato -- as would Descartes's classic separation of mind or self from body, which was essentially unchanged from the Greek view, only some two thousand years later. The soul, which is the essence of the person, is individual, eternal, and unchanging -- and of course separate from this material world, again by creation, which again closes off developmental or relational questions.

As for the particular creation myths and stories that go along with these positions, they too generally seem to start with the creation of some fully adult selves. Adam and Eve have no childhood or developmental history: on the contrary, their move into self-awareness, relationship, and humanity is a *fall from grace*, not an achievement. Then when their own children come along they too enter the story as adults, and fall further. We may see in the garden of Eden story, or in the parallel Greek myths of a lost golden age, a deep nostalgia or a longing for a greater sense of connections and belongingness in the world, and with each other -- a memory of pre-uterine life, as Freud interpreted it, which again denies that this could be a real sense and a real experience here and now, yet something which is hard to articulate and own under the dominant paradigm. The essence of humanness, in the West, is always this radical separateness of one adult self from another. (Even in Christian mythology, where a divine child figures at the center of the story, that child too, being divine, is a complete adult right after babyhood, lecturing and teaching from early childhood on, and never needs to go through any developmental process on the way to becoming or having a full self).

This Christian tradition, which then eventually comes to dominate in the West, is itself a synthesis of the Hellenic with the (already Hellenized) Hebraic, along with a certain admixture of Near Eastern mystery cults (particularly the Dionysian theme of the dying god who is slain and then born again). In the process much is changed and many innovations come to prevail -- the proccupation with sin and redemption, the diabolizing of the body, the idea of history as progress toward a glorious future (rather than a falling off from a golden age, as Greek mythology saw it): yet the profound individualism of the Greeks (and the Hebrews) remains. The focus of Christianity is on salvation, but that salvation again is only and always a matter of *individual souls*, saved (or lost) individually, one at a time -- never the redemption or realization of all being, say, as in certain Eastern worldviews.

Individual development in this picture is then not a matter of the self growing toward full selfhood, but rather the pilgrim's progress of individual souls, which are already fully-formed selves by Creation, moving toward or away from God. In traditional Christianity my salvation (or damnation) has nothing whatever to do with yours, but only with my relationship, or lack thereof, with God (again, direct relationships between individuals are not ultimately real). Far from our humanness being something we need to develop or grow into, if anything humanity here is more a condition to be recovered from, tainted as we are from birth by the original sin inherent in biological reproduction, which is to say in our bodily nature, and by our own desires. Any suggestion that these individual soul/selves are aspects or manifestations of some larger Soul or Self, or of the Deity itself, has always been regarded as dangerous pantheism in the Church -- as it has for that matter in mainstream Judaism, -- an anarchistic heresy that threatens to undermine church or temple authority. The philosopher Spinoza, some four hundred years ago, was anathematized and then excommunicated by both the Christians and the Jews for just this suggestion, as we mentioned above; and in our own century the same issue has been revived and debated passionately within Judaism between the Kabbalist Gershom Scholem and the more conservative-minded Martin Buber, who insisted on the dualist/individualist position. There is no room in Jewish tradition, Buber maintained, for the notion that individual selves are ultimately a part of some greater whole, or that creation in general is an aspect or expression of the Godhead (see Weiner, 1969). To be sure, this debate managed to unfold without anyone's being burned at the stake, as in former times (Spinoza narrowly escaped lynching). Still, the issues were bitterly fought, and widely understood as going to the heart of a Jewish worldview. Creator and created are utterly separate from each other, as is one individual self from another -- despite Buber's famous insistence (1965) on a subject-subject encounter between these separate adult selves (a kind of encounter, as we will try to show in later chapters, which is really not possible under the terms of the strict individualist self-model).

Practical Implications of the Paradigm

All this would be no more than academic semantics, the material for theses in sociology and cultural studies, were it not for the fact that these propositions and this paradigmatic worldview have *direct, important, and at times controlling consequences and implications for our lives and work with people*, and our conception and experience of ourselves. First of these consequences is the presumed contradiction, or inherent tension at least, between the *needs and desires of the individual,* and the *needs and desires of the community, relationship, or group* -- two presumably polar values which then tend to be pictured, in the way of linear polarities, in a zero-sum relationship with each other: the more you have of one, the less you get of the other; each exists at the cost of the other, by paradigmatic definition. The countervailing idea that these needs might be largely or ultimately congruent, or even mutually contextualizing, the kind of relationship that the Gestalt model calls "figure-ground," where each is dynamically necessary to the other -- much less the idea that the health and welfare of the community or relationship *belong to* the inherent primary needs of the individual, as much as do our needs to express our "animal drives" -- all this is advanced from time to time, or lamented as being missing, but can never really take hold, because of the way it violates the paradigm of our basic cultural assumptions.

This presumably inherent tension is then the very heart of

Freud's system, which is ultimately a speculative philosophy or ideology of human nature, for all that he presents it as objective science: the id drives are utterly narcissistic, solipsistic, predatory, and blind. If they are softened or corrected at all, it is only by the direct menace of the group (represented for efficiency as the internalized superego), or by the cooler head of the ego, which prefers to hold back strategically at times, the better to live and attack again another day. We know we're on paradigmatic ground here from the way these propositions are presented not as figures of attention or arguments to be demonstrated, but rather as the *given ground of the discussion*, the stable assumptions to which other observations and explanations may be compared and referred, and on which they are built. Thus again relationships, for Freud, belong to the world of "secondary process," the corrective and self-protective realm of strategy and instrumental thinking, and never to "primary process," the domain of the real (and predatory) self-urges and drives. The consequences of this view for intimacy, relational process, development, and health are direct and overwhelming, as will be discussed at more length in the chapters ahead, particularly in Parts III and IV.

A corollary to this same theme is then the idea that politics is the enemy of the individual person. "The best government is the least government," said Jefferson, in a classic precept of *liberal individualism* -- which makes sense only given the prior assumptions that 1) the completely unrestrained individual is by definition the highest good; and 2) the even deeper paradigmatic "truth" that that individual is by nature antisocial, or at best asocial, and thus in need of restraint. This is the "social contract" model of classic liberal political theory, with its deeply individualistic roots: we each give up a portion of our individual freedom -- however much that goes against our nature -- in exchange for some minimal conditions of safety and civility (the result of everybody else giving up that same portion of *their* "freedom" -- necessarily meaning here the freedom to exploit and destroy, at least in certain ways not sanctioned by the state).

Thus government and community are necessary evils which can only be justified as a minimal safeguard against our own bestial nature. The result is a political theory closely parallel to the map of the classical Freudian psyche: id is the unfettered individual in a state of nature, superego the reciprocal threat from other individuals and society, and ego the wise but precarious government, negotiating and compromising (somewhat desperately) between the two. When repression is too severe, in either the psyche or the state, revolution or breakdown is the result; enter the analyst, as moderate liberal reformer, who relieves the pent-up pressure and at the same time saves the system.

But this tradition of regarding the "state of nature," which is to say our individual human nature, as something to be feared hardly begins with Freud and the liberal tradition in whe West. It was Hobbes, writing some three centuries earlier, who held that human beings are ruled by fear, that fear leads to bestiality and the need for power, and thus no despotism is too severe not to be preferable to a state of nature (1974). Practical politics in this tradition -- the tradition of North Atlantic rim liberalism -- is then a matter of adjusting and debating the exact terms and boundaries of this trade-off, between individual freedom and collective safety and welfare, with contemporary "liberals" tending to favor more attention to the collective welfare -- under the justification that in the long run more individual freedom for more individuals will be the result (the "leveling the playing field" argument). But all the mainstream parties to this debate agree on the paradigmatic assumptions which lie behind the argument: the only ultimately valid good, the only value ultimately real, is *individual expression*; whereas the needs of any particular individual and the needs of the community or relational group are likely to be mutually opposed, by definition and by nature. The best point on the continuum between these poles is up for grabs, with various positions occupied by various parties in different eras (two centuries ago Anglo-American Liberalism favored less government, and the Conservatives more).

The reality of the poles, and the fact that political discourse takes place on a line between them, is assumed paradigmatically and thus is generally outside discussion.

Of course a countertradition has always existed, often voiced by poets and mystics (who at times have been persecuted for their heretical views). Thus the words of Jesus, "Inasmuch as you do it unto the least of these my brethren, you do it unto me;" or of his contemporary Hillel, "If I am for myself alone, what am I?" These words are echoed seventeen centuries or so later by Locke's contemporary John Donne, who wrote "No man is an island, complete unto himself" -- a concrete evocation of an alternative figure-ground or part-whole metaphor for the relationship of the individual to the collective. Indeed, we could make an argument that a central part of the function of the artist, and perhaps particularly the poet, is not just to "express him/her*self*," but specifically to give voice to *truths which lie outside the current paradigm*, and thus can't be rendered effectively in prose, which always belongs in some sense to the establishment way of looking at things. But this argument itself then rests on the kind of alternative view of the nature of the individual self and its relationship to the larger community of selves that we will be developing below, and then all through the chapters ahead.

There are other corollaries as well to the paradigm whose terms and history we're tracing here. As a basic belief system underlying philosophy itself, the paradigm tells us for instance where to look for the meaning of life, which is likewise found *deep within the individual self*. As long as God remains in the picture, that self is a self/soul, and thus the inner gaze leads through ourselves to the divine (again, the real relationship is between the individual self and its Creator, not between one individual and another). Later on, as we'll discuss in the next section, that same gaze leads us to the dead end of meaninglessness, which both Nietzsche and the Existentialists, as the ultimate exponents of atheistic individualism, will raise to the level of a noble truth.

Parallel to this is the paradigmatic belief that you can *never really know another person*. Again, being paradigmatic means that this is an article of faith, and not a matter of observation and experience (or disconfirmation or debate). In my experience I have to say that at times I do have a deep sense of knowing another person, even at times of knowing and sensing them somehow "better than they know themselves" (and of course vice versa). But this kind of knowing is held as less valid than inner certainty about oneself (however unreliable that "certainty" may have proved to be, at times, in our own lives and experience!); -- or if not less valid, then embroiled in a complex dynamic of power and authority relationships over who controls the relevant truth. Thus we don't like it when somebody else presumes the authority to "tell us our experience." We accuse them of "projecting," positioning ourselves in a right-wrong dynamic where one person's truth is in a zero-sum relationship with the truth of the other person (a topic and dynamic which will be taken up for exploration in Chapter Three). A different stance -- one where, say, each person is seen as having access to a validly different perspective on a common field which includes all of them, and each person is then making an interpretation based on that perspective -- is difficult to hold, because we don't easily regard ourselves as making self-interpretations in the first place. Our knowing of ourselves is supposedly "data," or a kind of direct knowledge: to think otherwise would be to relativize the sharp boundaries of individual self-definition.

When traditional religious authorities then want to challenge and invalidate certain individual thoughts, desires, and experiences, and still remain within the paradigm, they can do so only by positing some other entity -- the devil -- which has invaded the individual self/soul from the outside, or (in traditional Christianity) was passed down sexually, as the infection of original sin. Freud then tried to reverse these same terms, still without departing from the paradigmatic self-model: forbidden desires were relocated as originating within the true self, or even as the essence of that self nature (id now replacing original sin or the devil), while the harsh superego represented the voice of rigid authority, which now derives not from the self or from God but from outside pressure and control. Again, the individual is in inherent conflict with the community, and survives by compromising or betraying his/her true nature in favor of the demands of the group (a position we will find taken up as well by Freud's great modernist opponent, Jean-Paul Sartre).

What is not changed in this reformulation is the idea that he instinctual/individual drives are inherently antisocial and dangerous. Likewise the Freudian goal of sublimation, the delicate compromise of a socially acceptable outlet for drive energy, is not structurally different from the ancient Pauline dictum, "It is better to marry than burn:" "instinct" and "original sin" here are equivalent notions. Meanwhile the authoritarian, right-wrong structure of religious dogma is also preserved, with the result that classic Freudian session protocols of the early days of psychoanalysis sometimes read like debates or sermons, with the analyst urging a "resistant" patient to submit to a more correct view of him/herself, at the cost of felt, subjective reality. Thus the ultimate paradox of individualism itself: individuality is basic and irreducible; yet the *meaning* of individual experience is ultimately given by an outside authority (whether religious or "scientific.") This contradiction, which we already found in Plato at the dawn of our Western tradition, is an inescapable requirement at the heart of the paradigm, it turns out -- since as we shall see, if we begin constructing a self model based on *lived and felt experience*, the result (even when conditioned from the outset by the biases of our paradigmatic lens) will inevitably be far less rigidly individualistic than the ideology of the inherited paradigm itself.

Thus the paradigm contains some seeds at least of its own deconstruction -- seeds which we want to nourish and bring to life here. That is, a true phenomenology, the exploration of subjectivity which begins with the terms of experience as we live it, will always and unavoidably tend toward the *socially constructivist and developmental*, in the spirit of all the questions we are raising here -- because those are the terms of our real lives, which always begin with infancy and always unfold in and from relationship. Thus remaining as true as we can to the authority of individual *experience*, however we understand the boundaries of that term, will always be potentially subversive to the terms of the paradigm itself.

To summarize thus far, taken together the terms of our dominant cultural paradigm add up to an atomized universe, man (and woman) separated from woman (and man), mind from body, humanity from the natural world, art from science, and the individual soul or self from a larger spiritual whole. All thses are the kind of things which the later Gestalt writer and social critic Paul Goodman (1951) would term the "false dichotomies" of the modern worldview -- but which we are tracing here to their roots and branches running through the culture from its earliest coherent beginnings. This was and is a cold and fragmented universe, warmed (in theory anyway) only by the saving comfort of religion. If there were connections between those individual soul/atoms or among those separate worlds, which amount to discontinuous universes, then those connections could only lie, as we have said, in the mind of god. Today we live in the ongoing crisis and emergent deconstruction of that paradigm. The development and terms of that crisis, and where it leaves us now, will be the subjects of the next section, before going on in the next chapter to explore what kind of new understanding might be constructed out of the terms of our self-experience itself, in the opening left by the collapse of the old.

The Crisis of Individualism

Meanwhile, we left off our discussion of the evolution of the individualist tradition above with some of the assumptions and implications of the dominant Christian worldview. But the story doesn't end there. By the 16th Century the Christian synthesis had already yielded considerably to the (highly individualistic) terms of Renaissance humanism; by the 17th the Church was increasingly besieged, both by the Reformation and its accompanying wars and schisms and by the parallel growth of science, culminating in the new scientific paradigm of Newtonian physics and mechanics (which was earth-moving in a literal sense, as the very map of the solar system shifted to the Copernican view, but still without touching the deeper paradigm underlying it, of self and human nature). If anything, the individualism of the Reformation was even more extreme than the Catholic synthesis before, as private piety now tended to replace communal ritual and mystery rites, and the relationship between self and God was no longer thought to be in need of the social mediation of priests and sacraments.

In this atmosphere the older problem of reconciling soul or self and body began to seem considerably less urgent than the pressing need to reconcile the new science with the old religion -- and to do it still without stepping outside the given terms of individualism itself. The various attempts to accomplish this must surely have reached their logical limit in the philosophy of Gottfried Leibniz (1714), the brilliant mathematician who had invented the calculus at the same time as Newton, and who like Newton then went on to devote most of the rest of his life to this project of trying to hold an integrated worldview together, in the face of a seemingly ever-widening gap between a personal god and a mechanized universe. In order to save the reality and validity of both individual souls and Newtonian mechanics, Leibniz argued, the philosophy of nature is forced to assume that the entire universe is made up of fundamental, irreducible units which he called *monads*, meaning singular beings, each one complete and indivisible, and each of them a separate and utterly distinct soul/atom, independent in its nature from all the rest. Each monad or self/atom is a complete world unto itself -- the isolated individual self raised to its logical extreme. Moreover, each one is "windowless," aware only of itself, with no way of knowing anything of the nature of all the others.

The activity of the universe then is a matter of all these atoms bouncing off each other like billiard balls, all in accordance with the strict physical laws of Newtonian motion, from the beginning to the end of time (which is to say, as long as it pleases the whim and plan of the deity, who as Master of the Game created both the monads and the laws of physics themselves). Of course, this is really just the explicit assertion of the terms of original paradigm itself, now spelled out in its own defense. Still, on the logical level at any rate, the system is preserved: the universe can be completely physically deterministic, as the Newtonian model called for, and at the same time the presumption of the prior existence of separate souls created by God is saved -- at the cost, once more, of subjective experience itself. For Leibniz as for Descartes, and for that matter for Freud, ultimately, as well as to Skinner and the pure behaviorists of our own century, subjective experience again is not really real, but rather is a side-effect or "epiphenomenon," as we saw above. Thus to Leibniz we only *seem* to be in relationships with others, mediated and organized by meaning, intentionality, and mutual subjectivity. *Really* all that is only another kind of maya or illusion in this most individualistic of systems, the mind inventing a reality and then declaring it to be real, when in actuality the world of thoughts and feelings is an entirely private universe within us, parallel to the outer world in some way but utterly disconnected from it, neither of them influencing the other, while the whole thing is magically synchronized by the Great Clockmaker to be in perfect harmony with both physical effects and the reactions of other people. That is, to Leibniz the two worlds, inner and outer, which ultimately have nothing to do with each other, still work in magic parallel by the divine hand of God. (Jung would later posit something quite similar [1964]). Just as to Freud and Skinner two centuries and more later, to Leibniz our experience of this world and of other people is not what it seems, and not to be relied on as a key to self-understanding. In all these widely divergent systems alike, we must not think of our experience as actually affecting that of another person (or even of ourselves!) -- however much that seems to be the case -- because to do so will begin to challenge and undermine the basic terms of the individualistic paradigm itself.

To be sure, there is no free will or meaningful intentionality left in the picture of the self drawn by Leibniz, but where for Freud, as for most atheistic determinists, these were deeply pessimistic realities, here we have a complete determinism combined with a sort of relentless optimism. This Leibniz achieves just by keeping God in the picture -- albeit in a somewhat more remote position than before, since God no longer intervenes actively and personally in our day-to-day lives. Inasmuch as God made the whole plan and set this somewhat bizarre game of isolated souls in motion for reasons of His (as Leibniz certainly would have said) own, it follows that whatever happens is for the best, by definition. This is then the "best of all possible worlds" (Leibniz, 1714) -- the seemingly mindless optimism satirized by Voltaire in his popular novel of the times, *Candide* (Leibniz was himself the model for the hapless Dr. Pangloss, or "Everything-is-dandy," who is Candide's cheery tutor and mentor in the book through one horrible disaster after another).

But foolishly optimistic or not, the basic terms of this account of self and self-experience -- arbitrarily created, outside question in its uniqueness and boundedness from other selves and the world, and ultimately irrelevant to behavior and action -- were deeply in harmony with the cultural paradigm we have been tracing here, and in fact became the basis of the dominant scientific view of subjectivity right up to and including the present day, even after the removal of the deity from the picture as even a remote First Cause. Even today the Western self-model is sometimes referred to as "monadic," meaning that the individually separate self is irreducibly given that way by nature. The reference is to Leibniz, whose fanciful-sounding worldview may be easy to satirize (much as Heidegger's "Dasein" or pure being would be later on), but who nevertheless gave us the sharp image and explicit language of the self that still dominate the culture today.

The optimism of Leibniz's synthesis, however, was not to prove nearly so durable as the rest of his positions, which were the ultimate codification of the premises of the separate, individualistic self. This is of course because the "whatever is, is right" conclusions he comes to depend on positing a benificent Creator-God. With the rise of Enlightenment scepticism and then Nineteenth Century atheism, that position itself was becoming shaky. With the growth of science, it seemed that the only logical need for God to remain in the picture at all was as that very remote First Cause, to explain how we got here in the particular shape and form we are in. Evolutionary notions were already current, to be sure, but as explanatory systems they were still weak: we do resemble monkeys, and it's not hard to imagine them as primitive forms of ourselves (or perhaps degenerate souls who were punished or just spontaneously devolved out of their own sheer wickedness). But how would you get from one to the other, if not by a prior intervention, blueprint, or additional act by the Creator? Darwin's theory of natural selection seemed to fill that gap in a satisfying way, and science (meaning biology now, not just mechanics) for the first time became more philosophically respectable, in an ultimate sense, than religion, since the the last unanswerable argument of the religious objectors seemed to have been neatly taken care of. To be sure, you were still free to imagine an original Creator if you liked, who long, long ago set biology and chemistry themselves in motion, and then you could add an immortal soul to the given self if it pleased or comforted you to do so. But the position of that original Creator was no longer right at the beginning of historical time -- just a bit before, say, the beloved Greeks. On the contrary, it was now unimaginably distant, seemingly long before life or time itself; and the suspicion had to cling that the evocation itself was an act of weakness, mostly on the part of women or certain men who were not unblinking rationalists or brave action types, and who just couldn't weather the harsh chill of the vigorous new winds of scientific truth.

For this was a harsh picture indeed. Remember that as long as we assume an absolute individualism as the bedrock of reality, the only connections, the only thing that can possibly weave these separate threads into a common tapestry for us all to belong to and feel a part of, is the Creator Himself (sic). Take away the deity altogether, and what you are left with is the cold robotic world of 17th and 18th Century physics -- or the unforgivingly competitive biological jungle of 19th Century social Darwinism,[3] every man (sic) for himself and the survival of the fittest. At the same time, this is the heyday of 19th Century European imperialism, which sought and claimed to find justification in Darwin's doctrines in the form of popular ideology -- as it is the world of Nietzsche, who raised individual

[3] It is only fair to note here that the Social Darwinists themselves, much led by Darwin's cousin and follower, the eugenicist Sir Francis Galton, represented a considerable distortion of Darwin's theory. Darwin himself emphasized the competition among *species*, for ecological niches, not just among individuals. This competition, to be sure, would select certain individual contributions to the species gene pool over others, which is the foundation for modern sociobiology. Still, within one species, and particularly the human one, the emphasis was at least as much on social communication and cooperation, which were presumed to be encoded in some way genetically to favor the survival of the species as a whole. Thus Darwin devoted a major book, *The Expression of the Emotions* (1873), to the exploration of the proposition that our emotional lives and social expression are crucial parts of species as well as individual survival characteristics. The assumptions of this book in turn became the foundations for the 20th Century sub-discipline of affect theory (see for example Tomkins, 1960).

self-assertion and dominance to a whole new ideal of nobility, reversing conventional moral values by insisting that strength itself was the only criterion for judging actions or moral systems, and therefore sheer energy and aggression themselves justify any destruction that might be caused in their expression[4]. For that matter this Darwinian jungle is the world of Freud, who took up Nietzsche's privileging of the unconscious over the conscious, and of the individual over the social and relational, as well as his debunking of religion and social convention as anxiety defenses, all of them the Nietzschean cornerstones of Freud's system. In our own century Nietzsche's "perspectivalism," his insistence that all systems of knowledge are really ideologies which serve some power interests, would then become the creative foundation of the now-dominant post-modern schools which are loosely grouped under the heading of "deconstructionism" -- still without ever turning that powerful deconstructive lens on the most fundamental cornerstone of its own most basic ideology, which is the *assumption of radical individuality itself.* Once again, the most powerful analytic tools of the dominant paradigm -- reductionist analysis and deconstructive or "geneological" critique (which is to say, looking at a proposition in terms of its history and origins, as we have been doing here) -- have generally proven inadequate

[4] Despite the protests of Nietzsche's partisans down through the years, it is quite hard to see how the Nietzschean doctrine of power for its own sake, which is nothing more than the ultimate expressin of the individualist ethos, is meaningfully different from the worldview and self-justification of the Nazis, which were finally that strength and force of will were themselves the the highest values, completely apart from how and where that force is applied. Both celebrate the "triumph of the will," apart from any content values; and both rest on the unacknowledged paradigmatic assumption that the essence of that will is the drive for individual expression and dominance. To be sure, Nietzsche is full of contradictions, and no doubt would have abhorred and rejected the Nazis, who took up his doctrines so enthusiastically and applied them so literally. Still, his philosophy, and indeed the individualist paradigm of which it is the ultimate logical expression, offer little or no challenge to the Nazi program. If the individual is the ultimate reality and the highest value, then the choice of how that self-expression is targeted has to be ultimately arbitrary.

to call into question the most basic terms of that paradigm itself.

Meanwhile another of the great philosophical systems of this past century likewise owes its fundamental impulse to Nietzsche, and is likewise marked by his radical and unrelieved post-Darwinian individualism. This is of course the movement we know as Existentialism, which has roots in Kierkegaard and a tradition of introspectionism, as well as Husserl's phenomenology -- but even more in Nietzsche's emphasis on the lone heroic individual, brave in facing hard truths, who is the new source of meaning and values (an image which also directly inspired Freud). Philosophically, this is the challenge of the Nietzschean superman, unflinching in facing the absurdity of existence, disdaining the comforting fictions of religion and the transpersonal, always unafraid to create his own meaning and to own and live out his own truth, however harsh and unattractive in conventional terms.[5]

This challenge was taken up by Jean-Paul Sartre, among others, who undertook to extend and revise Heidegger's analysis of "being," which we touched on briefly above, but very much taking it in the direction of the personal responsibility and political integrity so lacking in Heidegger's own account, and in his life (Heidegger, as is well known, was himself a Nazi party member and led the expulsion of his own mentor, the elderly Jewish phenomenologist Husserl, from the University of Heidelberg). In the process, Sartre gives us the last and perhaps the best illustration we will find here of the way our inherited paradigm of self puts blinders on our inquiry about that self, and about the terms of human existence. Because of this, it is worth taking a moment here to examine what Sartre includes in his own analysis of being -- and what he leaves out.

This expression and these blinders we find in Sartre's classic existentialist text *Being and Nothingness* (1944), in which he describes the possible categories or dimensions of "being," which we might also call *aspects or modes of self*, ways of "being there" (to take again Heidegger's term). These he gives as "being *in* itself," "being *for* itself," and "being for others." The first, *being in itself*, refers to the state of "pure being" Heidegger posited (and Koszinzki mocked): the given conditions of existence "in itself," or "just being here," as Sartre saw them at any rate, *before* we undertake any activity, which always then involves mobilizing our being for some purpose or goal -- very much like the imaginary "pure individual," prior to any relational context. "Existence precedes essence," according to the famous Sartrean dictum which gave the movement its name-- meaning that we should look at our being in its own terms, as we hope to do here, without prior values and assumptions about that existence such as religion and ideology provide, which prejudge the inquiry. (To be sure, to Heidegger this state may preexist individuality as well, and thus may seem offer some kind of theoretical connection in a universe of individuals without gods -- and indeed some commentators have accused Heidegger of sneaking god back into the picture under the name "Being," while others have remarked on how the emptiness of the concept seemed to offer a natural space for his shameful embrace of Nazism. At the same time, from the more pragmatic or experiential point of view we want to develop here, we may well question whether this abstract term has any referent at all, since we may be hard put to locate the state of "pure being" in experience: even where we do find something like it, as in meditation, a kind of existence before or beyond individuality, the state is more often characterized as one of "non-being" or at least non-individuality).

The next term, "being *for* itself," is more real-feeling, in the sense of being close to our felt sense of ourselves and our lives. The word "for" here implies purpose and direction, either what the existentialists sometimes called "becoming," or in more everyday terms just "doing." This is the state we are in most or all the time, when we are engaged in the ordinary life processes of managing, arriving, avoiding, maximizing this, minimizing that, and generally trying to organize the field of experience in the service of survival, growth, satisfaction of desires and goals (and perhaps even that elusive wider goal we call *living well*, which we already met in Plato as the "good life"). Most of psychology and psychotherapy, and in particular the rich tradtion of Gestalt psychology and psychotherapy which we will be drawing on below and in the chapters ahead for a new take on some of these old questions, is located in this domain, which we associate with *organizing our worlds*, our subjective fields of experience -- the ongoing process experience of living, working, managing and mobilizing things (and fending off and demobilizing others), and above all *relating to other people*.

Curiously though, still remaining within the terms of Sartre's system, we don't yet encounter any other people at all in this realm, "being for itself." This is the world of desires, to be sure -- but of *my* desires, *my* goals, without reference to yours, or your experience and reality (Sartre set himself up as the major philosophical antagonist to Freud, yet here the resonances between them seem deeper than any differences they may show over smaller matters like the analysis of motivational process). The world of other people only shows up in the next category of being, "being for others," which turns out to be all those areas of life where I have to *give up* my own desire, impulse, and judgment (which were all found back in "being for itself," meaning for *my*self), and defer to those of others -- always envisioned here as a kind of "selling out," a compromise of my integrity and authenticity. For Sartre, this is not a realm of compassion or responsibility for others, but rather one of *abrogation of self-responsibility*, a failure to be true to oneself. Again, self and relationship, or self and other selves, are posited as lying at opposite poles of a linear continuum, in a zero-sum relationship to one another: the more I have one, the less I get of the other.

Taking this analysis of our lives and the conditions of self as a whole, what we then have is the interplay of two dimensions or criteria here -- *being vs doing*, and *self vs other*. If we then schematize the model into a visual array, using this two-way sort, as in Figure 1 below, then the individualist biases or ideology hidden in this "essence-free" analysis come to light in a curious way:

	self	other
being	"being in itself:" the domain of"pure being," or just "existence"	
becoming	"being for itself:" the domain of doing things, reaching my goals, satisfying myself through my actions, being true to my own desires	"being for others:" what happens when I give up my goals and yield to the desires of others; the domain of group-think or selling out

fig 1: Sartre's model of being and becoming, self and other

What emerges from making the model visual in this way is that in its own terms, being/becoming and self/other, there is a *missing term*, an empty quadrant in what is structurally a four-way window, whose absence is not so immediately obvious as long as we stay in a linear/sequential, or purely verbal mode of analysis. That quadrant, were it to be filled, would hold something we would then have to call "*being in others*," a being-with or inherent belongingness of one self with another, even the possible interpenetration of self-experiences, which would likewise precede and underlie action "for" others, or on behalf of their goals (that place where the self always betrays itself, to Sartre) -- just as "being in itself" is part of our nature, and precedes "being for itself," at least in this model. That is, not everything we do with or for others would be looked on so suspiciously, even phobically as it is here, as something inherently posing a threat to the self or to our own integrity. (And note too the implicit privileging here of the linear/verbal mode over the visual/holistic).

In other words, for all the Existentialists' insistence that "existence precedes essence," what we have in the top half of the array *is* "essence" (or "essentialism," as it is fashionable to say today, meaning that certain groups, certain "races" or ethnicities [or genders or "orientations"] inherently are thought to have certain predetermined qualities, just by virtue of their group membership). In this case, the group is all human individuals; and the essentialism is that of the individualist paradigm itself, which asserts this inherent threat or tension by definition, between the integrity of the separate individual and the demands of the larger community. This is the hidden or out-of-awareness meaning of the Sartrean analysis, brought out by making the model visual in this way.

Thus we can better say, this missing term, "being *in* others," is what the empty quadrant *would* hold logically, in the system's own terms -- *if such a thing were imaginable to Sartre and his readers*. That is, if only we could imagine or assume that one aspect or pole of our existent self *is* this interpenetration or inherent identity with the selves of others (complementing or corresponding to the other given pole of the model, which is individuality). But that's just the point -- the quadrant is empty because to Sartre, as to his readers and to the dominant voices of three thousand years in the West behind him, the point is *not* imaginable. We do *not* live in and through and with each other, in the dominant paradigm -- or if we do, it is only in a derivative, instrumental way (ie, the lower right quadrant of the array), and never in as fundamental and real a sense as the way we live in and as our separate selves. It is not imaginable because the *frame* of imagination, the paradigm, doesn't allow for it. Not that we never feel such things. We certainly do feel them, often and often intensely; but they are "just feelings," illusory, not real. That's the premise of the whole system, as well as the seemingly logical conclusion that was actually predetermined by the terms of the paradigm itself.

The point for our discussion here is not to say that Sartre is now "wrong," just because if we map him in a certain way the picture looks incomplete (though we will argue here that he is far from our felt reality, in discounting and leaving out of consideration real experiences and dimensions of living self-process). Nor is it any surprise, writing as he was under Nazi occupation (and under the disturbing influence of a distant mentor who was himself a Nazi), that Sartre himself should have regarded the whole arena of ceding one's own judgment to the standards and truths of other people with deep suspicion, or should have found the lower right quadrant dangerously problematic, preferring to take refuge in the lower left -- perhaps in the conviction that no one individual, no matter how self-centered or Nietzschean, could ever commit as much dangerous evil alone as a mass of people in concert, each of whom had given up "thinking for himself" in exchange for the seductive pleasures of belonging to the group. All that is at least arguable, and understandable in historical context. Rather, what is more important for us here is that to Sartre, *the upper right quadrant doesn't seem missing at all*, in a system which after all was of his own devising. Far from condemning experiences which might fall here -- experiences which we might call "intersubjective" or even "transpersonal," and which range for many or most of us from spiritual states to sexual merging to gazing at one's children or beloved or dear friends, to various other kinds of trans-individual exhaltation or self-boundary relaxation on the field of sports or battle or just quietly in contemplation or elsewhere -- Sartre doesn't appear to recognize them as real at all, or to consider them as calling for any comment. As with Plato, to bring the discussion here full circle, the questions that interest us most and perhaps seem most urgent to us today -- questions of how our own individuality relates to and belongs to the whole field of other selves -- just don't seem to come up.

The neurologist Oliver Sacks (1990) writes of a type of blind spot or "scotoma" associated with damage or experimental deadening of certain spots in the visual cortex, which results in a gap or scotoma in the visual field -- but without the subject's being aware of anything's being missing. That is, if your visual field extends itself in about a 170 degree sweep from left to right in front of you, then an object transversing this field in that same direction may just disappear at, say, 90 degrees (depending on the exact location of the lesion) and reappear at, say, 135 degrees -- but without your being aware of any break in the field itself, or any "join" between the two sides of the gap. The part of the field that just isn't there to you, phenomenologically, doesn't "feel like" it's missing -- even though the subject may know well that it is, and be able to prove it to herself by rotating the head, which has the effect of moving the scotoma around, so that all kinds of things keep popping out of the picture and then popping back in again, still without any "split screen" line in the seamless field of vision. Sartre exemplifies a "thought scotoma" of this kind on the question of the individual self, as does the Western tradition in general -- and as do we all, in various places that by definition it takes a carefully structured intervention, and the support of an experiential dialogue, to make us aware of at all.

If we believe Thomas Kuhn on the operational dynamics of paradigms, this kind of impasse and this scotoma should not surprise us. A given lens is not necessarily completely unable to see itself, but the exercise is difficult at best, and probably requires the use of other lenses or mirrors, to support other perspectives. In the sections of the book to come we will rely very much on other, less purely verbal approaches (yet still verbally mediated and reported, of course) to get a fresh take on the questions of self, self-process, experience and relationship, always seeking to find and exploit the terms of feeling and behavior, how we actually organize to approach the challenges of living, to power a fresh perspective and energize the deconstructive process.

Meanwhile, in the following chapter, we will stop to take a look at the alternative model we spoke of before, growing out of the Gestalt psychology movement, and like that movement in general, capable of generating and organizing a radically fresh approach to the question of human behavior, experience, and the self.

Chapter Two: Looking for an Alternative Paradigm

But suppose we were to begin our exploration of self in a different place, and pitch the discussion on somewhat different grounds. In place of looking for some "thing" we can identify or define as "self" -- which after all means accepting the extreme separate-self paradigm we have said from the beginning we want to question or deconstruct, -- suppose we begin with what self and self-experience are *like*, the processes that go along with and make up our experience of being selves in the world, and see what kind of understanding of self we can construct or arrive at, and what kind of language can then best serve us as we live out that self-process and self-experience, possibly in a new way. As we saw in the previous chapter, the legacy of the individualist paradigm runs through our culture and our language so deeply and pervasively that any purely abstract discussion about human nature and "the" human self is almost bound to end up in the same place it started -- missing important parts and dimensions of our own experience in the process. Therefore let us start with that experience itself, in process terms, as we live it and feel it -- again with the idea of creating more "wiggle room" or play in the system for a new kind of understanding, even as we use the limited tools of a language already shaped and colored by that paradigm and that system.

This kind of approach is what is called "phenomenological," meaning that we start with the processes or phenomena of life and awareness, the perceived events and felt actions of our lives *as we perceive and experience them*, and then look out from that experience to explore who we are, and what these things have to tell us about our separateness and/or connectness with the world and other selves. As we do this, it is important to note that this way of approaching "truth," and this valuing of felt experience, violates and contasts sharply with much of the Western tradition we inherit, which has tended to insist that feelings and subjective process were the last places we should look, to build any useful and reliable understanding of ourselves and our nature. To Plato, as we have seen, feelings and even "objective" sense impressions were too variable, too ephemeral to serve as the basis for organizing anything important: this was the whole reason for making up another realm, of higher truth and authority. To the writers of the Christian synthesis, building on this Greek split between ordinary experience and the Ideal, anything that rested so squarely on *embodiment and desire*, as a phenomenological approach must do, was immediately suspect at best, if not actively evil. And then to Freud, the classical behaviorists, and other writers of the materialist tradition, consciousness itself was deceptive, and again in need of an outside explanatory system to tell us which of the experiences we think we're having are "real," and which are just self-comforting fictions. All these widely varying and contrasting models alike, we have been arguing, flow from and then support the basic individualist paradigm, which posits a separate, isolated self, created or biologically given and real *before* self-experience, relationship and development themselves.

Today, in place of the implicit creationism of our inherited model, we live in a post-Darwinian world that assumes that our nature and our capacities have evolved in interactive response to natural conditions and context, and serve problem-solving and survival needs in the "real" world of experience and learning. Along with that shift goes a new interest, all through this past century, in the active, creative role of the perceiving, experiencing subject in understanding and dealing with that world and those problems of living. And yet self-theory, our concept and our models of ourselves and others, has not accomodated to these transformations in any basic, paradigmatic way. Thus it is to these conditions and processes of awareness and action-in-the-world that we need to turn now, current cognitive theory and brain/mind research, *how* we experience our world and how our own awareness and self-awareness are constructed, to create and explore the terms and the nature of a self that has evolved out of a natural history and development, and out of the experiential field itself.

Our first step in a new approach is to begin with *awareness itself*, the same questions of perception and knowledge that intrigued Plato -- but in their own terms now, without all the prior assumptions about who it is who is "having" this awareness -- which we can then try to derive or define as we go along, out of those terms. What are these processes actually *like* for us as we live them, how do they work, and ultimately what they are *for*, in a living Darwinian or sociobiological sense? To be sure, this is what the Existentialists wanted to do: to consider "existence" without so many inherited givens about "essence," and then work out the terms and meaning of living from there. But as we have seen, they too were hobbled by hidden cultural assumptions about the self they meant to be analyzing and redefining. Here we want to go much further than they could with their quest for a self defined in its own terms, by drawing on what we now know about the nature and processes of awareness and self-experience themselves -- those processes which create us, define us, and enable us to connect with a world of other selves.

The Structure of Awareness

Surely there is nothing more astonishing, in this staggeringly complex and variegated universe, than all those functions and processes we know as "awareness" itself -- all that remarkable equipment and elaborately integrated interplay, partly inborn and then developed, for *apprehending* the world, resolving what we might well think would be an overwhelming level of bombardment with stimuli at every moment, into some kind of coherence and workability -- all of which must serve in some way to enable us to *deal with* our world, or else plainly we wouldn't be here now, considering these questions and their implications. What then is this awareness? how does it work, and what are its component processes? These are enormous questions, but for our purposes here certain features, particular aspects of awareness processes stand out, as directly related to our exploration of self. Our goal, as all through this extended discussion, is to point at least toward a model *and a felt sense* of this elusive notion, "self," which is not entirely biased from the start by a prior cultural assumption that each self is its own created archetype (Plato), or self-contained monad (Leibniz), or isolated little universe of drives separated by nature from every other self (Nietzsche and Freud), and therfore the connections and relational feelings we experience must only be illusory, if not imposed on us from some other, divine realm.

First of all there is the most fundamental and salient general feature of our awareness experience, quite remarkable when you think about it, which is that the world we are aware of seems to come to us *already organized*, "prepackaged" as it were, into the objects and events and patterns and sequences we know and see, and then take up and interact with as our given, known world. That is, the world of our experience, very much including "internal experience," is a world characterized by *articulation and boundaries*, and not at all a field of "booming buzzing confusion," as James put it (1983). Rather, the world as we know it is one of things, identities, and those meaningfully linked sequences we take up and use as "cause and effect," -- all of which is in some way the very essence of our predictive, problem-solving activity in living. Indeed, despite our linguistic distinctions between "just sensing," or "pure awareness," on the one hand, and proactive or creative behavior on the other, it is hard to know just what we would mean by "awareness" at all, without some element of selection and structuring of what we are "aware of." How does this happen, and how do we make use of it in "real life?"

As we have seen, Plato had one kind of answer to account for this question -- the imagining of another world of Ideal Forms, which exist both in some Ideal realm and in our own minds, -- a solution which had the tidy virtue of explaining both how the world got that way, and at the same time how it is that we can know it as it "really is." This kind of explanation doesn't satisfy us today, basically for two reasons which are in a sense opposites. One is the success of *scientific materialism*, which would seem to constitute a clear argument that the "things" and unseen forces of this world are real after all, since we can manipulate them to such powerful technological effect; and the other is an *attitude of relativism* about how we make meaning of things, growing out of our exposure to different cultures, ethnic and religious subcultures, gender or sexual orientation identities, and family and personality styles, all with somewhat different worldviews and values, none of which may strike us as either completely "right" or completely "wrong." In a social field of such powerfully diverse voices as the field we live in today, it is more and more difficult for most of us to uphold the old cultural assumption that meaning systems themselves are "given in the data," rather than created by individuals and groups.

These two viewpoints -- "positivist" materialism and deep cultural relativism -- don't sit very well together (a characteristic of periods of paradigmatic decline, where people oscillate among several basic views in rapid alternation), but we handle this by saying that these domains, the physical world and the social world, are *different kinds of things*, so different *kinds* of truth apply. Thus we all become uncertain constructivists -- unsure where the boundaries are of these different kinds of "truths;" and uncertain because on the one hand a wide range of different worldviews, different cultural or personal constructions may strike us as equally plausible, given "where you're coming from;"

while on the other hand our inherited tradition of individualism, with all the hidden authoritarian implications of that tradition discussed in the previous chapter, doesn't seem to offer us any ready language for talking about *how* we go about constructing these meaning systems, what they serve, or where we might find any useful criteria for comparing one of them with another.

To begin to understand these constructive awareness processes, and point the way at least toward an approach for comparing and evaluating different meaning systems, we will draw heavily here on the results of a century of research and model-building in the field of *Gestalt psychology* -- a body of work, as we said in the Preface, which has been so radically transformative to cognitive, affective, perceptual, and self-organizational models, and so completely integrated into the field of psychology as a whole, that it is no exaggeration to say that there really is no psychology today which is not fundamentally Gestalt in nature, while Gestalt psychology itself scarcely exists anymore as a distinguishable sub-discipline of cognitive/affective and brain/mind research, so completely has it been absorbed and integrated into cognitive/affective psychology and brain/mind research as a whole. Meanwhile, the derivative tradition of Gestalt therapy, now a half-century old, which has applied these insights to the experiential processes and issues that concern us here, has had much less direct impact on the fields of psychotherapy, self theory, and developmental and related models, which have generally lagged behind psychology itself in integrating cognitive/affective brain/mind research into the field (no doubt because psychotherapy, as the branch of applied psychology closest to philosophy and the study of values, has remained the most mired in the old philosophical heritage of individualism).

By drawing on both those related traditions and bodies of research here, we aim to ground our phenomenological exploration of self on a foundation of modern and post-modern cognitive/affective theory and research findings, and at the same time to tie it to the kind of therapeutic work which is closer to lived experience, and less constrained by individualist assumptions, than some mainstream therapeutic models (and the self models they both grow out of and give rise to).

What does the tradition of Gestalt psychology have to offer to our exploration of self and awareness here? The fundamental problem the early Gestaltists took up was this very question of the *organization of experience*: how *does* the perceiving subject make sense of the experiential field, so that what we see and know is a coherent whole picture, and not just a flood of discrete stimuli? The old positivist answer of the Associationist school in the 19th Century, which tried to stick to "objective empirical data" free of imaginary or "ideal" assumptions, rested on the idea of just stringing all the sensory stimuli together till they somehow "add up," by a process of "association," to what we see and know and retain. But this only seemed to beg the question, which is *how* do we add them together, synthetically and in an organized way, to arrive at the *organized wholes* we see and know, which are more than just a series of unrelated parts? The answer proposed by the early Gestaltists was that the fundamental, relevant unit of perception *is a significant, meaningful whole*, and not a discrete individual stimuli themselves at all, most of which are ignored, discarded, distorted to fit, or otherwise screened out. That is, we register and take in *whole forms*, which the Gestaltists sometimes called "figures," sometimes "gestalts," and not just a series of details -- much as Plato said we did, in a sense, Only here instead of accounting for this by imagining Ideal Forms behind the ordinary ones we see and recognize, the Gestaltists set out to explore in the lab just how our perceptive apparatus manages to accomplish this (as for instance by "selective inattention," by being "prewired" to attend more to edges and sharp differences in the field than to low-contrast areas, by blurring or discarding what doesn't fit, completing or filling in what's missing, and generally interacting with and in the experiential field, to produce the "best available gestalt," and so on -- all of these being experimental findings of early Gestalt research (for review and discussion of this kind of work, together with its problems and implications, see Wheeler, 1991, especially Chapter One).

Perception, that is, is not just "reception" at all, but *is always an active process*, a constructive interaction between the unified properties of the environment ("affordances," as the later Gestaltist James Gibson would call them [1969]), -- and our own active, constructive process of resolving incomplete, partial, ambiguous, overwhelming, and/or unuseful field energy "inputs" into *meaningful wholes* that we can register, retain, and then *manipulate and use*. And by "meaningful" here we mean, again, not the "ultimate reality" that both Plato and the contrary Western tradition of materialism alike both insist on, but rather *pragmatic reality*, a picture that is recognizable and usable -- which always and necessarily means *relating the perceived form or gestalt in some way to a wider context of purpose and meaning* -- i.e., resolving or referencing a larger whole, which contextualizes the "figure" at hand (because otherwise we wouldn't know what to do with it). Thus it is that the gestalt process of perception and meaning is open-ended by nature, not discretely episodic, one "thing" after another, as both the Platonic and materialist models would imply. That is again, we are "wired" to keep on doing this resolving process continuously, to keep on finding, forming, and resolving wholes, as each previous "whole" or gestalt becomes potentially an integral part of some larger whole, or at times broken down into significant component wholes, in the widest field of perception or experience that seems relevant and important to us at the moment.

The organized whole picture or gestalt is the relevant unit of our experiential process, and *our role in that process is active, selective, and constructively engaged*. Whenever that natural organizing process is thwarted or too ambiguous -- i.e., when wholes are chronically broken or not available, as in perceptions that are borderline recognitions, ambiguous, contradictory, or just too strange for us to make meaning of them in this sense, of fitting them into a wider scheme -- then our nature is to stop, puzzle, show signs of trouble, and invest *more* perceptual energy into the situation, until we can resolve it in some satisfying way.

At that moment we become aware of our own perceptual process -- aware, that is, of awareness itself, as a constructive or creative act. Or as Gestaltist Kurt Lewin (1926) put this same idea, the act of perception and the problem-solving process are not essentially different: perception is not a passive state, but is itself a kind of active problem to be solved. Thus we are drawn by nature to the incomplete gestalt, the unfinished problem, the anomalous or contradictory picture. And the more important the case, as when we are recognizing and assessing some possible menace or attractive possibility, the more energy we invest in that "incomplete gestalt," until we can achieve that resolution and take action or move on. If the problem is important, and we can't resolve it meaningfully, some of our active perceptual energy may remain chronically invested there, constituting a long-term or habitual drain on the energy and attention we have available for other perceptual tasks and the business of living, in the widest sense -- an insight which lies at the heart of the derivative application of this work to issues of life adjustment and creativity in the theory and methods of the Gestalt therapy movement, which will be discussed in the chapters ahead.

Implications of the Constructivist View of Self

This fundamental insight, which amounts to a radical shift in how we conceive the "person in psychology" in Allport's (1968) phrase, then has a number of corollaries and consequences which bear on our exploration here, of self and self-experience:

1) The first of these insights is the realization that the traditional absolute distinction in much of Western culture,

between "objective data" or "reality," on the one hand, and "interpretation" or the meaning of those "facts," on the other, just doesn't hold -- or at least, doesn't hold in any traditional, absolute way. To be sure, we may sit back and reflect on the "wider meaning" or best interpretation of some fact or finding -- which is the ongoing gestalt-making process of fitting that datum into larger and increasingly more inclusive whole pictures. But -- and it's a major "but" -- *large doses of interpretation and contextualization were built into our perception of that "fact" in the first place*. This follows from the very terms of our given perceptual nature: we simply *can't perceive anything* without identifying it or locating it in a context or giving it at least some provisional, implicit wider meaning in this sense. We don't *first* perceive and *then* interpret. Rather, *perception is an interpretive, constructive act*, an active process of synthesis out of the flow of sensory stimuli "coming at us" -- but already selected, screened, edited and *organized into* the the world we know, which is at a level removed from the "world as it is," in some sheer physical sense. The two acts, receiving and resolving, "seeing" and "interpreting," occur together, in the same perceptual act and moment.

That "world as it is," as Kant pointed out two centuries ago (1781), is ultimately unknowable to us: all we have to work with are the constructions of our own bodymind -- themselves of course constrained in wome way by environmental conditions and consequences, which will act to limit not our possible constructions, but rather the *viability* of those constructions, in an ultimately evolutionary sense. It is this that makes constructivism in general, and Gestalt in particular, a model of *evolutionary psychology*. In the end it is this fact -- that certain kinds of constructive process will be favored, and others disfavored, by selective evolutionary pressure -- that accounts for why we are "wired" in the gestalt-making, problem-solving way that we are. But that still does not mean that we know that "real world" in the objective, direct, "purely empirical" way that the individualist/

dualist paradigm of our cultural tradition insists we do. All we have are our interpretative pictures, themselves negotiated socially and evolving both culturally and ultimately physically, which are themselves creative hypotheses or "fictions" which we use to apprehend/interpret, evaluate, and hopefully manage our worlds.

This point is so important to everything that follows -- and so often misunderstood as we try to make the shift to an evolutionary psychology perspective -- that we will repeat it here: every perception is in a real sense a *hypothesis*, a *trial* organization of data (literally, "givens"). We're "wired" to make this kind of estimation, and to integrate it into an ever wider, ever more complex and coherent picture of the world: this is our gestalt nature. But there is no bedrock of absolute, clear "givens" that *are* the objective data of experience, ultimately, behind or beneath our interpretive process. We never get there. To be sure, as Kant argued long ago, we may assume there is a "real world out there," consisting in some way of the energy inputs that we are building our experience out of. But we can never actually know this "real world" -- again, other than inferentially. Again, we can reasonably suppose that the "real world" in some way constrains or limits and informs our *range* of viable interpretations, at least in an evolutionary sense. I have learned, based on my prewiring together with cultural experience, to interpret the roadway of life, literally and figuratively, in certain ways -- incuding the notion that certain collections of visual stimuli constitute an impending obstacle that I have to turn or stop so as to avoid. And if I don't learn and resolve meaning in this way, then no doubt I'll tend to drop out of the gene pool, in favor of others who can manage that kind of situation more viably. Thus in an evolutionary sense, at least, not all interpretations of reality are equal, and we may even go on to infer features of the kinds of pictures that are going to work better or worse, and use all kinds of secondary tests and instruments and social consensus processes to support or cast doubt on this or that subjective picture, this or that hypothesis (again, we can think of this pattern literally or figuratively, as a metaphor for a wide range of environmental adjustment moves and problems). "Reality" then in some sense tests or limits our inferences and perceptual interpretations. But those inferences or perceptions remain what they are, inferences or hypothetical interpretations, always potentially subject to revision -- and always shaped in some way, as we have already seen, by cultural assumptions and processes, starting with the level of basic paradigmatic assumptions we will be referencing and investigating all through these chapters.

This insight about our inevitably active role in seeing and knowing anything, which is the crux of the Gestalt model and movement in psychology, is then itself at the heart of all the various movements in psychology, psychotherapy, and philosophy (and increasingly, modern and post-modern physics) which go under the general heading of Constructivism -- the idea that we *construct* the reality we know, which by definition includes the idea that there could be *other* realities, other ways of construing and knowing the "same events" (remembering that "events" themselves, in the usual sense of happenings as we know and identify them, are also constructs or interpretations, a way of putting boundaries on the flux and flow of stimuli). And Constructivism in turn contains and underlies the somewhat diverse panoply of related perspectives known as "Deconstructivism," or "Deconstructionism," -- which is essentially the Constructivist position about reality, together with the investigation of *the social conditions of power and influence that lead to this or that particular view gaining or losing in currency and dominance.*

Taken together, these various movements of Constructivism and Deconstructionism then amount to the even wider collection of views and tendencies we now call (for want of a better term) "post-modern," meaning the period we are in now, a time when we have lost faith in the certainties of the last few centuries of modernism -- including pure scientific materialism, the ultimate reliability of "objective" data, the neutrality of the detached expert observer, the secure superiority of Western culture, and the inevitability of progress, under the banner of science and the Western tradition.

In the argument of this book, the reason our own age has not yet taken on a name of its own, beyond identifying it as "post," meaning coming after something else, has everything to do with the fact that the *culture as a whole has not yet appreciated the depth and significance of the paradigm shift going on at an even deeper level*, having to do with who we are and how we understand and define ourselves. This deeper level integrates and contextualizes Constructivist, Deconstructionist, and other post-modern movements like field theory and chaos/complexity theory alike, as well as the loss of faith in the whole range of older modernist certainties. This is of course the deconstruction of the *paradigm of individualism* itself, which is going on all around us, and which this book aims to be a part of and to advance in some constructive way.

Meanwhile, we live as we have said in a transitional time, on our way to something still emergent, which when it is more fully formed may be characterized first as post-individualism, then perhaps as the Age of Community, the Age of Intersubjectivity, or more generally the *Age of Complexity* -- in the sense of the field-organizational and complexity theory models which are emerging around us now, and which have the potential of unifying the fields of psychology and physical science once more. This new unification will then be not on the reductive level of the old biochemistry, as Freud imagined, but on the new grounds of the *complex interactive organization of fields*, which we resolve in our usual meaning systems into physical science, psychology, experience, behavior, and so on -- and even ethics, philosophy, and religion or spirituality, -- but which actually interpenetrate and contextualize each other, in ways and at levels our minds are only now learning to express and imagine. All these are the far-ranging implications and articulation of the constructivist perspective, which is the heart of the Gestalt model of psychology and psychotherapy in general, and which integrates Gestalt and constructivism into evolutionary theory.

The self we seek, then, that essential part of our nature which makes us who and what we are, that which we *cannot not do*, is a *synthesizing self*, an agent of the construction of *meaningful views and points of view*, an organizer of the experience we have or are, which is the same as our knowing of self and other and the world. We *cannot not* organize our experience, at the widest level available. And synthesizing or organizing in this sense means meaning-making: *our self-nature is that of a meaning-maker*, and however we define ourselves, this activity of creative meaning-making must be central in the definition, from the given natural terms of our being. This is our first conclusion, from taking up the terms of the awareness process itself, in relation to self and self-experience. Continuing now with that exploration, what else can we say about our self and our self-experience, out of the terms of our being and their implications, still starting from and going back to our nature as experiencing beings, and the nature of that experiential process itself?

2) A second corollary to the constructivist view, closely related to the argument above, is that in a real sense *we live in our imaginations*, in the images we construct and hold (especially visually, as we are evolutionarily a species heavily reliant on visual processing -- but also images of sound, touch, smell, kinesthetics and other sensory or intuitive processing). This has to do not only with the notion that we "image" or construct our experiential worlds, but also with how we are able to *manipulate* that world, to learn and think abstractly, as we are doing here -- and in general to problem-solve at such an amazing, flexible, and efficient level, compared with other natural species we know of. All of these things flow from a particular feature of our awareness process, which seems to set us qualitatively apart from the other animals: our ability to hold, activate, compare, and actually reach in and modify or "morph" *multiple images in rapid alternation,*

or at the same time.

The human after all is the problem-solving animal *par excellence*, the animal who is not particularly good at anything else except this rare, precious multiple-imaging capacity. This is what enables us to "think ahead" or predict, to try out solutions by running thought-experiments in our minds, before applying them to the more costly and risky world of the outside environment. And this ability, this feature of our awareness process, is central to how we do it, which always involves constructing and holding images, comparing one to another, modifying them freely, and imaging the results of the modifications. This is what "thinking" or planning *is*. Essentially, this ability is not just a central component of consciousness, self-consiousness, and creativity, the generation of novel combinations and solutions: rather, it *is the same as* those capacities themselves. We think of images as a sort of memory bank, but actually it is this active and predictive feature of imaging or awareness that is the key to our survival as a problem-solving species in a changing environment -- one in which other species with more elaborated specific instinct patterns are constantly defeated by major environmental shifts (even our closest relations, the Neanderthals, as current thinking has it, may well have vanished because of their highly specific adaptation for living as scavengers in an ice-age environment of semi-frozen meat, which favored a massive jaw structure, but perhaps fewer social planning skills.

Again, this feature of our awareness equipment and learned skills in handling it has implications and consequences. Among them, and important for our discussion here, is that looking at ourselves in this way causes us to lose the clear and absolute distinction between imagination and "hard reality." This closely parallels the loss of the rigid difference between fact and interpretation discussed above, but with the additional dynamic feature of a time dimension. That is, the fact that we can hold and modulate images in this way, and run thought experiments on them (indeed, once again we *can't not* do this) means that in a very real sense we live in the future, and not the present or the past, by our nature. That is, we manage a shifting environment, with quite limited tools other than this awareness process itself, by *estimating and assessing outcomes*, and then adjusting our own actions (and the environmental conditions, to the extent that we can) accordingly. We are able to do this, again, by virtue of the strength, cohesiveness, and malleability of the particular images or "figures" we can form, bound off, manipulate and hold, and "run out" as thought experiments, all in the world of imaginative awareness.

The self we seek, then, is not only a constructor or synthesizer of the world, but an *imaginative self*, a self-process that ranges and lives in and by a world of images, in a fluid and creative way. In the individualist paradigm, where the self and the world were both already fixed and given, we learned to think of this kind of creative imaging as the province of the artist, or possibly the visionary scientist or leader, a special kind of person whose existence and nature were either mistrusted (Plato and the materialists alike) or celebrated (the Romantics discussed above) -- but whose nature was set apart from other people. This was the romantic myth of the lonely genius. In the different perspective we are developing here, all this, in the words of Gestaltist Paul Goodman (1951), is one more "false dichotomy." Rather, we are all artists, of our lives and of the world, creative image-makers of reality, including ourselves and others.

With this much said, what further implications can we continue to draw, out of our original propositions about awareness itself, themselves drawn from Gestalt psychology and its implications for deconstruction of our inherited "essentialist" views about the "individual self?"

3) A third sharp distinction that is softened, at least, by all these considerations is the traditional one between emotion and

cognition. Again, if our reality is a fixed, given "thing" -- whether determined by Ideal Forms or by materialist facts, -- then it follows that cognition, like "pure perception," can be exercised and evaluated, ideally at least, apart from interpretation and subjectivity -- the point that we took up and discussed above. As we have seen, this notion was the basis of Plato's hope that "pure reason," or cognition supposedly independent of mere sense impressions and feelings, would give us the reliable guide we need to knowing, judging, and acting in accordance with "the (objective) Good." Likewise with Aristotle, whose rules of syllogistic or deductive logic were meant to be the complete guide to reliable thinking -- i.e., the inherent and objective rules of cognition itself, which would ultimately be like thinking about mathematics (on this Plato and Aristotle agreed, for all their differences on the reality or significance of the physical world).

In the view we are exploring and developing here, all this is radically different. If our reality is always a selective construction, an interaction in and with the field, and a kind of imaginative play, then plainly subjective factors will enter in and play a heavy dynamic role. In the dictum of Kurt Lewin (1936), "the need organizes the field" -- meaning that in any selection and construction, the *concerns the perceiving subject feels and attends to most will inevitably be orienting and organizing*, making certain features of the world and the self stand out and be more salient than others, in the particular creative resolutions that are our reality at a given moment. This is no more than to say that our selection of salient features is not going to be random, but rather will have to do with the particular problems we're trying to deal with at the time. Again, this follows really from the idea that the evolutionary meaning of our awareness is inseparable from our flexible problem-solving strengths. Obviously for survival, the problem we organize around will tend to be the one that "feels" most urgent and controlling to us at the moment -- given the whole picture or context which, again, it is our basic nature to construct.

But this then means that we can't keep feelings out of thinking. As Lewin said (1917), the world of a hungry person is a world of food (or the scarcity of food, or the instrumental steps in solving the food problem, and so forth) -- while the "same" world, to the soldier who is dropped, say, behind enemy lines, is not the same world at all. Their "maps" are entirely different: salient features on one person's map are less important, or have an entirely different meaning ("valence," Lewin would have said, meaning emotional charge or value), or just don't register and appear at all, on another person's map of the same environment. *And the map is the relevant reality*, not in a fixed or final sense (things that are "really there" but unnoticed may always surge up as resources, problems, or obstacles, and then have to be taken into account in a revision or updated version), but in the sense that the "version" itself, the subjective construction, is all we have to go on, and thus will govern our actions, reactions, feelings, and new understandings of meaning.

This perspective differs from, say, a classically Freudian positivist way of understanding the same insight, which is that we tend to "see" what we already expect and believe -- and then oftentimes to enact a sort of self-fulfilling prophecy. In the psychodynamic model this is thought to be true particularly in interpersonal relations, but also in the dynamics of phobias, say, where apprehension leads to avoidance, which lessens anxiety, which seems to validate the phobia, which in turn is then never actually tested out for confirmation or disconfirmation. All this is quite valid, but the difference here is that in the older positivist/individualist perspective, the accent was naturally on *correcting* the erroneous misperception, from a point of view of expert authority. In the view developed here, the accent is rather on "getting inside" the perspective of the person whose reality construction is giving him/her a problem in some way, as in much clinical or psychoeducational work. Of course in practice we may still feel concerned at times to get people to see what seem plainly to be distortions in their own thinking or perceiving. Still, our emphasis will more likely now be on supporting him/her to develop his/her own "experiment" for testing those beliefs out -- if only because we recognize that since it is our nature to construct an understanding of the world, a whole meaningful picture, and since these "gestalts" are all we have to go on in dealing with the world, this means that these subjective understandings are often fiercely held, and in extreme cases may feel like life and death to us. You cannot simply talk a person out of a strong, important phobia, one in which the "irrational" cognition is supported by intense affect, in a unified "schema" or gestalt. What you can do is to work together with the person (from "inside" the phobia or other problematic beliefs) to construct *experiments* -- virtual or "thought" experiments, or "real world" ones -- that will change the affective experience, and thus free up a space for a different interactive construction of reality.

This kind of thinking, which assumes that cognition is and must be grounded in and shaped by affect, is extensively supported nowadays by a new generation of brain/mind research, which among other things finds the direct involvement of the amygdala region of the brain, for example, long recognized as an emotional processing center, in most or all higher cognitive processing (see discussion in Damasio, 1994). If the Gestalt model of perception and cognition is as valid, as it appears to be after a full century of research and elaboration, then this has to be true, and must then be supported by brain structure and process. That is, again to take the evolutionary point of view, the organization of attention, and thus of cognition, necessarily depends on emotional orientation and value, which tell us what is important to attend to, and which organize perception and cognition in relation to everything we are managing and trying to arrive at or avoid.

Once more the constructivist view, that our relevant reality is something we construct actively, has to contain the idea that that construction will be colored by what seems most important to us. And "what seems most important to us" is in turn a process or evololutionary psychological way of talking about affect, which is our evaluative orientation in the experiential field.

The self we seek, then, is an *affective self*, a self that orients and finds itself and the world through emotion or affect (from the Latin *affectus*, disposed or influenced in some particular *direction*). Our constructions are directed in some way, which is to say colored by an implicit notion, at least, of going toward or away, of valuing, affirming, or rejecting and wanting to change. In other words, feelings are a kind of compass or directionality, always moving us potentially toward or away, lifting us "up" or casting us "down." This understanding of the evolutionary or evaluative/coping aspect of emotionality, which has long been the perspective of the subfield of affect psychology going back to Tomkins (1963) and deriving from Darwin (1873), emerges here as a necessary dynamic dimension of self-process and attribute of the self we are trying to find and understand. What we call "data" (again literally, the givens), can never be completely given to the self by the environment, but is always a creation of the self, in interaction with the environment. Our "thinking about" always rests on and is grounded in a "feeling about" (a proposition with implications which take us right back to the social policy question of "intelligence" discussed above). We feel and evaluate as we perceive and think: the processes are inseparable. Indeed, in an evolutionary sense this has to be the whole reason why and how we have the problem-solving awareness and cognition that we do.

4) This in turn then tends to collapse the rigid distinction between "mere feelings" and "higher principles," or *emotion and value*. We have already seen how in a creationist, individualist self model, we are accustomed to thinking of "values" as something higher and more significant than "mere feelings," something more in the realm of "mind," which is quite distinct from affect and sentiment. To be sure, we may not seek value and meaning in "pure reason" alone, as Plato did; still, we

hold the notion of values, ethics and morality as somehow apart from the rest of life, and from the natural world. Understanding nature is "objective," and "value-free;" whereas values rest ultimately on faith, which is to say some subjectively-derived (or divinely revealed) criteria which are not demonstrable in the same way. Thus in the old paradigm "values" are located somewhere close to "the self," which is to say deep in the innermost and private recesses of the individual person -- whereas perception is more "out there," given "objectively as the self itself was seen to be given objectively, before any interaction between them.

It then follows that through the past four centuries, approximately, of the modernist era, since the last grand (and failed) attempt by Leibniz to unify these two realms, which we looked at in the previous chapter, the two central concerns of all philosophy, *understanding "being,"* which includes the self and "higher values," and *understanding the world,* which means nature or "objective reality," including how we know that world, have just been assumed to be irreducibly separate and ultimately beyond hope of meaningful integration. Here, by contrast, with a different view of affect as the *evaluative dimension of cognition*, and of cognition as the working out of an evaluatively-charged problem in perception or knowledge, we find that values are not essentially separable from cognition and perception, but like emotions, are integral to all thinking and perceiving, which are themselves inseparable from subjective and group preferences and problem-solving.

In other words, rather than deriving from some other realm, apart from nature, here values are something more like a kind of relatively stable preference, that tends to hold across situations and countervailing considerations (see discussion in Wheeler, 1992). This brings us to begin to question the deep modernist assumption that the worlds of ethics and natural science can never be related to each other (Russell, 1964) , which we can now see more clearly as one more artifact or precipitate of the individualist paradigm. If the self and the world are not preexistent, separately given things; if we construct the world we see and know and move in; if those constructions cannot be held as meaningfully separate from our affective evaluations which enter into those cognitions themselves, then the old dream of a meaningful whole view of human nature, including a new human ethics derived from that nature, may come to life again.

The self we seek here, which is constructive and imaginative, always interpreting and oriented by emotion in a problem-solving field, is thus an *organizer or agent of values*, an evaluative being or process not in some "added-on" or supernatural way, but by its evolutionary, gestalt-forming, meaning-making nature. Feeling and value are not separate parts of the self, nor are they meaningfully separate from thinking and perceiving. Rather, all of them are implicated and integrated in taking in, interpreting, understanding, and acting on and with the world, and other selves. And since values are such relatively stable preferences, absorbed early (though they may change later) and making reference by definition to group identification rather than the immediate situation, this means that the question of values implicates the question of the social construction of self and self-experience, a question we will take up below, after talking about what kind of knowledge and certainty the self we are picturing here can have and use.

5) Another implication of the picture of self and self-process we can build up out of the terms of our own nature as aware beings has to do with the kind of knowledge we can have, its relative certainty or uncertainty, and the ways we can go about getting it and using it. As we've already seen, this was the problem that preoccupied Plato -- how do we know things, and then how can we possibly rely on that knowledge? If we take the kind of constructivist view we are building up here, we're led as we've already seen to the idea that our knowledge of anything is always provisional, hypothetical, and pragmatic: we construct as

whole a picture as we can, under the given conditions as we understand them; we work with the limits on completeness that we seem to be dealing with; and then we use that picture as the basis for other understandings, other plans and actions. These actions, together with the results of them (again as we imagine or understand those results) then become the basis for ongoing revisions in a constantly-changing picture.

To be sure, many of these constructions are so stable, so often confirmed, and so universally shared (at least within one culture or subculture) as to seem bedrock, and qualitatively different from the shifting hypotheses we make and use about day-to-day affairs, about people, even at times about ourselves and what we think we know ourselves to be "like," or capable of. But this can be tricky. A case in point would be the kind of assumptions and distinctions we were just discussing above and may also hold to be "obvious" and "bedrock givens:" namely, the sharp or absolute differences, say, between and among thinking, feeling, imagining, valuing, and "real scientific knowledge." We said that the rigidity of these distinctions flows from the individualist/separate-self paradigm. Indeed, the perspective we have been developing here makes it more clear why and how it is that paradigms themselves are so controlling, and so important: if our reality is a construction, and if that construction rests on fundamental assumptions that are themselves outside full awareness (or full "objective" verification), then there will be whole ways of seeing, and whole realms of "things to see" that just remain invisible to us -- like the possibility of an essential identity between and among the cognitive, affective, and evaluative/ethical terms above.

In other words, the self we are looking for is an *experimental self*, by its/our nature. We make a picture, test it out, use (or fail to use) the (interpreted) results in some way to influence that picture itself, make another action which tests the whole thing again, and so on. We do this all the time; again, we *cannot not* do it, or at least not for more than brief and protected spans of time. All this isn't just to get ready to think clearly about something, or solve a problem, or start living: this *is* thinking, problem-solving, and living. In this sense one of the crowning cultural achievements of the West, the "scientific method," which has been both the glory of the Western intellectual tradition as well as the key to Western domination of the globe, is really no more than the formalization of our basic gestalt cognitive/perceptual nature and process flow. That nature, that inherent "wiring" for the making of gestalts or whole pictures, and then the attention to the fit or misfit of parts and sequences -- all of which we have said is in the service of problem-solving in a changing and challenging field, -- is the natural sequence of scan-synthesize-test/act-revise, the generation and testing of hypotheses which make up our inherent self-process. These are not basically different from the classic sequence of steps in scientific inquiry, of collect, induce/hypothesize, test, and confirm or disconfirm the experimental hypothesis -- steps laid out by scientific writers since the time of Francis Bacon. The codification of this natural process into procedural rules and the formal collection and classification of data, which have been so enormously powerful and fruitful for Western technology, are our own self-process spelled out in formal steps and stages for the sake of maximum clarity -- steps which, as we shall see in the next chapter and then all through the more experiential chapters to follow, are naturally unified and tend to happen, most of the time, all at once in a single cognitive/perceptual act, of scan-imagine-assume-evaluate-act and then move on. Science, like psychotherapy, seeks to deconstruct this holistic process, intervening especially to stretch out the feedback/results step, which is often neglected, as well as to lift out the unexamined assumptions which lie behind the first scan, and then are present at every stage.

But this examination of assumptions is itself subject to the same rules of our awareness process -- and to the influence and limits on that process which result from the dynamic prestructuring of the whole inquiry by out-of-awareness assumptions, including most centrally those controlling assumptions contained in the paradigm we are inhabiting at the time. Again, the assumption of a qualitative difference and separation between thinking and feeling discussed above is an example of just such a limitation: as long as the individualist/materialist paradigm was still in full force, brain and mind research tended to be set up in a way that already contained the assumption of that separateness, and then seemed to confirm it in its results. When a brain researcher such as the Gestaltist Kurt Goldstein (1939, 1940) argued that these processes were inseparable, that argument was generally brushed aside, while physical research continued to focus more on what specific regions of the brain were responsible for what specific functions, not how those regions and the whole interacted and informed and communicated with each other.

Later on in this book we will develop an argument that the key to healthy self process lies in this inherent experimentalism, which will become our main criterion for evaluating and diagnosing self-functioning and dysfunction. At the same time, it will be well to remember that even the healthiest self and self-process still will never have perfect access to its own assumptions and blind spots, and that in our own discussion here, as we labor to bring old hidden assumptions to light, there are always inevitably others we are not seeing, that will stand out to other readers in other times, other cultures, looking at the "same" material from a different point in the shared experiential field.

To summarize the places we've been so far, we can say that the self we are exploring and seeking, the understanding of self-process we are trying to find and articulate here using just the terms and conditions of our own living awareness process in the experiential field, is a *creative constructor of reality*, building its relevant world in imaginative interaction with the given conditions as subjectively perceived; a *meaning-maker and a synthesizer* of whole pictures; organizing, selecting, and acting on that world through the orientation of *feeling and value*; always *interpreting* and then acting to test, strengthen, or possibly revise those interpretive pictures and meanings in a natural, organic exercise of experimental method. These keys -- *construction, interpretation, meaning, feeling, value, and experiment,* the hallmarks of the awareness process and the process self, -- will be the themes we return to again and again in the more experiential chapters that lie just ahead.

Meanwhile, there is one more process key, even more radically deconstructive of the inherited paradigm of individualism than all these, and central to all of them, and to the revision of our understanding of self that is the subject and the goal of all this discussion. This is the crucial fact that *none of this takes place individually*, in the strict sense that we have been taught to assume it does. Our construction of reality is always and everywhere a *co-construction* with other people, and this is as true of "solitary reflection" as it is of public discourse and debate. Our interpretations and meanings are shared interpretations and meanings -- not in the sense that they are identical to everyone or anyone else's, but in the sense that we make them in and out of a shared and co-constructed field of experience. Our feelings and values are culturally conditioned, and the experiments we conceive and make, formally and naturalistically, are those that are in some sense afforded, or offered preferentially, by the cultural field, and those whose results can be communicated meaningfully somehow to other people, within the terms of our given paradigms at the particular time and place.

We "know" all these things -- which is to say, we feel them in some way, even recognize them as truisms -- which are then held in a way that doesn't quite disturb the individualist paradigm itself. We may hold the widespread cultural notion, for instance, that while we are inevitably influenced by society and by other individuals, this influence always and necessarily represents a compromise of individual integrity, a failure of independent judgment -- the perspective we found, for instance, in Sartre in the previous chapter. To see these same insights in a different light, and to see how they are transformed by a shift of self-paradigm, we need the help of a different theoretical view of where and how self is *located* in the experiential field -- as well as the felt experience of exploring the implications of looking at self-process in terms of those hallmarks or keys outlined above. We will close this theoretical discussion, for now, by turning next to that different way of locating self and self-process, on the way to taking up the question of felt experience all through the remainder of the book.

Goodman's articulation of self

Gestaltist Paul Goodman (1951) took up some of these same questions and concerns, and attempted to sketch the direction at least for a new way of thinking about self, without recourse to the "little man in the machine" or "homunculus" theories and models that we talked about in the previous chapter, and which we have said follow directly from the premises and assumptions of the individualist paradigm of self. Drawing on the work of Dewey (1938), James (1983), and others in the American pragmatist tradition, and writing very much in the Existentialist spirit, Goodman suggested that what is essential about human beings is not some preexistent spark or kernel which is separate from the physical body or from everyday life, but rather is *this awareness process itself*, with its natural gestalt drive to make unified wholes of experience, which we have been discussing and elaborating through the previous section. The essential self, in living practice, is not a "thing" or a hidden aspect of us, but is best understood as this natural process itself of unifying the experiential field, the synthesizer or "gestalt-maker" of experience (or better still, the gestalt-mak*ing* process itself). This dimension or activity of "me," which is always going on, is what we are looking for when we talk or think about the essence of a person's existence, the process which defines us and enables us to survive, learn, and grow.

We may restate part of Goodman's argument for our purposes here in this way: since our nature is *actively constructive and synthetic*, always elaborating whole pictures of meaning in some kind of interaction with what is "there" (the process Goodman called "*contact*"), and since this constructive process is *inherently affective and evaluative* (as it has to be, to meet the evolutionary survival needs of our own nature) -- then there is no need to look for a self that is hidden away somewhere in the innermost recesses of our being. Rather, in this perpective it makes more sense to see self, metaphorically, as occupying some superordinate position or "place," as the *integrator of the whole field of experience* (or better, again, as the integrat*ing* of the whole experiential field, to make it even more clear that we are not talking about an additional "thing" or "little person in the big person," but a process, which is living itself. In Goodman's language, still using the spatial metaphor, self is "at the boundary," the "place" where that part of my experiential field I know as "me" meets that part of my field I think of as "out there."

After all, it doesn't help really help me to understand or integrate either of these two "self-realms" -- the subjective "inner world" or the (also subjective) part of the field that I see "out there" -- in isolation from the other one. Plainly it is not enough, for surviving and living well, just to know and articulate my own "inner" realm of needs, desires, wishes, plans, fears, dreams and beliefs, if I cannot connect this with the "real world" of resources, obstacles, and most of all, *other people*, the realm of fulfillment or frustration of those desires and needs. And then the same thing of course is true the other way around: it is the integration of the two experiential realms, which interpenetrate and structure each other interactively, that is the goal and the process of living, and the operation of the self. To have only the latter -- a well-managed environment with no inner life -- is the position we call "schizoid," meaning split, in recognition that this separation of one realm from the other is unnatural, and represents a self-disorder, a breakdown of the natural integrative self-function. To have only the former is the common lament of some early patients after classical analysis, that now "I understand myself (meaning my inner world in isolation), but nothing has changed."

To experience this boundary or difference, the distinction Sullivan (1953) called simply "me/not me," is essentially what we mean by self-awareness, the sense that there is an I who is here, and is somehow not identical with the world. Your pain, your pleasure and joy are not exactly the same to me as my pain, pleasure, and joy (yours may conceivably be *more* intense to me at times than my own; still, they won't be the same). This is what we mean and know as existing (from the Latin *ex-stare*, to stand out): an inherent bifurcation or polarity in the experiential field, around and along an experienced "me-boundary." The rigid separation of the poles, the inflexibility of the boundary around an impenetrable "I," is a cultural artifact in the West; but the sense of some distinction is inherent, and implied in our ability to be here and talk or otherwise be in contact with each other at all, as opposed to everything just being an undifferentiated constituent of everything. Indeed, we can think of this inherent bipolarity, the "two domains" of the experiential field, as an evolutionary necessity: it is by resolving the field first and foremost into a realm identified in some sense with my "organism" and another realm identified as "other," that my field-resolving process can integrate the two realms viably in some way, and the organism can survive. Thus *self is our ultimate survival process and structure, as vulnerable problem-solving animals in an ever-shifting physical field.*

But conceiving or metaphorically locating self "at the boundary" in this way (to use Goodman's metaphor again), as a superordinate process of integration of both these experiential realms, then *radically changes our understanding of our relationship with other selves*. Rather than each self being self-contained and self-referential, possibly relating outward in some way to the deity but otherwise essentially cut off from other selves (the "monadic" view we talked about in the previous chapter), here each self is an active organizing agent or process of integration, integrating the *"same" field.* If my natural self-process is to integrate the whole relevant field, to the degree possible, and if you are relevant in that field, then you and your "inner life" *are part of the "material" and the relevant domain of that integration*. To be sure, your inner world may be largely unknown to me, in which case I may "fill it in," if that is what is necessary to complete a meaningful gestalt -- the process we generally call projection or interpretation, which we'll be taking up in detail in the next chapter. For that matter my own inner world may be largely unknown to me, and thus extensively unarticulated and undeveloped. Still, my living task and nature is to integrate the whole field meaningfully, as well as I can, and as much of it as seems relevant and available for understanding and use. (And at this point we'll generally drop the quotation marks around *inner* and *outer* from here on, but without forgetting that these two realms, the "me" and the "other," are interexistent, and not rigidly separate places as the old model had it)

In other words, in a world of multiple subjective selves, far from being self-contained, each self potentially *interpenetrates all the others*, in every direction. My inner life is a part of your field, and thus of your self-process -- and vice versa. This is much more than to say that each self lives "in an environment" of other selves -- as if each self were a "thing," apart from that environment. Rather, the model that results from all these considerations so far, and from Goodman's simple shift in the metaphorical location of self-process, is what in current language is called *intersubjective.* And not only intersubjective by assertion or intention, in the way of some current relational self-models, but necessarily intersubjective, at a level of theory, from the basic terms and constituent processes of self that we have been exploring and building up here (for further discussion of this point and distinctions between and among models, see, for example Miller, 1986; Stolorow et al., 1987; and discussion in Wheeler, 1995, 1996a). As we will see in the chapters ahead, these considerations and implications will be crucial for a revised view of development and a new understanding of what we mean by healthy self-process. That new understanding, we will try to show, is one that is much closer than the old model, to our own felt experiences of ourselves, other people, relationships, and our sense of our own best experiences of living, learning, and growing in a world that we can know and make use of and share as a meaningful whole.

Conclusions

As we come to the end of Part I, the more theoretical part of our exploration of self and self-process, we have moved in one sense a long way from our intial questions -- and in another sense circled right back to them again. To the question what do we mean by self, we have been developing a process answer, out of the terms of our own awareness and experience-creating nature -- an answer which centers around the constructive themes and dynamic dimensions of *meaning-making, interpretation, imagination, feeling, value, and experiment* -- to which we have added the overarching dimension of *intersubjectivity*, the inherent interrelatedness of particular selves in a shared social and experiential field. There is much more we could say in this vein, about these and related topics, which are not only vast but also key to our understanding of everything else, since who we think we are and the implications of our self-understanding have profound, structuring consequences for our views of every aspect of our lives and our worlds.

At the same time, there is a kind of diminishing return in "pure theoretical" discourse of this sort, and perhaps especially when the theory issues in play go to the heart of our controlling paradigms of how we conceive and relate to ourselves and the world. The longer we stay in "just theory," the more we may court the risk that our inherited language and established, out-of-awareness habits of thought will exert a pull on the discussion, back in the direction of the assumptions of the dominant paradigm we are trying to critique and deconstruct. As we've already said, there is never a way to avoid this risk entirely. What we can do, in the interests of loosening the grip of deeply-held cultural assumptions and patterns of thinking, is to try shifting to another mode, which we may find closer to feeling and living, to give ourselves still more "play," more open space for constructing and experiencing a new view. Thus as promised, the chapters ahead will shift to more emphasis on exercise and experiment, to get more of the feel of these and related new ways of thinking.

In the first of these, we will start with the kind of living problem that we deal with many times, most days of our ordinary lives: namely, how do we take up interpersonal contact and relationship, in our living social field. If the self is a constructive self, always interpreting and evaluating and feeling and evaluating, always in the shared field co-populated with other selves, how do we organize the social situation itself? Out of this simple yet profound question, and on the basis of a simple opening exercise that we can follow together here (and the reader can replicate at any moment of life, just by looking around and paying attention to her/his own process), we intend to begin fleshing out some of the abstractions of the discussion up to this point, and to ground ourselves in the assumptions and implications of an entirely different way of feeling and understanding ourselves and other selves in our shared experiential world.

Part II -- The Self in the Social Field: Relationship and Contact

At this point we turn to the more experience-based, directly practical part of the book -- still with the idea of finding and understanding a kind of self which is based in our living experience with other people, and still with the idea that these two ways of approaching our subject, "theory" and "experience," should be intimately supportive of each other, and should lead us directly to the same place. That new place, we have said, is a new way of sensing and conceiving ourselves, which in turn gives us the ground for a more effective, more integrated experience of living and working with others.

Up to now we have been tracing the theoretical outlines and the active path of the kind of self that is given in the terms of our living processes of awareness, perception, and action -- a constructive self that is an active meaning-maker, always interpreting and imagining out of a ground of feeling and values, and then testing those constructions and images out in the imaginative theater of the mind, or the experimental crucible of living. This is the self, as Goodman said, that is the ongoing, living resolution of the whole field of experience, inner and outer, across a "me-boundary" which both defines me and at the same time integrates me in a liveable way into a shared world. Finally, this self is intersubjective, in that it constructs its own process out of a field which includes the inner worlds of other selves.

This construction and this integration are what the Gestalt model calls "contact," the resolution of meaningful wholes of understanding and action (or potential action) in the experiential field of real life. But how do we go about making or finding this "contact;" how does this process act to integrate the "whole field" of ourselves and others? What processes of awareness and organization do we use to know what (and who) is "out there," (which immediately implicates the inner worlds of other people, as integral parts of our own experiential field)? We are born into a relational field, which in some sense was already there before we got there, before this living process of our own subjective self-experience and self-articulation as a distinct part of that field begins. How do we get to know that field, make meaning of and in it, and join in on that ongoing web of relationship? How do we actually take up contact in any social situation -- a problem we must confront and resolve continually in the process of living, and particularly that process we call "living well?"

To examine all this in a new way, we will leave off our "pure theory" discussion at this point, and turn instead to an exercise, which the reader can follow along with in active imagination, or actually recreate at almost any place and moment just by looking around at other people, and then taking a moment to attend to her/his own processes of awareness and meaning-making -- processes which are going on all the time within us at nearly every moment of life. The exercise itself is one that is widely used, and may be familiar to the reader -- and at the same time, it can yield some rich and perhaps surprising new insights, when we view it with the different lens of the new perspective we are building up here, on self, relationship, and the co-construction of experience.

Chapter Three: The Self in Relation -- Orienting and Contacting in the Social Field

Imagine an exercise, of a familiar type often used in training groups in counseling, management skills, conflict resolution, and other courses in "human relations training" and process dynamics -- anywhere people are formally engaged in learning to understand themselves better and work more effectively with others. The setup of the exercise is quite simple: a group of people sit around in a room, while one group member at a time, the "subject," walks up and down and around in front of the others without saying anything, and the others take turns saying or writing down *what they see*. The task the observers are given is a deceptively simple one as well: just to be as concrete and as descriptive as they can, noting only that data which they can actually *see*. Oftentimes a specific additional caution is given with the instructions, about not adding any interpretations or judgments of the observers' own. The idea here is that everything said by any one person should be non-controversial, readily visible and verifiable by others. For example, sample responses might be:

I see a firm step, heels coming down hard
I see shoulders a little hunched, neck forward
I see an even gait, head doesn't change level
I see arms hanging still, not swinging, etc.

The exercise at this point probably feels a little artificial or somehow incomplete, even trivial -- for good reason, as we will be seeing below, since this is not at all the way our integrated awareness process normally or naturally works. And yet despite this seeming triviality (or maybe because of it), the experience can be surprisingly difficult, at first at any rate, for a great many people. Over and over, with the best will in the world, people will offer responses that go way beyond the instructions in the direction of interpretation, opinion, judgment, or other "subjective" material, in violation of the simple "objective" task rules. For example, people may say:

> I see a *determined* gait (an interpretation on "firm step")
> I see *tension* in the neck (a sort of borderline interpretation, a kind of guess about musculature that may have physically shortened by this time from habit, so that this is now actually the relaxed position)
> I see a *calm* pace (an inference about an inner state)

and so on. At the same time, the subject being observed (or "target," as some participants have ruefully put it) may well report some palpable level of discomfort, enough at least that teachers and trainers usually know not to try this kind of thing until the group has developed some beginning level of comfortableness and trust.

Both these reactions may be puzzling if we think about them. Why should it be so difficult to "just say what you see?" And why should it be uncomfortable to be looked at, especially when you consider that we're looked at almost all the time, often pretty judgmentally, whereas in this case at least the onlookers have been specifically enjoined *not* to interpret, judge, or otherwise make any meaning at all, really, of what they are seeing? The answers to these questions take us a considerable way further into our inquiry about self in relationship, and the operation of our self-experience and awareness processes in the all-important social field.

The Goals of the Exercise -- "Behavioral-Descriptive Feedback"

First of all, let's look at what the exercise is manifestly about, and then see what we can say about what else is really going on. As it is usually conceived and presented, the goal of the activity is to learn to give (and receive) something that is commonly called "behavioral feedback," or "purely descriptive" information about someone else's behavior, output, performance, and so on. Clearly the capacity to do this is important, even essential, to our ability to manage, help, control, or just get along with other people. Take an everyday example: if you tell me, say, that I frequently interrupt you and correct what you are saying, and that this is a problem for you, perhaps even makes you reluctant to talk to me about anything real, -- *and you stop there*, -- then you are offering a particular attentional focus (my behavior, in relation to your need); and that offer will tend to organize our shared field, for a time anyway, in terms of that attentional figure. Of course, the situation is still quite fluid at this point, and may be more or less difficult for me to manage and bear. I may respond by joining that focus, listening and even agreeing, or perhaps offering another interpretation of the same events (saying for example that this happens, but it's only because I can't get you to listen, or maybe in my view you interrupt me first, and I'm only trying to finish, and so on). The observations of others may be invoked, to support your or my perceptions. Maybe at this point I will enact what you are saying, interrupting you right now, which would add some interesting present data to the conversation. Or maybe all I can do is "resist" or deny -- which is still a way of joining your focus. Situations of this type are seldom easy, and may go well or ill. Either way, the demand on me is to deal somehow with the organization of our shared conversational space that you initiated. I may try to deal with it by brushing it away, or changing the focus to some other subject altogether (your behavior, say) -- in which case I may well still end up influenced by your bid and your feedback, perhaps trying to adjust my behavior in some way, all depending of course on the nature of our connection, our goals, the power dynamics between us, and what all is at stake for both of us in the relationship.

On the other hand, suppose you try to open the same discussion with an outright interpretation of my inner states and intentions, most likely with a negative spin, as in: "I hate it when you always try to *control* me like that," or "You *never have any respect* for what I'm trying to say." Maybe you go even further than this, linking the interruptions to my childhood experiences, my presumed or known relationship with an overbearing parent, my feelings of impotence and frustration in life, whatever. These are suppositions and imputations about my "insides," and while they may well hold some merit and some learning for me, they are almost bound to be quite different from the internal experience I'm aware of at the moment, which may be that I'm anxious, or *you* weren't listening to *me*, maybe even that "people never do listen," and so on. What probably happens next is that we now find ourselves embroiled in (and perhaps mystified by) an argument about my intentions and inner state and overall mental health (and perhaps yours as well, which I may introduce here) -- which after all *are the topics and attentional focus you proposed*, perhaps without quite meaning to. All of which carries a very low probability of any satisfying outcome or useful learning for anybody involved -- as we all know only too well from personal experience, as supervisors and supervisees, as teachers and students, and perhaps most poignantly as partners in any kind of couple or other intimate relationship.

In other words, we're all familiar with this kind of distinction, between "describing" and "interpreting," and know the importance and the effects of it -- at least on the receiving end. Which means in turn that all those on the "dealing" end of the feedback loop -- not just managers, teachers, counselors and therapists, parents, and so on, but also any of us, whenever we engage in relationships that are important to us -- will do well to understand and sense the difference from the delivery side of the transaction as well, and become more skilled in the supple and easy application of these distinctions. And sure enough, with a little practice most people do get much better at all this, learning to suspend or suppress interpretations and judgments in favor of (more) pure "behavioral-descriptive" messages --however odd or incomplete that may feel, at the beginning at any rate ("lame," as one participant put it). And perhaps it's not surprising either that the discussion at this point may tend to take on a certain judgmental flavor of its own: it's *good* to be descriptive, *bad* to interpret -- or even worse, "project" (an accusation which often carries a sort of double interpretation, that I'm indulging in a fantasy about you and at the same time denying something uncomfortable about myself). "Objective" data are true and reliable, we're taught to think; all else is "just imagination," which is to say, a kind of fiction, not "real." The one leads to the possibility at least of learning and behavioral change; the other generally leads to a small or large disaster.

We could leave off the discussion -- and the exercise -- at this point, taking satisfaction in a new skill learned or an old one sharpened. Indeed, this is what generally happens, as the training program moves on to the next topic and some new skills practice at the next level. And yet a couple of nagging questions remain, as potential contradictions, at least, in everything we've said so far. The first is, where do the interpretations and projections *go*? Are they just wiped out? Just a moment ago we were making them liberally -- presumably in answer to some need. What happened to that need? In the previous chapter we spoke of how *seeing* and *making meaning* are actually integrated aspects of a unitary process, for sound evolutionary reasons: we see as well as we do, and in the particular selective, bounded, "figure-ground" *way* that we do, in order to problem-solve in a challenging field, where problem-solving always means assigning ("projecting") some *predictive value or meaning to the data in relation to the context.* Do we really learn to "just not do" this anymore, after a single morning's practice in a training exercise, simply unlearn something we have been calling an integrated feature of our self-process and awareness itself? Or does the behavior rather "go underground" -- which would then go a long way toward explaining one of our original questions from the exercise itself, the one about why it can be uncomfortable to be looked at by people even when they've been formally instructed to "just see," not judge or make any meaning. After all, if we know from our own (private) experience that this is next to impossible, then it could well be more uncomfortable, not less, to have those judgments and meanings just denied, effectively removing them from the discussion and holding them privately somewhere, in a place where we can't even find out what they are.

The second problem is the absoluteness of this "seeing/interpreting" distinction itself, which the whole exercise seems to rest on (small wonder if we can't manage the distinction absolutely, if it doesn't really exist in fact in the first place). In the previous chapter, we questioned whether this distinction was even tenable anymore, in light of everything we know today about the constructive, selective, highly contextual and evaluative/contingent nature of perception and awareness themselves, which always seem to rest on assumptions, examined and unexamined, which prestructure and color our reality in ways we can never completely step outside of. Given all this, what do we even mean by "seeing vs. interpreting," "objective vs. subjective," and other right-wrong distinctions of this type, which seem to come out of another paradigm entirely, and rest on assumptions about "objective reality" that we no longer have much confidence in? And yet some felt differences here do remain in practice, and remain important in our living experience of communication, "feedback," and relationship. What are we to make of this? What is the nature of the "seeing/interpreting" distinction, in this new view, and of the source of the different effects we get from those two kinds of overtures or interactions, if it's no longer the old, absolute distinction between "real data" and "imagination" we once thought we knew and could rely on?

There's much we could say, and will say, on these puzzling topics. But instead of going on in this fairly abstract vein, let's go back now to our exercise, adding another step to what must now seem like it was too simple by at least half, by way of exploring these and related questions about self, awareness, and relationship in a more hands-on way.

From Seeing to Interpreting -- the Dialogic Link

This time, instead of asking people to say "just what they see" (and keep the rest to themselves, as their own little secret), we'll legitimize what was excluded and perhaps stigmatized before. Now the instruction is to say, "I see," and then follow it with "I imagine" -- as in:

I see --	I imagine --
firm step, heels down hard	determination, confidence, anger (or insecurity, over-compensation, etc)
shoulders hunched forward	worry, resignation, burden (or eagerness, energy, far-sightedness, etc)
even gait, head level	calmness, relaxation, openness (or cockiness, control, indifference, etc)
arms not swinging	awkwardness, self-consciousness , anxiety (or serenity, balance, ease, etc)

In each case, we've taken pains here to include some more or less opposite, perhaps equally plausible interpretations or imaginings that participants have actually supplied in this kind of activity, to illustrate some of the possible range. Most striking, of course, are those instances where people see the "same behavior," but offer sharply contrasting meanings to account for it. (We put "same" in quotes here, because even when people give the same name to the behavior observed, they may well be selecting and putting boundaries on the "same figure" quite differently, with quite different implications, as will be discussed below).

Curiously, the subjects of all this scrutiny will often report that they feel more comfortable, not less, with this stage of the exercise than they did with the "purely descriptive" phase. This may seem surprising, since by and large we tend to object to "being interpreted:" most of us do prefer to speak for ourselves, at least most of the time. But if you ask them, many participants will say they'd "rather know" what people are thinking and imagining; it can make us anxious, at least under some circumstances, *not* to know. In other words, they do know that people *are* still interpreting and making meaning, instructions or no instructions! When asked how they know this, participants may say, "well, because everybody does it, it's just human nature;" or else perhaps "I know *they're* doing it, because *that's what I do myself*" (an interesting use of "projection," not to deny anything about the self, but just to imagine one's way into the inner world of other people). And are the other people really saying what they really think and imagine? "Well, pretty much," many subjects will reply. "Maybe they're pulling a few punches," said one participant, "you know, toning it down, -- saying it, but in a nice way" (laughter from the group). Again, how do you know this? "Because I do it myself."

At this point we're a far cry from a world of "objective data" and "pure description" -- and yet, subjects will still report a marked difference in their own feelings and attitudes, between "being described" and "being interpreted." Only now the difference is more nuanced, as we can see from the greater comfort most people will feel in the second part than in the first. The difference -- and this point is key to everything else -- lies not in whether people are interpreting (everybody pretty much assumes that everybody pretty much is interpreting and judging, at least potentially, most or all the time). Rather, it lies in *how the interpretation is held*. In the first part, either the interpretation is held privately (because its a "wrong answer," given the exercise instructions), or else it "slips out," in which case the task is to learn how to suppress it more vigorously. Either way, people may feel "seen into" -- either rightly or wrongly, and either way this is an uncomfortable feeling, even at times an invasion or outright violation.

In the second part, "people are saying right out that it's 'just their opinion,' or 'something they're imagining,'" as some participants have explained this difference. This follows from the second instruction, which was specifically to *imagine* the inner state of the subject -- i.e., presumably (though this is left open) something that might account for the behavior observed. Some observers will take this injunction quite playfully, purposely offering projections and theories that are far-fetched or contradictory (and thus perhaps non-threatening -- an interpretive projection on our part here): a "firm step" because "he'd really like to be dancing, but this is a serious training course;" "neck forward" because "she's a visionary person, she's seeing all our auras, and knows everything about us" (a mock-menacing projection which may cover a real fear, since seeing and revealing are now "up" as themes in the group). The atmosphere generally lightens, tension in the room seems to relax -- and at the same time people will still report, if asked, that they find in themselves (and imagine in others) a sort of cautiousness, a kind of unspoken agreement to "be nice," and "not say something that might hurt somebody," be offensive, provoke too much reaction, and so forth. Plainly the whole business of seeing and being seen, interpreting and being interpreted, and generally making sense of and to oneself and others is a serious and potentially charged process, which goes on constructively around us (and in us) all the time, whenever we're in a social group -- and at the same time may erupt into antagonism or conflict at almost any moment (indeed, if you ask people at this point the defining hallmark of a "real friend," the answer will generally include something about not having to worry about "being misinterpreted").

By this time we can begin to see the outlines at least of an answer to the second of our questions from the end of the previous section, where we asked what accounts for the difference in the effects we get, from "seeing" as opposed to "interpreting" (or, as we are calling it here, "imagining"), if not the old idealized distinction between "objective" and "subjective." Perhaps the best way to understand that answer is to ask where we would go to *defend or validate a claim*, in either of these two areas. That is, if two or more observers -- or the subject and one or more observers -- disagree on a response, what happens next? Where do we go, to bolster or just explore a response of either type? Plainly, in the case of "I see," we would simply *turn to other observers*. When we do, we learn a couple of things (in addition to whatever we learn about the observed behavior itself). The first is that "just seeing" or "objective description" is not so "objective" after all: rather, myriad personal, cultural, and other assumptions are built right into "pure observation," just as we were saying they must be, in the previous chapter. Take "firm step," for example. True, by saying "firm" we've backed off, at least, from imputing or attributing "determined" to the subject. But what makes a step "firm?" Isn't that description itself something that is going to vary enormously, depending on what I ordinarily expect from a subject of that particular categorical membership -- gender, age, perhaps size, race and culture, and on and on? My 90-plus-year-old aunt has a remarkably "firm step" -- which is to say, everybody remarks on it. But the same gait, in, say, my 18-year-old son, would hardly look "firm" to me: I'd more likely call it "cautious," "hesitant," even "shuffling" (in that casual mix of description and interpretation that characterizes most of our ordinary conversation). "Firm," that is, implicitly means "firmer than I expected" or "firmer than *normal,*" -- where "normal" is an evaluative/predictive, not just descriptive designation, deeply dependent on cultural assumptions and group membership of the subject and the observer, in interaction.

Nor is it going to solve the problem -- and save "objectivity" -- if we decide to quantify the data, so that it becomes measurable, and thus presumably "sanitized" of all the contaminating subjective factors. This is because behind the numbers, behind the "objective measure" of inches-per-stride, or pounds-per-square-inch of heel pressure, lie any number of hidden prior decisions, all of them still subjective, cultural, and evaluative. What counts as "firm," for instance? -- we still have to make up a benchmark, and agree on it. And what are the boundaries of the thing we want to measure: are shoulders part of "firm step"? is arm swing? do "swishy hips" invalidate a designation of "firm," no matter what the heel pressure -- and if so, is that equally true for both genders, or is it just men who look "vacillating," even "feminine" if their hips swing during an otherwise "firm" stride (and note too how that word "otherwise" seems to prejudge the question)? The numbers themselves may look "objective" and value-free;" the decisions behind the numbers, about categories, boundaries, and criteria for scoring, as well as about what was interesting and worthwhile to attend to and measure in the first place, are, again, subjective, evaluative, deeply colored by culture and personal history -- *and most often hidden from view.*

So much then for the "pure objectivity" of "just seeing," which turns out to be something very much held, constructed, and negotiated (or imposed) *between people,* in ways that are both implicit and explicit, both aware decisions and deeply embedded, out-of-awareness assumptions carried in cultural or personal history. This leads us in turn to our second observation about how we validate "descriptive data," which is that in the end, there is *nowhere else to go*, to determine what's "really out there," *other than to other people*, whom we can invite to look at the "same scene," and share what they make of it (and even more importantly at times, *how* they make what they do make of it). We hold a deep cultural fantasy that somehow, as we do this, the "objective facts" will speak to us, jointly and univocally, for themselves. But "facts" don't speak: they must be interpreted, by particular subjective persons, with particular personal and cultural histories and contexts. Or if they do speak, they speak very differently, inevitably, to different people, different groups, different times. And the "seeing" that results is still a construction, an interpretive inference on data that are themselves evaluatively selected and weighted, and not "direct reality," unadulterated and unmediated by all these evaluative processes.

If we appeal to an expert authority to make the call, then we are merely substituting his/her assumptions and evaluative categorizations, intentional and unawares, for our own. Of course, it may make eminent sense for me to do that in some area, on some occasions (the entire germ theory of disease is riddled with obvious and unexamined assumptions that run in a non-holistic, anti-ecological direction, which means that it cannot be more than a partial truth; but this doesn't mean I don't want a doctor to make the call, as to whether my child has strep or not). Still, whether I attend to it or suspend my awareness of it (or am simply blind to it, for paradigmatic reasons), the fact remains that what we call "objective reality" is a consensual, negotiated convention between and among people, constrained to be sure by material limits (whose "real" outlines we can only infer, never know directly) -- people who are all of us subjective beings, with our own constructive nature and evaluative self-process. And the determination of what that reality is has to go back, ultimately, to *discourse and dialogue among people* -- a dialogue that has no other authority than itself, in the end, to establish what we mutually agree (or disagree) to treat as "real."

And then what about that other kind of organized perception, the kind we have been calling "interpretation?" What makes that any different from "seeing," -- and what about that difference then accounts for the different effects we get when we lead off with the one as opposed to the other, -- again, if not bedrock "objectivity" and "pure fact," untainted by subjective/evaluative factors? Here too, we can approach the question by looking at how we go about validating a claim or settling a dispute in this area. Suppose I see "firm step" as meaning "resolute, decisive," while you see it as indicative of "pushy, aggressive," perhaps even "ruthless, controlling." Where do we look, to see who is "right" in a dispute of this kind? To more observers (but then how do we weight their varying opinions)? To an "expert," who knows the "real meaning" of the behavior (priests have often claimed this kind of authority, as did an earlier generation of classical psychoanalysts)? Or don't we rather go, sooner or later, *to the person him/herself,* who after all knows something at least of the experience, if not the final meaning of the behavior "from the inside" (the "ground of the figure," in Gestalt terms, from which the observable behavior is constructed and emerges). Not that we are prepared to concede, necessarily, that the person her/himself knows *all* there is to know about the determinants and intent of her/his own behavior. On the contrary, we know all too well from our own experience (of ourselves as well as others, if we are honest), how often somebody else's perception or insight about our own action may open up a door we hadn't even considered. "You *say* you're just angry, but you *look like* your feelings are hurt," we may say to someone, or they may say to us -- and the remark may change not just our understanding but our *actual experience of ourselves* and others at the moment, somatically as well as psychologically and interpersonally.

Or perhaps, in the middle of a reaction, an intimate friend or partner may say to us, "you know, you're really tense -- are you remembering that today is the anniversary of your father's death?" -- and suddenly the reaction we were sure we were having is gone, and another feeling entirely in its place. This is the power of the experience we call "insight" -- a new gestalt of meaning -- to reorganize not just our cognition, but *our affective state as well.* Just as we couldn't look "to the data alone," or to the other observers alone for that matter, for an absolute answer about "seeing," so here we can't get the final truth about a person's inner state and organizing motives, just by asking that person him/herself (though we can hardly approach it without asking him or her at some point). Nor do we get absolute answers from expert authorities, in either case. Rather, in each kind of case -- "description" or "interpretation" -- the answer is a provisional, not a final, truth, co-constructed in a dialogic process. *But the dialogue starts in a very different place, in the two kinds of cases.*

This then begins to answer our deeper question above, of what the difference ultimately is between "seeing" and "imagining/interpreting" -- a difference we have said cannot rest on the old shibboleth of "objective truth" versus "mere imagination" or subjectivity. The answer is, these two things are different *kinds of truth*, different ways of knowing the world. Neither of them is absolute; both are provisional, and both are dialogically constructed. But the particular kinds of dialogue needed, the places and processes we need to go to, to make these ways of knowing the world work for us, are very different in the two cases, and take place in different parts of our experiential field.

To see how this distinction plays out in process, and what that means for the kind of self-model we are seeking and constructing, let's now add one final step to our exercise, taking it almost the whole rest of the way in the direction of "real life," and shedding some further light in the process on the questions of why our perceptual/evaluative/cognitive selves and nature are the way they are, and how a different notion of self and human nature may support us to live and experience this unitary process in a new and more empowering way.

From Projection to Relationship

At this point we're ready to bring in an element which may have begun to feel as if it were missing, or perhaps held somewhere just outside the terms of the conversation, to both readers and participants alike. This element is the *feelings of the observer*. Up to now we've been doing some speculating about the feelings of the subject (or target) observed, but without revealing much about our own. To fill this in, we add two new instructions to the series: first "I feel..." and then, to make that fully concrete, "What I might *do* with the person I'm observing, given everything I've seen and imagined, *and* given my feelings about all that now." If you do this with a group of people and then put it all together, you'll begin to get a table something like this:

I see	I imagine/interpret; (and then I feel...)	I/we could then do...
a firm step, heels coming down hard	decisiveness, firm purpose (feel comfortable with this, at ease)	I'd avoid you (or I could rely on you, I'd come to you in need but not for fun, etc)
shoulders down, mouth drooping	depression, sadness (feel hesitant, lonely)	I could take care of you, but you couldn't take care of me
hesitant step, eyes glancing down	insecurity, uncertainty (feel reassured, you wouldn't compete with me)	I'd have you on my team, and I'd be the leader

chin up, rising step	good mood, confidence (feel joined, but maybe a little apprehensive-- you might intimidate/overwhelm me)	I could rely on you, you wouldn't run out of energy/ get depressed
big smile, meeting people's eyes	genuinely happy, or maybe faking it (not sure how to feel)	we could have fun together, or I couldn't trust you -- *I'd have to know more*

and so on. These examples are actual responses given by workshop participants in exercises of this kind, again with some suggestion at least of the range and variation people can come up with, in reaction to the "same figure."

Along with that range itself, perhaps the most striking thing about responses like these is *how immediately and easily most people are able to supply elaborate and coherent statements for the fourth question* (Column 3). It's almost as if the answers to that last question were somehow already contained and prepotently available in the first two columns (as indeed they are in a sense, as we will be discussing below). Only rarely does anybody ever have to stop and think hard to come up with scenarios and reasons, and when they do, even then the hesitation usually comes from perceived contradictions in the subject's presentation (big smile but halting step, and so on) -- or possibly because of a strong "transference" reaction on the part of the observer (something about the subject that calls up a very charged association for the observer, perhaps without awareness). Again, plainly we're "wired" to do this, and do it in such a way that the interpretive and action/experimental "steps" are not really separate from or subsequent to the "seeing" and "feeling" steps: each fuels and informs the others in an ongoing, recursive, and very nearly simultaneous loop.

In this sense, taking the exercise to this next level then

serves to clarify or illustrate more concretely something we have been arguing all along about the nature of awareness and the meaning-making self. This is the fact that the nature and enactment of our basic awareness and gestalt- or meaning-making process do not just "happen to be" the way they are, spontaneously willed or divinely created outside of any functional context (though we may of course regard the whole context as divinely inspired if we are moved to do so). Nor are they driven directly by the immediate environment, unmediated by our constructive processes. Rather, our perceptual nature has evolved, just as the shape of the hand or the action of the liver has evolved -- and that evolution, being contextual, necessarily has a functional or adaptive aspect. Specifically, we perceive as we do, in wholes of understanding embedded in context and shaped and colored by evaluations and feelings, *so as to estimate and plan what to do in the real, concrete situation*. Column 3, that is, is in a sense the *reason for the existence* of columns 1 and 2, which in turn ground the action in meaning, as a response that relates our felt need to the perceived conditions of the outer field. To cite Lewin again (now turning his observation around), perception is an integral aspect or dimension of problem-solving, and vice versa. The activity is unitary -- unless and until it runs into a problem, or until we take it apart laboriously in the lab, as we are doing here.

This in turn is part of the blurring of the presumed sharp distinction between "seeing" and "interpreting" in the first place, which we discussed above from a perceptual process perspective. Here, in the living situation, we can see the same "leakage" from one column to another in a more practical light. The whole "business" of life, after all, is the process of *dealing with what's around me*, both immediate and long-term -- resolving the whole field, of inner needs and desires on the one hand, and outer conditions and resources on the other, into coherent, workable wholes or gestalts, not just of seeing or knowing, but of *predictive understanding and action*. This, together with reflecting on it (plus the exercise of these faculties for their own sake, which is definitional of pleasure in an evolutionary sense) is what being alive *is*, and how it works. When this is done well -- which is to say fluidly, with suppleness, and in a way that takes the whole field into account (inner and outer, self and other), then these things are what satisfaction, happiness, and the processes we know as *living well* consist in. We know all this, and we come "wired" to act in accordance with it. In practice this means that as I scan the field (column 1), my selective, bounding-off, and evaluative/weighting processes are *already colored* by some notions of what I may likely need to *deal with* here, especially now and in the immediate future. That's how my scanning is energized and organized, not randomly but always with implicit or potential purpose, -- because, again, that's what it's *for*. What I can do, how I feel, and the interpretation I make, that is, are already "feeding back" into what I "just see;" and this happens not just after the fact, correctively, but also during the seeing, with seeing and interpreting interpenetrating each other, in a supple problem-solving strategy and whole. Each of these distinguishable sub-processes -- looking and seeing, interpreting and predicting, feeling and evaluating, and acting or planning a potential, possible, or reserve action -- interpenetrates and colors all the others, ongoingly.

Each one can also be influenced or deconstructed in a particular targeted way (seeing by consensual validation, as we have seen; interpreting in part by dialogic inquiry with the subject; feeling/evaluating by the self-deconstructive processes we call therapy, as well as by the first two methods just listed; acting by the perceived practical constraints of the external situation, and so forth). But each of them is also a dynamic aspect of a process that is unitary: we see *because* we may need to act; we interpret *to predict* the future course of what we see; we feel *so as to assign preference and value* to what we see and imagine; we act so as to realize or else test out our hypotheses, which are predictive interpretations held together by the "glue" of affective evaluation and feelings, telling us which goals are worth pursuing, which experiments are important to run, and how to assess the value of the outcomes.

Here we begin to have the outlines of a set of criteria for evaluating healthy and dysfunctional self-process -- no longer in the oversimplified, right-wrong terms of a false dichotomy between seeing and imagining, "objectivity" and projection. On the contrary, in the model emerging here, projection begins to take up its rightful place in the organization of awareness, as our *essential orienting skill in an intersubjective field.* That is to say, in a field made up of other subjective beings with internal process and self-awareness like ourselves, who organize their reality on the basis of affect and value as we do, and must be known in this "inner" or projective way, in order for us to deal at all effectively with the whole challenging field of living. And affect and value are another way of saying *preferentially*, on the basis of the overall fit between and among these related activities of seeing, understanding, feeling or desiring, predicting, and ability to act to unify these things, in the whole field of awareness and relationship. Thus the criteria of health and dysfunction that emerge from all this will have to do with the fluidity and coherence of each of these aspects of self-process, and how they work together to make a liveable whole: seeing that is not dogmatically blinkered; interpreting or meaning-making as *hypotheses to be dialogued and tested,* not as absolutes to be imposed on the rest of the field; feelings and values that serve as a compass to action and meaning, not a dead weight or a reactively destabilizing force; and actions that are based on the experimental organization of the whole field, including especially relevant others, for support. In short, all those process dynamics and components we will be discussing later on as the "experimental stance" -- by which we will mean an approach which is deconstructive without being destabilizing, relativistic without being random, and intersubjective without the sacrifice of a coherent point of view.

Meanwhile, there is one more feature of our table of

responses which stands out, and which further supports and organizes this unitary perspective. This is the fact, curious too if you think about it, that there's never any need to instruct participants to *link their responses from left to right*, making the interpretation serve as a (provisional) explanation of the behavior observed, the feeling response a basis for evaluating and choosing a possible action, and so on. This isn't necessary, because people will just automatically do this on their own, from seeing to imagining to acting across the table of data, unifying their seeing, interpreting, affect and action plan spontaneously, in just the way our understanding of our own constructive awareness process would predict.

Not that everybody is equally good at doing all this, of course -- in the sense of creative, flexible, with a self-process serving to ground them in responses and actions with a good probability of getting them to satisfying outcomes (or at least avoiding disastrous ones). On the contrary, when we said that nobody has any trouble with the exercise, we meant people always seem to have *some* response ready for each column, and to take it for granted that the columns are meaningfully related to each other in the integrated ways we've been outlining here. But that response, for some people or with some observed behaviors or contexts, may well be constricted, fearful, stereotyped, even phobic or paralyzed. That is, within each section, people will vary widely in the breadth or constriction of their response capacity -- and this breadth or constriction will likewise feed across from one column to another, in the same necessary, integrated way, basically from left to right (in this culture) but with some backfeed or interpenetration in the other direction as well.

If a given participant says, for example, that she can see "firm step," but has "no idea what that might mean," just "isn't good" at imagining the inner states of other people, -- then the consequences of this constriction will be considerable hesitation, if not a kind of outright paralysis, in response to questions 3 and 4 as well. *Not* projecting, in other words, can mean not estimating what the person may do next; and this in turn means that I can hardly afford to take much of a risk or make much of an overture with that person at all! After all, if I don't have even so much as a good hypothesis about the person's inner state, then I'm lost as to how to proceed, even to gather more information. I might like to make a small overture, say, some fairly safe gesture just to "test the waters" (though how do I even know if I'd like this or not, without some provisional working notion of what the person is like "on the inside"); and then how do I begin to select, design, and safely test any such overture, even as a trial gesture, without some working hypothesis -- a projection of his/her inner state, what we may often call "first impressions," -- to guide me? Again, far from being a "mistake" or a "failure of objectvity," *projection is our essential orienting strategy, in dealing with people*. The problematics of projection and interpretation, as we have seen, lie not in our habitual dependence on these skills and strategies, which is built into the very nature of our awareness and self-process -- but rather in our failure or lack of skill in the particular kind of deconstructive dialogue and intersubjective inquiry which serve to complete the projection, by taking it and us on to the essential corrective and experimental phase of the whole projective/interpretive/evaluative act and process.

The more common problem people may exhibit, if any, in doing the exercise tends to be at the "confessional" level: that is, people may sometimes be reluctant to reveal just how far they really have already gone down the track with their first impressions, elaborating them into whole little scenarios almost before the starting gun went off -- and how extensively they may base their actions on the expected responses of others. This is because under an individualist paradigm, where maximum autonomy and "field independence" are the ideal, it may feel inappropriate or shameful to admit the amount of field orientation and careful, calibrated reading of other people's imagined intentions that we really are doing, typically and by our very nature, much or most of the time -- and how much we actually do adjust our own actions, constantly and correctively, to those readings. This very activity clashes with the individualist ideal of "autonomy," and may even be hard to explain and talk about, under an individualist model (where others are "objects" to us, remember). And yet we go right on doing it, indeed must go right on doing it -- for all the reasons discussed above: because if we didn't, we wouldn't know where to begin to base our own actions and reactions in relation to those others, as we work to manage and accomodate and meet our needs in the social field.

None of this is to say by any means that we are totally constrained by the reactions of others (though some people may be, because of hidden assumptions of danger or self-worthlessness they are integrating right into the seeing-imagining-assessing unit). Rather, we are constantly taking the (interpreted, predicted) field into account -- if only to estimate how much self-energy we are going to need to marshal, to deal with a social environment that we expect to be supportive or resistant, as we imagine the case may be, to one or another particular way of organizing the shared field.

But this then brings us into the topic area of systemic conditions and systems dynamics -- those field patterns or process rules held between people, that favor or disfavor particular actions and patterns of action in the field. To see where these topics and these dynamics fit into the perspective on self and experience we are building up here, and to see what "system" itself means in this unified perspective, we now go back and add one last step to our exercise, moving now across the personal self-boundary, from imagination to living interaction and relationship in the high-stakes theater of "real life."

The Self in the Social System

At this point we are ready to add one final thing to our step-by-step process, to finish bringing it up out of the lab and into the living situation. We do this by adding a *response*, to everything supplied so far on the flip charts of people's "see/imagine/approach" tables, on the part of the endlessly patient figure still walking around in the middle of the room. It goes something like this: "*if* you see me with firm step, heels coming down hard; *and* you imagine decisiveness, *and* you approach me in cases of need, but not for fun, then *my* response might be ________________." And then the person in the middle fills in the blank, for each of the sets of feedback/ interpretation/approach up on the charts. Of course, this response will differ, depending on the person, and also on the situation and context -- and then too, the same person in the same context will have a different response to each different observer (a difference based on his/her own perceptions of that observer, interpretations of those perceptions, feelings and action estimations about that, and so on). In other words, we now are dealing with the *interaction of two sets of awareness/construction and meaning-making processes*, two projective/evaluative/experimental systems, in a rapid and fluid process of mutual influence and reciprocal co-regulation. Our table now begins to look quite crowded, and by the same token more lifelike -- something like this (remembering that the third column could be quite different, to the "same" stimulus):

if I see/imagine	and if I feel/do	then you see/imagine/ feel and offer in response
firm step/confidence	relaxed/approach	smile -- joining -- warm welcome -- we can work or play together
firm step/overbearing	fearful/make nice	half-smile -- insincerity -- tight, anxious -- stay in control in response
shoulders down/ depressed	overburdened/try to fix it	wrinkled brow -- warm concern -- safe, dependent -- leave everything up to you

hesitant step/ shyness	safe/approach trustingly	vigorous approach -- unsafe, menaced -- become guarded -- stay at a distance in response
big smile/sign of insincerity	unsafe/try to control danger	tight face -- dislike -- hurt, rejected -- become controlled, suspicious in response

and so on. Note how easily sequences like these can settle into a set of mutually self-fulfilling prophecies, assumptions that are never tested or dialogued any further. In the first sequence, where each person "reads" confidence, relaxation and availablility (rightly or wrongly) into the other, the interaction this gives rise to seems likely to promise a beneficent circle, one where positive projections may promote good outcomes, which lead in turn to more positive interpretations and attributions and so on. Indeed, this may well be the case -- as long as the projections were well-grounded in the first place! But what if the initial subject is a "cruiser," a seductive person (male or female) who smoothly radiates an attractive confidence which draws trusting others in, sexually or otherwise, -- but masks a deep fear of intimacy, even a need to control or punish later by abandonment. Positive projections as well as negative ones may profit from being checked out in more intimate dialogic inquiry.

In the second case, the initial projective interpretion, "overbearing," may or may not have been accurate -- which is to say, congruent with the "real" inner state of the person observed (but note too that that state itself may be fluid, and may shift from defensive overbearingness to relaxed confidence, if only it is somehow met with an interpretative reception that reaches "beyond" the surface behavior and strikes a congruent chord at a deeper level). If the projection "overbearing," right or wrong, is then responded to as in the table, the result, for a time anyway, will very likely be a familiar kind of vicious circle, with mistrust breeding mistrust, and defensive efforts to mask, placate, and/or control leading to more of the same. As above, events may happen that change the interpretation, and thus change the emergent "system" (a shared task or emergency, for example, or other new information about the other person). But for a time at least, the likely outcome is a mutual self-escalation of negative effects (what in information theory is called, actually, a "positive feedback loop" -- that is, one in which each response heightens the triggering event, in an escalating round that may eventually spin dangerously out of control. Ethnic prejudice and inter-group violence come to mind as instances of this kind of escalating mistrust and enmity, with possible violent consequences).

In the third response sequence, the interpretation of "depressed" led to the kind of response we may think of as "codependent:" i.e., feelings of being burdened or stressed, accompanied by efforts to "fix" the other person. In this case, the other person (the initial observed subject), becomes "confluent" (as the Gestalt term has it) with this proposed set of process "rules," and gives up some measure of initiative and self-responsibility -- the posture known as "learned helplessness." In the next case, however, a somewhat similar interpretation of shyness or anxiety is met not with a "fix-it" approach (or avoidance, hostile contempt, exploitation, dismissal, or other possible moves, each depending on the personal history, cultural underpinnings, and expectations of interactive possibility on the part of the observer), but rather with a kind of relaxed identification: "you're shy and anxious *like me*; we could relax safely and do something pleasant together." And finally, the last response seems on the way to a kind of self-fulfilling prophecy, where a projection of insincerity and a hidden agenda may well lead to masking and managing, much as the observer imagined and feared.

Thus the same person may seem to be or present a "different self," or at least a different aspect of self, a different possible self-organization, with each different set of projections and overtures from others -- because with each set, the person is operating in and integrating a different interpersonal field. And in each case, the dyad may then be then off and running, for good or ill or some combination of the two. The course the twosome would follow is not set in stone, of course: depending on what happens next, and how they are able to dialogue about it, they may self-correct in their projections, learn more, make new hypotheses and new experiments with each other. They may get help, formal or informal, from a supervisor, a consultant, or just a colleague or friend who offers a different interpretation, with deconstructive effect. On the other hand, they may well polarize and escalate, each one reacting to her/his own interpretation of the other's behavior, which of course was itself based on an interpretation of the first one's gesture, and on and on. Even without escalating, they may well just settle in to a particular way of dealing (or not dealing) with each other, a sort of steady or frozen state, of avoidance or other fixed or limited possibility. Indeed, this is probably the most likely outcome, for a great many of our relationships in life, where we simply don't have or take the time, or have the skills and the social support, to deconstruct our own projections, or help in the deconstruction of those of the other person.

Another way of putting all this is to say that each person, while not absolutely constrained by his/her interpretation of the other's apparent motive, will nevertheless be making and using a *mapping of the field*, to use Gestaltist Kurt Lewin's image (1936). This map, or whole field picture (inner and outer worlds in relation to each other), serves to show what courses of action are likely to be easy in the given context (in the field, that is, of relationship at the moment with that particular person), and what will probably be hard. Again, we have to be doing this, as best we can, if only to have a sense of how much energy to muster, or whether we are going to need other help and resources, to get where we want to go and accomplish what we need to get done.

In the chapters ahead, we will be calling this kind of

survey or field-scan a *map of supports*, needed and available or missing in the field. What we mean exactly by supports, in the new paradigm view we are building, will be more clear in Chapter Five, where we take up support and development in detail, based again on a concrete exercise and our own experience. For now we can say that we don't just mean those people or features of the field around us that are "friendly," to us or our purposes, but something broader, a general estimate or mapping of how much the job at hand (of influencing you, say, or moving you in some way, getting your attention or agreement on something) will be easy or hard, and what is available or not, in the environment and in ourselves, to move toward our ongoing goal, which is some kind of satisfying living in the field of relationship.

This map of supports is then by definition the *system* that I am living in, as I try to understand and negotiate (and influence) a given field. Again, how this has to be true will be spelled out in more detail in the chapters ahead, where we will focus developmentally on the meaning of that familiar yet tricky word "system," and how that meaning and understanding change, with the change from the individualist paradigm. At this point we can at least point out that if we think of "system" in an informational sense, as many schools of "systemic" therapy do (as a set of rules and patterns, say), then our own *subjective understanding* of those rules is exactly the same as the term "map of supports" as we used it above. And remember that it is not the "rules themselves," but *my understanding* of the rules, that will govern and influence my behavior in the field, as we have seen all through this chapter. That is, as with any perceptual construction, the system I react to, the one I am influenced in and by, is the system I think I'm in, not the one I'm "really" in, in some "objective" sense (a point often neglected and thus troublesome in some systemic therapies). This perspective on system and support, viewed from somewhere outside the individualist self model, will then serve to link the often separate domains of *systems analysis* and *subjective experience* -- which is just the kind of link we were hoping for, out of the switch to a new paradigm.

Summary and Conclusions

Where does all this leave us, so far? In the first two chapters of this book we critiqued, first of all, the history of individualism and its vicissitudes down through the 3000-plus-year reign of this dominant paradigm of self and human nature in our Western tradition. From there we turned to the outline of a new way of viewing and experiencing self, based not on the "essentialist" assumptions of our dominant individualistic paradigm, but on the organization and process terms of our *defining self-functions in real living,* which are the processes of awareness or existence (*ex-stare*) themselves. Starting over in this way gave us an accumulating and coherent picture of a self and self-process that are inherently *constructively organized, affectively oriented, image- and imagination-based, meaning-making, evaluative, experimental by nature, and intersubjective,* in approaching and understanding the field of experience and action. These process characteristics, again, were not characteristics of "self" that we wished for or posited only, as has often seemed the case in our philosophical tradition, and indeed in much of the psychological tradition that derives from it. Rather, our argument throughout has been that these are the *necessary functional aspects* of a self that is in any way distinguished from, and yet can perceive and participate in, the whole existent field. Given our nature as perceiving beings, these are the features we can derive and discern, as we look and feel our way into our own self-process and definitional self-experience.

In the course of this chapter we've taken up these features and inherent processes, in the real, dynamic (albeit staged) arena of *living with other people*, which we have said is our first and most basic task and ongoing challenge in life. Using that exercise stage, we've then walked our way, along with some of the participants in the training exercise we've been using as our data lab, from first sighting to dyadic system formation, from first impressions on up through interpretation, estimation/prediction, the evaluative self-readings we call "feelings," and on to gesture and overture, then response, assumed possibilities, and the beginnings of "stable system," for good or ill. Note how these dyadic "proto-systems" can seem to arise spontaneously, without the intention or awareness of either party. Rather, they arise, in the felicitous term of relational psychologist Alan Fogel (1993), by a process of *co-regulation of the shared field*. Such patternings, and the stable interpersonal systems they often harden into, may then of course be a good or a bad thing, supplying either positive attributions which carry the participants through injuries and misunderstandings -- or negative ones, undermining sincere overtures and good-faith reparative gestures.

In the process we've both explored and taken for granted that most defining self-property of all: *our capacity and necessity for experiential field-integration itself*, for forming the "best possible gestalt" out of all the dynamic elements and processes available to our understanding at the given time, and in and from the given place, a particular moment and point of view. Once again, this is our self-nature: that which we cannot not do. Meanwhile, not only have we glossed over, to some extent, the question of *how* we integrate, but up to now we've also been emphasizing more the momentary, situational aspect of this integration -- which is to say, we have in some sense neglected, partly for clarity's sake, the integration of *memory*, persistent image-patterns of past meaningful field-resolutions or gestalts. In part, we treated the exercise as if the participants walked in fresh (though certainly if we think about it, we do know that the interpretations we bring and construct do come from somewhere, and bespeak a history). But in real living, we're never starting fresh, with the new situation, the new relationship, the new moment. Rather, the crucial interpretative stage or aspect of awareness and meaning-making is by definition a process that involves the *holding and comparison of images from the past*, in and along with the organization of images of the present (that capacity of the human brain/mind to hold multiple images together, which we said in Chapter Two is fundamental to everything else we are and do).

The result of this capacity, and this necessary part of our human nature, is what we may call the *narrative self*, self as story, in the sense of our everyday use of the word as roughly equivalent to identity, person, "who I am." This accumulating narrative is built up out of the interpretive integration of defining moments in the whole field, or what Gestaltist Paul Goodman (1951) called *creative adjustments,* our spontaneous need and act to make and find the best solutions and resolutions we can, out of all the elements at hand at a given moment. But one of the elements at hand, more and more importantly as time and development go on, *is that self-narrative itself*, which integrates and encapsulates in shorthand, message form the essence of what I need to know about me-in-the-world, as I look for and make the creative adjustment of the present moment. That is, our creativity is always constrained in various ways, no more "completely free" to combine and recombine the available "elements of reality" than our perceptual process is "completely free" to perceive "objectively," what is "really there." Both are informed and prestructured in certain ways by *expectation*; and expectation, about what I am and can be, and what the world holds and can (and cannot) hold for me, is another way of saying self in this narrative or self-in-the-world sense.

But then how does all that get formed? Where and how does that coherent "sense of self" arise? What are these integrative processes over time, that yield and then rely on self-narrative or identity -- and then which are themselves the crucial informing structures of ground which we bring to the new figure of potential relationship at first encounter (and then all through), which we have been tracing and deconstructing in detail through this past chapter? How does self-process in the field become *personal self-structure* in the individual person (however conceived), formed or standing process -- which in turn becomes part of the template for the next ongoing process stage or flow? The exploration of those themes and questions will be the material of Chapter Four, "The Self in Contact: Integration and Process in the Living Field."

Chapter Four: The Self in Contact -- Integration and Process in the Living Field

From Self-process to Self-narrative

Consider another exercise, in our ongoing exploration of self and self-process. This time, as you read you can either just follow the exercise along as it develops in stages, through the tables of responses and the discussions which follow -- or better yet, you can take a few moments and a notebook or your laptop and give your own responses to the exercise questions, adding your material to the tables given here. In this way, your exploration of your own process and your interaction with the theoretical and clinical/developmental discussion here can inform and support each other, in the way that we have been saying that theory and lived experience should do, if we are on the right track with this new approach to the question of self (one that takes us into, not away from, our own experiences of living and working in relationships with people).

Here is the exercise, which begins with private personal reflection, the present organization of memory as part of the dynamic construction of self:

> Sit back, close your eyes, and let your mind roam back over your life, all the way back to childhood, and then floating freely over the years. Let the images and memories just float till you come to a time when you had a *problem* in your life. Not just any problem, but one you experienced as something *wrong with you*. You know the kind of thing --you're too much this, too little that, too intensely something else. You can't seem to do

something, or stop doing something, that you need to be able to do, or stop doing, or change in some way.

Take your time. Don't worry if more than one thing comes up -- just let the images play till one of the things stands out more strongly, and then go with that one. Maybe other people were telling you about this problem, trying to shape you up. Or maybe you were covering it up, or trying to -- it was your secret, and you were hoping no one would find out. Use sounds and your other senses, as well as images, because we store things in memory in multiple ways. Feel what's it's like to be you, in that situation, at the age you're picturing. What feelings come up? What does it feel like in your body?

When you feel you've got it, and you feel ready, open your eyes and write it a few sentences down about it -- your age, the problem you were up against, and what it all felt like. It helps to use the present tense. Write as much as feels lively and important to you -- for example: "I'm ____ years old, and I have this problem. I'm too ________. I'm not _________ enough. I always seem to __________ , or I never can _________," -- and so on. Add the details that make it real. Remember to include your feelings, and your *body sensations*. When you feel you've written as much as you want to for now, put down your pencil or your laptop, and we'll be ready to go on with the discussion here.

The vignettes below are responses some people have given to this stage of the exercise, which will have several other parts that follow. The names of course are fictitious, and some details are altered or combined for privacy, but the issues and feelings are real, and the wording for the most part is the participants' own. Space is left at the end of the table to hold a place for your own story -- whether you choose to write it down here or not.

A word of support: since some quite difficult or painful personal material may come up at times for some people, the group is always given the proviso that no one has to share anything of what they have written. Group members are also told, as an alternative, that for purposes of learning and participation it is just as useful to report only the feelings of the story in the course of sharing and discussion, and not the concrete content issues and events themselves, which may feel private. Interestingly, while people often report that having this option frees them up in the processes of memory, in the end no one in our groups has ever availed him/herself of it completely in practice -- though the offer is sincere, and the alternative legitimate (participants may of course be screening some details of their narratives, which would also be appropriate). By the same token, if the group is large, or doesn't already know each other well (or if trust level is low for some reason), then the sharing (with the same caveats) takes place first in dyads, and only then is reported out in part to the larger group -- again with the option of keeping the content or any details within the boundary of the dyad.

table 1: a time in my life when something was "wrong with me"

Jake: I'm nine years old, and I have a big problem. My problem is that I'm too sensitive -- way too sensitive, especially for a boy. I get tears in my eyes if anybody so much as looks the least bit stern at me. If I'm scolded or just spoken to coldly I may actually cry. This is mortifying to me -- and it's very distressing to my father, I can tell that, even if we never talk about it (of course talking about it would make it happen). I feel completely hopeless about this -- I'll never be casual and confident like other people, and there's nothing I can do about it.

Eleanor: I'm eight, ten, any age, and I talk too much. Way too much. My mother tells me constantly that I'm too full of myself, nobody is interested. I'm too smart for my own good, she says, and if I don't shut up, I'll never get a husband. I do try, but it makes me feel like I'm bursting. I honestly think that's why I don't write today. I hear my mother's voice -- shut up, who do you think you are, nobody wants to listen to you chatter all day.

Barbara: I'm five or six years old, but also even older, and I still can't go *anywhere* without my mother. I don't even like to play out in the courtyard, right outside the kitchen door. She's always sending me out, but I just hang around near the door till I think enough time has passed, and then I go back in. I'm dreading the start of school in the fall.

Kathy: I'm ten years old, and I fight all the time. I don't even know why it is that I end up in so many fights -- many of them physical. My teachers hate me, I can see it on their faces -- my mother is at her wits' end. I just seem to fly off the handle all the time. This is hopeless -- I'm hopeless. My sister is so perfect, and I can't do anything right.

Ricardo: I'm afraid of people -- especially men. I'm not sure what I think they'll do to me, but I avoid them as much as possible. I don't have any friends, except the girl next door, and she's a girl. I could be any age, up to about twelve or fourteen -- this goes back as far as I can remember. Then it changed, in a way, although now I'm not so sure --

Jane: I always feel left out. I'm about nine or ten. All the other girls have friends, they're all so tight, sleeping over all the time and everything. I don't have anybody. I hate myself, and I hate my life. My mother tries to make it up to me, but she doesn't understand, she was always popular. My father doesn't even try.

Sam: It's simple, I'm stupid. I can't read, can't pay attention, can't concentrate. Whatever the teacher says I can't remember it. Everybody knows it -- Sam's stupid. My parents don't care. My father's always in front of the TV with his beer, yelling at everybody. My mother is dealing with my father. I'm going to be a total failure in life, and they won't even care.

As with the last exercise, the first thing that stands out about this one is that no one ever seems to have any difficulty in coming up with responses. Out of some hundreds of participants, in various workshop and course settings over some years, no one has ever yet reported that she/he just can't seem to find her/himself in the instructions, or find anything to write about that would fit the instructions. Apparently the myth of a carefree and thoughtlessly happy childhood is just that, -- a myth. While there certainly are childhoods and children that are developmentally healthy and basically positive in tone, the truth is that the world is a difficult place, growing into it in a robust and well-grounded way is not self-evident in the best of cases, and no childhood or children are free of periods of doubt, challenge, or struggle -- nor perhaps should they be, for healthy lifelong development in adulthood. (This of course is not to say that real stress and abuse are good for children: the unassimilable challenge may indeed lead to a kind of strength, but that strength will inevitably be rigid and constricting, not supple and growthfully robust).

Rather, it seems that pretty much everybody has had whole periods of life, at the least, where they worried about something being wrong with them. The nature and severity of the situation differ greatly, of course -- from the well-supported child with peer insecurities of some kind, all the way to tragic loss and even more tragic abuse. Still, even when we put the task in the fairly depressive, self-condemning way we've cast it here, we've never had a participant who put down pen or computer and said he or she just couldn't find any way to relate to the question.

Of interest too is how often the problem seems to hinge on something that is gender-dystonic, which is to say, contrary to traditional social expectations for our own particular sex. Not infrequently women will report being "too" assertive, dominant, or aggressive -- or if not that, then too asocial or shy, not able to make friends and get along with people, "the way a girl should be able to." Men for their part may often report doubting that they were aggressive enough, or competent enough, or thick-skinned enough, or feeling sure that they weren't. People may or may not make that link consciously -- that the perceived inadequacy is something that violates gender norms -- as some did and some didn't among the responses above. Later on in life, among the presenting problems of psychotherapy, again it is remarkable to notice how often the life problem also involves a misfit with stereotypical gender expectations in the world, which have been internalized by the patient. This is something we will take up further in Chapter Five, in the discussion of support and development, in light of the new self-model we are developing all through these chapters, and then again in Chapter Eight, when we talk directly about gender and the gendered field.

The feeling tone people have after completing this first step of the exercise is often one of sadness, helplessness, perhaps mild depression and some sense of shame. Typically people report feeling small and fairly isolated, sometimes irritated at the workshop leader for putting them back in touch with a time and a state that have been left far behind (and yet still may seem disturbingly close and familiar). Some will have a stronger reaction -- a feeling for example of "hating themselves," or of shame that burns -- and you can see the flush on their face as they tell it. Other body feelings too may be those associated with shame -- shrinking, sinking, hot, wanting to disappear. As one workshop participant put it, "This had better be going somewhere, because I don't go back to feelings like this for no good reason."

It is going somewhere. Here's part two of the exercise (again, if you haven't yet done part one for yourself and still want to, this is your last chance to do it *de novo*, without yet knowing all the discussion, and where we're going with the material from here):

> Once again close your eyes, and picture the same scene, that time and place in your earlier life where you have the problem you've just been writing about. Only this time, instead of being inside yourself, the child looking out and around at the world, pull back and survey the whole scene from above, or some other vantage point a little way off. Before, we were looking at the child's world, your world, from the inside. Now let's look at the same scene from the outside, more from our perspective now.
>
> Viewing at it this way from the outside, look around the whole scene for what's *missing* or wrong *in the environment outside your child-self*, that makes or helps make this behavior or characteristic of yours into such a problem. The behavior characteristic itself, whatever it was, was just that -- a fact, a characteristic (if it was even true). Something outside you made that characteristic, that fact or challenge, into a big problem. What was that something?
>
> What was it that was too much, or not enough, or maybe missing entirely in your world, back at that age, that made your problem worse -- or maybe made it into a problem in the first place, instead of just a descriptive fact? What made it all feel so hopeless, so insoluble, back then?
>
> When you've got the scene, again take a few moments to write it down, in a few phrases or sentences. Use the present tense, and remember to include your feelings and body sensations now, from this new vantage point, which may be different as you view the scene from outside. When you're ready, look up, and again we'll share it out.

Table Two gives some sample responses to this stage of the exercise, from the same people who responded in Table One. Again participants are reminded of the option either not to share out at all, or to share only the feelings, without any reference to the content of the scenes per se. And again, no one has ever yet availed him/herself of the first option, though we hope and believe that people do adjust and accommodate level of exposure to level of comfort, holding back some details that feel too private in a given setting, at a given moment.

table 2: the environment of the "problem"

Jake: it's easy to answer, they were so *preoccupied*, so wrapped up in themselves, and I don't know, so rough, so impatient. All except my grandmother, who died. But there again, I was too close to my grandmother, it made my father uncomfortable, I could see that. Too close for a boy. But nobody was interested in the kind of boy I was -- you know, sensitive, bookish. The irony is, my father was sort of like that too, under the surface. I guess that's why it was so hard for him. Why I was so hard for him. But of course I didn't know that then.

Eleanor: you know it's funny when you think about it, why *didn't* they want to listen? what was the matter with them? If I had a little girl like that, I'd be in seventh heaven. And they weren't so downtrodden and over-worked or anything -- I mean, we were poor I guess, but no poorer than anybody else. We had family parties, and dinners and things. What was the matter with them, that they couldn't listen to this bright, serious little girl who really was trying to figure the world out? I don't get it!

Barbara: this is incredible -- my father was an alcoholic, and he left the family. He wasn't abusive I don't think - he just left. and the incredible part is, I don't think I ever made that connection before. It almost makes me mad-- no, it does make me mad! It's so obvious. I've made the connection that my mother was depressed, and I was taking care of her, clinging to her and all. But it was more than that -- the world out there actually was a dangerous place to me, it was where people went off and drank, and never came back. How did I know what it was -- my mother practically never went out, today you'd say she had agoraphobia. So how was I supposed to be -- happy and outgoing and full of confidence??

Kathy: look, my sister and I were just very different people -- we both know that now, and we respect each other, even if we're not really close. But back then -- back then it was like there just wasn't any room for a person like me. Not a girl like me anyway. This was a small town, it was the fifties, you wore dresses and black patent leathers to school. That suited my sister fine, she still lives there, and she's a good person, led the fight to integrate the schools 30 years ago, marched and everything -- in her stockings and her black patent leather pumps and her black patent leather purse, that was part of it, she makes all that work for her. I just wasn't like that. Actually I think if I'd had a brother it would have been better, it would have been a bridge to my father, or my mother, or somebody. I was such a tomboy, and I hated, just hated my sister. because I thought they didn't love me, or love me as much. I think they did love me, but I don't think they liked me very much -- I made them uncomfortable. They like me better now, my mother does. The world has changed so much, even there--

Ricardo: well, if you put the question like that it answers itself. There just wasn't any room for a person like me. of course I was afraid of men -- I didn't *know* any, till I was in junior high school, and then they were these weird gym teachers. and of course I hung out with girls -- they were the only ones who had the same interests I did. I'm a fashion designer for chrissakes. For a long time I thought that meant I must be gay. Then I wasn't so sure. Now I don't care -- I mean, I care, but I don't try to define myself. That has some problems too, but *I live in a world where there's room for people like me* (underlined twice).

Jane: I don't know why I was so shy, I think I was just born that way. I still am, but I handle it better now -- a little better anyway. I try to look at the other person and say "he's shy too," or "she's shy too." You know, like people with stagefright are supposed to visualize the audience in their underwear, or something that humanizes them. The funny thing is, I don't have stagefright. But why couldn't somebody have taught me a few of these strategies back then? I was miserable, I hated Brownies -- and nobody even seemed to notice. Well, my mother, but she wouldn't talk about it -- she'd just buy me a dress or take me to a movie, if she thought I needed cheering up.

Sam: look, does the word ADD mean anything to you? What do you have to do to get psych testing, kill somebody? I wonder now if my father didn't have it too, and just was self-medicating. I do believe it's hereditary, at least in my case. My little boy has it, and lord the resources the school has he's doing fine, really just fine. But that's because he has support. and different parents -- I almost just said "parents," period.

Again, this exercise question is not a step anybody seems to have any trouble taking, once you suggest it. The environmental side of the child's problem, and the way this environment, this context, made that problem the crisis or inner torment it may have been, seem right there at hand as soon as our attention is turned to them -- even for participants like Barbara who never made this connection before. At this point in the exercise, the feeling tone in the room usually shifts dramatically. Before, with identification of the problem in language that located it "inside" the individual person, the feelings were mostly sad, depressive, hopeless (but remember the old clinical wisdom that says depression covers rage, and turns it against the self). Now the mood shifts, as some of these vignettes already suggest, with many people reporting angry feelings (which come through in some of the written reports), ranging from exasperation to bitterness to outright fury. And where the depressive, shameful feelings from the first stage were held privately (and then magnified by the group resonance), here the impatience or anger may well cross the individual boundaries between participants, with many people reporting outrage or exasperation at other people's situations, as well as their own (a number of participants, for example, spontaneously expressed resonance with Eleanor in the vignette above, assuring her that they too would be ecstatic with a bright "nudgy" little girl like that, and it was her parents' great loss not to appreciate that). Compassion for the young girl or boy that one was back then replaces some (not all) of the shame and self-condemnation felt before, often accompanied now by judgment or incomprehension at the world around the child, and the people whose job it was to provide a liveable environment for growing. "What was *wrong* with those people?" more than one participant has asked, "Couldn't they see, didn't they care?" Or, with more compassion for them, as one young man put it, "They were doing the best they could, I can see that now. I probably could see it then, that was part of my problem, I always made allowances, never made any demands. But lord, they just didn't get it."

The shift in how we frame things, then, leads to a shift not just of understanding but of *feelings and actual sensations and body states as well* -- just as we saw in the previous chapter on projection and relationship, and posited in the earlier theoretical chapters of this book. This again is because our activity and reactivity in the field of experience is a whole -- and because our feelings and even our sensations, as part of that whole, are not just received events that we register passively, but active, (self)-interpretive constructions like any other perceptions, differing from other perceptions not in how we organize and hold them, but in what *part* of the experiential field they refer to. And thus they will differ too in the particular deconstructive processes we might go to, to validate them or change them, or just know them at a deeper level.

This simple shift of vision, from "inside" to "outside" dimensions or "places" in the experiential field, then has important implications for our understanding of our particular topic here, which is how self-organization operates as a process, and what all this means for our notions of self and human nature. But before going on with that discussion, let's look first at one more stage of the exercise. Here are the instructions for Part Three:

> At this point you've looked back now on a child or young person -- yourself -- who had a problem, who felt there was something wrong with him or her, something she or he just couldn't seem to fix, for a time anyway. You spent some time looking at this child from the inside out -- his/her feelings, frustrations, hopes and fears or even despair, that trait or incapacity that felt like a danger or a block in living. Then you pulled back and looked at that same child, your childhood self, from the outside in, with an eye broad enough to encompass the environment, the world your child self was living in and dealing with. From this perspective you could see what it was in the environment that made this trait, this problem so serious for you back then -- what it was that was too little, too much, or both, in your world then, that made the thing you're talking about feel at times like a desperate, insoluble problem.
>
> Insoluble -- and yet somehow we solved it. We know we did, in some sense at least, because here we all are today, grownup people in a professional setting, functioning pretty well, at least, and looking back and doing this exercise. In other words, somehow or other we've come a long way. Not without stress, maybe even damage -- and yet most of us would probably say that we're doing better now than we might have expected back then, at those low points we were just looking at, and feeling in our bodies and our emotions, and writing and talking and thinking about together.
>
> Our question now is, *how did you do it*? You had a problem, as you framed it back then anyway; and in some way you solved that problem. You found some way of dealing with it, or else we wouldn't be here together today, in as good shape as we are basically in. Or if not solved exactly, then you compensated for it in some way, managed it, made the best of it, maybe even turned it into a strength. How? What was the strategy you made or found for dealing with that problem, and how did you make that work for you, to get where you are today? As before, think about this, write it down -- and then when you're ready, share that solution with your partner.

And again some sample responses, still from the same people who responded above, so we can begin to draw people's stories together and look at them as a whole: the problem "in me"-- the environmental conditions that created it or made it worse -- and then my solution or strategy for dealing with it:

table three: strategies and solutions

Jake: well, that's an interesting question. I guess I did two things. One was, I figured I'd become an academic star. I mean I was smart, but a lot of kids were smart. But somewhere back then I made the decision that if I wasn't tough, I'd get respect another way. So I maxed out on the academics -- I just had to be the best, the first, whatever. If we had to learn a poem, I learned six. If we wrote a report mine was illustrated, I read whole books, that kind of thing. And the other one was -- I mean, I couldn't have put words on this back then -- but I think I figured out how to use my sensitivity to psych people out, and protect myself. I learned to read people, really really well, you know, for a kid. First my dad, but then everybody else too. I became sort of famous for it: you wanted to know how to get around a certain teacher? -- you just came to me, and I could tell you, or else I'd handle it for you. My brothers and even my sister were tougher than I was, but if it was a matter of confronting our father, they always got me to handle it. Same thing at school -- everybody just knew, get Jake, he can handle it. And I still do that today, in the clinic. If they can't deal with this certain principal, or judge, or school superintendent -- they all just call me. That's how I got respect, without being tough.

Eleanor: I went on stage! literally, in plays, in school and college - but also figuratively, student politics, and in a way my job now, as a consultant and lecturer. On stage, other people *wanted* to listen to me, which actually impressed my mother. She made cracks about it, which sort of hurt, but I knew she was proud all the same. As long as it was somebody else's words, like a play, I never had a bit of nervousness. With my own words it's harder -- I have to have a prepared talk, I still can't speak off the cuff at all well. And I don't write -- if I sit down to write, more than just a talk, I'm paralyzed, I still hear my mother's voice: "who do you think you are, who wants to listen to you?"

Barbara: well, of course I became a caretaker. I was already my mother's caretaker, and somewhere along the way I found out or figured out that all these other girls needed caretakers too. Everybody needs a caretaker, and believe me, I'm good at it. I can make you feel listened to, and I'm not threatening, I don't compete, I'm a completely safe person. People are always surprised to find out that I'm a vice-president of a bank, and I did have to show I could take a stand now and then, to get where I am, but mostly that was faking it, really I got there by being a caretaker. The customers adore me, the president of the bank adores me, I'm just the world's most helpful person. Maybe that sounds sarcastic, but I really am. The only thing is, I can't get married. Every time I get in a relationship I get panicked, about being drained and all, and I break it off. And you can imagine the guys I get involved with -- always needy screwups. You know, really dysfunctional -- now there's a part where I just want to tell you the feelings, not the details! (laughter) But the other ones I don't know how to relate to, I can't believe they need me. So everything has its plusses and minuses--

Kathy: tennis. That was my answer -- tennis. It was the only sport a girl could play back then, and compete in. There was swimming, but no girls' swimming team. But girls were supposed to learn tennis, you know, to meet boys, and to use at the club, so they had a little so-called team. I took it all the way to state, in girls' singles. My mother couldn't believe I could keep those little white miniskirts so clean -- my clothes were always dirty before that. At 14, I was teaching tennis to girls and then women -- at 16 I was the women's tennis pro at the country club. They didn't call it that, but they paid me, and that's what I was. That got me through, and then I got out of there, to college -- on a tennis scholarchip. I'm not sure I ever changed that much, but I did stop fighting. It even helped with my sister, because she wanted to learn tennis!

Ricardo: I don't know that I ever did work it out really, not back there. What I did do, and it helped, was to become the artist. I could draw things for people -- I drew caricatures for the school paper, and got a lot of strokes for that. it sort of gave people a label to put on me, and that helped too -- "you know Ricardo, he's an artist." It was an Italian neighborhood, and with Italian people that has some panache, even the macho types. The

Renaissance and all that, it's part of the self-image, we Italians are artists. I mean, in my neighborhood the guys thought Leonardo was a Ninja Turtle -- but they knew he was Italian! And of course I knew a lot of those Renaissance artists were gay, so it opens up a little space for you -- just in your own mind, which is so important.

Jane: I don't think I did get over it, really. I did find a few other shy girls to be friends with -- that helped. And then I got to college, and something amazing happened. I had these really sweet sorority sisters, and a group of them decided to take me in hand. I was their project, it was a big game, but at the same time it was incredibly sweet, because they made me feel like I was worth something to them. Oh, it helped them too, the way helping somebody does, but I think it also just really pained them that I was so distressed all the time. They're the ones who taught me that everybody is shy -- they taught me everything, how to talk to a boy, how to flirt, how to make out. And then I could play the piano, which was good at theatricals. I was always a different person on stage, because it's not personal. But I do still struggle with it today. I'm struggling with it right now, just talking --

Sam: it's interesting reading everybody's responses up on the charts around the room -- you feel like you could write this part for them, just looking at them. You can see what strategy they adopted, because they're still using it now. They can probably see mine too. I did two things, as I see it. I became the clown, everybody loved me for that. I couldn't get anything out of the damn books, the print just hopped around in front of my eyes. But I was really smart at tracking a conversation, and knowing what people were going to say next. And then I'd say it, but in a funny way, that would put everybody in stitches - even the teachers. But I also became the protector. I wasn't the mean type, so I wasn't a bully -- unless somebody else was being bullied, or put down -- and then look out, because I was big for my age. Boy, I protected the world -- and got a place for myself in the process. And then I finally learned to read -- that helped. but that was in high school. I never would have made it to high school, without, you know, that little bit of affirmation --

Again, space is left to make room for or at least signify the reader's own experience. At this point we can begin to summarize everybody's responses in a combined table, to see what stands out and what we can draw from it for our purposes here. It would look something like this:

Table Four: the solution in the whole field

problem in me	problem in environment	solution
Jake: too sensitive	no support, no listening, father uncomfortable with sensitivity	academic star, learned to "psych people out
Eleanor: talk too much	mother not interested	found others to listen, "took the show on the road"
Barbara: afraid to leave mother's side	father made world scary, mother withdrew	became a caretaker for others
Kathy: fighting, sister "perfect"	parents unable to relate to more aggressive girl	tennis
Ricardo: afraid of people, especially men	no acceptance of "feminine" no support for exploration of possible gay identity	identified with new group, then found new environment

Jane: terribly shy, no friends	no help with strategies, social skills, compensations, no models	found a few shy friends, later got "tutoring" from college friends; also music
Sam: "stupid" (ADD)	no supports for learning disabilities at school, no concern at home	became "clown," also protector of others

And the list could go on. Each participant, and each one of us, could continue supplying answers to each column -- sometimes with a significant "aha!" reaction, especially in column three, when we suddenly see something that is very much ourselves (or each other) today, as Sam did above, looking both at himself and around the room. The "aha" marks the link, between something we know about ourselves today, for good or ill (very likely both), a dominant or habitual strategy or style, and the *moment of creation* of that style or talent, developmentally, in the urgent crucible of real-life exigencies, as a strategy to solve or manage some life and developmental problem long ago. This is the process Goodman called "creative adjustment," discussed earlier, the constructive integration of the field, "inner" and "outer," into a new, more workable self-organization, a new gestalt. This is the operation of the self in process, in the integrated act of solving a problem in living, as creatively as possible, with the given elements at hand as we perceive and interpret them.

At this stage it is instructive to ask people the question, "Where do you see the operation of *self*, in Table Four? This is a significant slice of your living and dealing with the world, and your place in it: what dimension or process of all this would you call "self," or "self-process?" Where do you find *yourself*, as a living process, on this tableau?"

From an individualist perspective, the answer should be clear: "self" lies in the left-hand column. That is, if self is my innermost being, my private essence and core, then it is the left-hand column that comes closest to capturing my "self-experience," my most inward-looking place or part (and note how closely this way of conceiving self is tied up with the dimension of shame, a point which will be elaborated a good deal more in Chapter Six). Column two, after all, is the realm of the outside world, the "not me," to use Harry Stack Sullivan's more "experience-near" terminology. Column three is something more in the nature of an action or a behavior, the solution or strategy that is meant to bring that outer world more in harmony with the inner world of feelings, capacities, talents and so forth (that is, with "self," traditionally defined) -- and hopefully vice versa.

However, when you ask people where on the tableau they "see self," or "feel themselves," most people will answer, in contradiction to what the received tradition would seem to tell us, not column one but column three. And those that don't, almost without exception, will say again not column one, but "everywhere" or "the whole thing, it's all my self." Once someone offers this way of looking at it, oftentimes that response too will command a lot of agreement in the group, with other members saying things like, "well yes, that's true too, it's all my self, because it's all my perception, it's all my world."

Is "my world," inner *and* outer, (and not just my "innermost" world alone) the domain and raw material of my self? Experientially, which is to say in "real life," it seems that it is. Again, in both lived experience and the insights of the Gestalt cognitive/affective model discussed in the introductory chapters of this book (and a good deal more in the sections to come), the integrated process of living, what I know myself as doing (or know my "self," as doing), is the ongoing resolution of a workable, liveable map and "fit" of this whole picture, "inner" and "outer," in a "whole of meaning" (and remember, "meaning," in an evolutionary survival sense, has to mean a picture I can live with, and live in, and somehow rely on for some liveable degree of predictability and useful outcome).

But this amounts to a thoroughgoing shift in our understanding of what self is, or perhaps better, where it is, where it "happens" or operates -- exactly along the lines developed in Chapter Two and then illustrated in action in Chapter Three, only with the definition itself arising now directly from our own developmental experience. That is, the modern post-Freudian systems and schools of thought that have wrestled with this problem of defining self have tended to emphasize the integrative or organizational function (which Freud took for granted and thus neglected) -- but without necessarily questioning the *domain* of the self, what part of the field "belongs" to self, which remained much as it was given in the individualist paradigm that is our common heritage. Thus Kohut (1977) came to think of self as that which is cohesive and continuous about us, that sense of oneness in our experience that is the very definition of sanity (or at least coextensive with what we call sanity; as opposed to the disintegration we call psychotic). As far as it goes, this makes sense in terms of the picture we are developing here; but it leaves unquestioned the idea that self is something purely internal, private to me, and individually separate from the rest of the field.

Certainly Kohut recognized that we need the experiential/relational field to achieve this self-cohesiveness: he coined the somewhat awkward term "self-objects" to characterize those things we need (including people) to maintain this needed stability. In this way he manages to talk about our need for others, without departing too far from the terms of the individualist model: "self" is still a purely "internal" matter, while other people or even other things serve as internal representations, as props or ballast ("self-objects") to keep my inner core from flying apart. And there we are, where the individualist model always lands us: people as "objects," which means that the relationships we make and find, which for most of us are at the very center of our lives and meaning systems, are really in the end only a kind of self-indulgent fantasy, a comfortable fiction that enables or justifies our getting our own needs met.

But in real living we do not and cannot orient to people as objects only, as we saw in the exercise in Chapter Three. We orient to other people, more or less well, as *selves like us*, beings with an inner process like ours, which we *have to make some guess about*, at least, in order to deal with them. That is, in real life we assume an intersubjective perspective. Indeed, it is the degree of our ability to do that at all well which defines and determines our ability to *live well in the world*, in a practical sense of "getting our needs met" or any other sense. (To be sure, coercive political, military, ideological and family systems sometimes try to operate on "object" principles alone, relying on force and punishment in place of intersubjective appeal and real assent. But aside from ethical questions, such systems are famously inefficient and disastrously prone to "resistance" movements of every kind -- just as we would expect. As slave economies of all types have proven down through history, the attempt to control behavior through external pressures, as one would control an "object" or thing, is ruinously expensive on the sheer practical level alone).

Likewise the child psychoanalyst Winnicott (eg. 1965, 1988), surely one of the most gifted clinicians of his time, tries to accommodate relational needs to the old individualist model without going beyond individualism itself. Winnicott sees "self" as always arising in a relational context, and relationship itself as the fundamental self-drive (we've already made reference to his poetic dictum, that the infant self first exists in the "eye of the caretaker"). But that self, as the individualist Freudian tradition which Winnicott is a part of teaches, still seems to lie purely within the personal boundary; and those relationships are still with "objects" -- indeed, the school Winnicott is associated with goes by the name of "object relations," not "subject relations," which would be orientation to the inner world of other people in the sense that we were exploring it in Chapter Three.

The Contribution of Paul Goodman

It is here that the *relocation of self* outlined by Gestalt writer Paul Goodman, which we discussed briefly in Chapter Two, comes into play as a useful way of conceptualizing self and self-process, helping us to deconstruct at least some of the embedded linguistic assumptions of the old individualist model. Writing at around the same time as Kohut and Winnicott, Goodman's suggestion, as we have seen, was that once we conceive of self-process and self-experience not as the activity of some little agent or sub-person within us, but rather as our *basic process activity and tool for integrating the whole field of experience*, then it is more useful to think of this process, metaphorically, as taking place "at the boundary" (Goodman, 1951) of experience, and not somewhere deep within the private and preexistent individual. Rather, Goodman argued, it is that "boundary process" which *makes* the "individual person," in and out of the whole field. "Contact," as Goodman put it (the Gestalt term for that integrative, whole-field meaning-making process), yields the "self," and not the other way around. Outside of that ongoing process, which includes memory or the "narrative self," as we have called it here, there is no self: the integrative process in and of the whole field of living, is itself what self is.

But what does "boundary of experience," or the "me boundary" as we were calling it in Chapter Two, mean exactly? Subjectively (or phenomenologically), it means that by sensing my own existence, or "self-awareness," I register an experiential *difference* in the field, a sense of some experiences as "me" (and "me" as those experiences) in some way that is qualitatively different from others, which are "not me," -- or at least not in the same way (if they were mine in exactly the same way, then I wouldn't sense myself as existent at all, in any defined sense: I wouldn't "stand out." As the research of Stern and others (1985) demonstrates, we are born equipped with the prepotent capacity, at least, to begin to organize the experiential field around this fundamental dichotomy, this basic, categorical organizing principle of "me/not me," from the start. And this capacity itself rests on and comprises the building blocks of other, inborn component capacities (as for example the fact that we are wired to respond attentionally to differences: edges, corners, contrasts, shifts, and other distinctions in the field -- something that Aristotle noted long ago, and current research in perceptual neurology amply confirms (see e.g. Gibson, 1969).

Drawing once more on our evolutionary perspective, here too we can see how something like this almost has to be the case, or at least is one possible favored solution to our conditions and dilemmas as a species. Our evolutionary problem as a species, after all, is how to maximize flexible adaptability and problem-solving in a changing environment -- because we aren't good at anything else! But this necessarily means some mechanism or capacity for perceiving those changing conditions, making predictive estimates of that environment, evaluating those estimates in relation to survival needs -- which in turn means registering some distinction between the species itself and the rest of the field. In other words, awareness, coherent perceptions, predictions, evaluations, experiments, interpretation of all that -- all those hallmarks of self and self-process that are the characteristics of our species, and are our human nature itself.

Conceivably that problem might be solved with a "single organism" kind of species, rather than individual members. But if it were, that single organism would have to look something like the aggregate of all the individual members of our species now, in process terms anyway. Moreover, for long-term survival it would have to have component parts or sub-organisms that could be lost and regenerated without causing the death of the whole -- just as individual members of our species are now. And indeed, this is quite close to the perspective of a number of various traditional, Eastern, and mystic spiritual worldviews. In fact, looking at the species as a whole as a single organism doesn't really change anything in our self view at all -- except the idea that the individual precedes the relational whole, exists in a complete sense apart from that whole, and realizes its/his/her nature in some fundamental sense apart from relationships.

In other words, an evolutionary perspective, again, leads us to a clearer understanding of how we are perceptually evolved to have a sense of "me" as a difference in the field, and then to reintegrate that distinguishable picture into a new whole of meaning (which is the solution of a problem, and positions us to solve other problems). This is our evolutionary self-strategy for survival (species survival, not just individual), which in turn yields our evolved self-experience. The rhythm of attention/resolution, noticing a difference and then relating or resolving the parts of the experiential field again into a (necessarily new) whole -- the process the Gestalt model calls "figure/ground" gestalt formation, -- *is the flow of self-process itself.* And as such, it is the source of our sense of the world, and our sense of self. However much this "me/not me" distinction has been exaggerated and rigidified in our Western individualistic culture and paradigm (and we know it has been) -- and however careful we must be as we try to language this experience freshly without falling completely back into the self-vs-other terms of that cultural paradigm (and we must be careful, knowing at the same time that this will inevitably happen to some extent), we still can say that the "inner-outer" distinction is also at some level an experiential given of our evolved self-nature, the defining dimension of self-process itself.

If we then go to oral histories and anthropological accounts of "traditional" cultures, where people speak of their own childhoods (see e.g. Kenyatta, 1938), what we find is that a child's sense of having a personal, developmental challenge to solve, as in our exercise here, *is a universal feature of self-process and self-narrative.* The differences in our own culture, perhaps, lie in the extreme and sometimes crippling aloneness many children feel with these challenges -- a sense which follows from the rigidity and hyperautonomy of the "self-boundary," culturally conceived, which militates against the very sense of interpenetration of selves, of availability of the field for support in what Goodman called the "coming solution," that we found in the previous chapter, and which we are arguing all through this book is a dynamic part of our self nature.

This sense of the field as "my" field, as a vital part of me, and me of it -- and yet as a "place" that is different from the "inner me," -- as we are trying to demonstrate here and all through these chapters, is our birthright and our evolved nature. By contrast, the exaggerated indiviuality of our Western cultural tradition is a problematic distortion of one pole of that legacy and that nature. The "inner world," the sense of self as different and significant, so much emphasized in the West, and the "outer" or whole field, the sense of self as belonging to and not different from the whole, are *both experientially real*, both crucially part of our self-process and indeed of our very selves. Taken together, they are the crucial poles of awareness and self-process, both necessary for the solving and creating of something new. And as our exercise shows, sometimes humorously, sometimes painfully, that integrative process still goes on, and goes on creatively, no matter how deeply split that self-field is, or how isolated and unsupported the "individual" pole may feel, from our natural world of self-extensions, self-incorporations, and self-supports in the whole field. As the childhood environmental picture grows less and less supportive, the resultant creative solutions may well be more and more extreme, and less and less flexibly adaptable and applicable to other challenges in later life; but given the conditions as they were, we still can admire and appreciate the imaginative, creative quality of some of these "neurotic" solutions, which then may cause us such problems at times in later life.

The Self as "Boundary Process"

Granting this "inner/outer" terminology, this in turn means that when we say "at the boundary," or "boundary experience," we mean at that "place" or in that "space between" where inner and outer experience meet, and *must be integrated* for my life to go forward well, or perhaps to go forward at all. Again, as we discussed in the previous chapters, to resolve or perceive the outer world without reference to the inner realm of needs and desires, fears and memories, is at best a sort of passive registration of potentially relevant information for future needs; indeed, it is the inner world which directs and organizes my selective/deselective attentional processes, and thus informs the "facts" that I see. By the same token, to see and understand my "inner self," without then integrating and extending those perceptions and experiences to the whole field, does not in the end serve either mental health or evolutionary survival (which ultmately have to be the same thing, after all). There too, at best the "purely inner gaze" serves to clarify and reorganize that experiential domain, in the service of returning to the whole field later to make a better integration, a more articulated, encompassing gestalt, of the whole field of experience, inner and outer, each in terms of the other.

We can see these principles in operation in the responses to our exercise so far. The working solution each person made, flexibly and ongoingly, for well or ill or both, to the problems and challenges of development, was made up of a self-assessment (weaknesses and strengths, desires, antipathies, and fears) *together with* an assessment of the outside world (what's there, what's missing, what might possibly be done). Together, these two kinds of assessment go into and make up the integrated response which was our "solution" to those problems -- "creative adjustment," as

Goodman said, emphasizing that the solution is the creative life force in action, not merely adjustment in the limited sense of reaction. Again, in this whole-field, process view the "creative adjustment," the living integrative principle or process in action, is not just something done by a self that is preexistent: it *is the self*, the self which is "given in contact," again in the language of the Gestalt model.

To be sure, that solution, that creativity in action, is imperfect and may well be problematic, as we were saying above. Again, the more the creative solution to a past life dilemma was created and learned under conditions of diminished options, which is to say high personal stress and low field support (two dynamic dimensions of the solution which amount in the end to the same thing), the more that solution will tend to be both inflexible and constricted. Inflexible, because it was so intensely learned, under relatively desperate circumstances; and constricted in that it does not easily allow for seeing or adopting other possible field solutions, other possible ways of framing the same kind of challenge -- again because the conditions of the original learning and creativity were so limited. But looked at in this way, the solution itself is all the more creative for that, all the more sparked with the integrative power of making something new, the "best possible gestalt," which is still our self and our nature, even under the most disadvantageous circumstances.

If we ask our partipants now for a reading of the feeling tone in the room as they look at the whole tableau generated so far, we may get a mixed kind of feeling, which one group member characterized as "rueful pride," and another as "prideful regret." That is, looking around at others' creative solutions and personal styles as well as their own, people often feel both the admiration and appreciation we spoke of above, and also a head-shaking or heavy-sigh kind of feeling which can range from comic to wistful to downright bitter. All these are reactions to people's sense of the price they've paid, in terms of the limits of adaptive styles, for where they've gotten by riding on the strengths they created and cultivated back then (and oftentimes have maintained with remarkable consistency ever since). If we ask people to reflect at this point on how their particular adaptations have served them well or ill over the years, we will get a table that looks something like this:

table 5: how the old solution is a strength and a problem today

problem in me	environment	solution	serves/disserves now
Jake: too sensitive	no support, father ill at ease with sensitivity	academic star, "psych people out"	achiever, caretaker; hard to take a stand, ask or depend on others; lonely
Eleanor: talk too much	mother not available	found others to listen, became performer	became successful teacher, but can't write - frustrated
Barbara: too dependent on mother	father absent, mother withdrew	became caretaker for others	well-connected with work, friends, afraid intimacy, under nourished, drained
Kathy: fighting, sister "perfect"	parents unable to relate to assertive girl	tennis	self-sufficient leader, a little disconnected, hard to need/depend
Ricardo: afraid of men, people	no acceptance of "feminine," no support for sexual exploration	artist, identified with girls, later changed environ-ment	creative career, well-connected with friends, can't take a stand
Jane: terribly shy, no friends	no help with social skills, no models	found a few shy friends later music	well-liked, got some support from college friends; "still struggling"
Sam: "stupid" (ADD)	no supports for disabilities	learned to be funny by paying close attention to others; protector	high social skills, empathy; can't establish intimate relationship; defensive

Again, space is left here to accomodate or indicate and honor the reader's own challenges, circumstances, creativity, and results, both productive and problematic. Given the generally "rueful" or "heavy sigh" tone of the group by this time, possibly covered with considerable humor, possibly with more compassion for others than for oneself, it becomes important to support people here to stop, breathe, and celebrate, together and within ourselves, the power and positive impact those early adjustments and creative solutions have had in our lives -- for all that they may have settled or hardened now into what we call "character," meaning simply adaptations that are early and overlearned, and firmly supported now by corresponding adaptations of body, belief system, lifestyle, and the adjustments of others around us.

It used to be a shibboleth of psychotherapy that the "neurotic level" can be changed, but "character" cannot. This is probably true -- given the autonomous self in isolation. With a field-self view, where each dimension of the adaptation or style is seen as a *present dynamic in and of a whole field*, the issue of change becomes a question of *supports* for change in all the relevant domains of the whole field, inner and outer. This in turn will be the material of Chapter Five. For now we will just say that in the perspective we are developing here, of a self and self-experience built up out of the dynamics of our evolved nature, we can understand that to make a significant change in any given part of the field has demands, implications and repercussions for every part of the relevant field -- relationships, body, "cognitive" beliefs, values, feelings, and the resultant or summative behavior that integrates all these things. And that a change in each area means and requires a *new support in that area,* if it is to be both lasting and generalizable to other situations, other "places" in the experiential field.

But before moving ahead to that aspect of our topic, let's take another look back at the exercise and experiences of Chapter Three, the question of orienting in the relational field and taking up the beginnings at least of new relationship, quickly hardening, oftentimes, into a new dyadic or larger "system." With the added experience of this chapter's exercise and discussion, we can see perhaps more clearly how our orientation process in any new encounter is both a present example of this general "creative adjustment" or gestalt-making process here, and at the same time an expression of our personal or interpersonal "style of contact." That style will of course vary considerably, depending on the circumstances and stakes, and on what is evoked in the projective encounter and orientation process. But the basic dynamic rhythm, of inner scan and outer scan -- not in fixed sequence but in mutually informing alternation, the inner telling us what to look for on the outside, and the outer telling us likewise what beliefs, hopes, fears and memories to evoke and organize around on the inside (and then the integration of these into a whole of action in the field) -- is omnipresent in human process. Indeed, that basic dynamic rhythm, once again, *is* that process, and in that sense is the human self *in vivo*. Ideally, as we have said, that action is itself held as an experiment, a hypothesis which serves, always, both to manage the present situation and to gather new understanding for a next or distant moment. In this stance the new event, the new possibility in the outer world is also an occasion for the ongoing questioning and revisioning of inner beliefs and their associated feeling states, in a sort of continual living update of own attitudes, styles, and experience -- the self evolving as we live out and create the self.

Of course, as we know, all too often something quite different from the ideal happens, either just in the rush of circumstances (we don't get back to most of our projective interpretations -- the moment has moved on, and we with it), or because the rigidity of our own style and our own beliefs creates one of those self-fulfilling prophecies we spoke of and saw exemplified in the previous chapter. Think for example of the respondents and what may be their habitual (which is not to say unvarying) styles, in our exercise here, applying that to the interpersonal encounter of Chapter Three. What happens if Jake, say, the "achiever/caretaker" who can't ask or depend on others, encounters Jane, who feels valued for her skills but not for herself, and "not really respected." Depending on how they carry and display their own styles, masks, and compensations, the initial encounter may go well enough, since each of them seems to be used to managing him/herself, and Jane knows something about how to lead with a need, while Jake knows how to orient and relate as the caretaker and to that extent as the dominant member of the interaction.

But won't their own issues and solutions then likely just be reenacted, perhaps polarized and further entrenched, with little deconstruction or new learning on either side as the encounter goes on? May Jane not soon feel under-respected and under-needed (since Jake can't need anything), while he feels lonely as usual (since he can't display his real needs)? Whereas Kathy, Barbara, and again Jake, who all have this "self-sufficient" style in varying ways and might learn something from each other, may not connect at all, because the initial projections (in both senses, that of the actor projecting a part, and of the observer projecting an interpretation) don't offer them a ready "in" with each other. Each may turn -- very early in the encounter, or at any time along the way -- to other dyadic partners who know more how to use the other's self-sufficient strengths (at a price, as with Jane above), thus making the lonely partner feel somewhat connected (also at a price) -- only to end up feeling more alone with her/his real felt (or denied) needs for listening and reception, and valued instead only for his/her leadership and caretaking abilities, "as usual."

And so it goes, in the familiar relationship dance we know so well in our own intimate relations of all kinds, successful and failed and in-between -- and in other encounters and relationships at work, in school, with patients and clients, neighbors and family members and friends. Who doesn't recognize this kind of pattern, in ourselves and in others? All too often we tend to keep perceiving/imagining and then solving, the same relational problem over and over: how to manage this person who "looks judgmental," say (but may actually be feeling shamefully lonely or out of control), by recreating a relational "system," a schedule of fairly stereotyped and rules-based behaviors which conserve a particular belief system. And "systems" of this type, we are arguing here, are created and recreated around us (and by us) all the time, as our habitual presentations "pull for" or evoke this or that habitual projection, which we then may interpret in a habitual way driven by our own belief system and interpretive process (people who make a joke out of everything are too light-hearted; males with a firm step are reliable/menacing/faking it/safe/competitive, etc., etc.) -- in a stereotypic round of "projective identification" (as the neo-psychoanalytic schools call it), or what we may simply call a self-fulfilling prophecy.

What can we do about all this? So far we have focused on how the interpretive self gets "up and running" in relationship, how the integrative process works, and how all that can be crystallized developmentally into the creative solution of certain kinds of challenges and problems -- but also into "character," self-rigidity, and self-fulfilling prophecies, in at least some parts of our lives. What can make a difference? If our self-process is holistic and integrated, where does change come from? To examine and explore all that, still building on our exercises and making use of a hands-on approach, we will next take a look at what could have made a difference to the child self that we were (and in some ways still are, or are the heirs to), and then at what can make a difference and foster a change now, in psychotherapy, in other modes of working with people, and in our own lives.

Part III -- Support, Shame, and Intimacy: The Self in Development

In Parts I and II of this book we have been exploring and developing a new view of self and self-experience, radically different from the pre-existent, isolated, and ultimately passive self-model of our inherited individualist paradigm. In this new view we understand self to be an active process of meaningful field integration -- making sense of experience as a ground for action, -- with a recursive or continuously back-and-forth sequence of scan-evaluate-interpret-integrate-act, all in an ongoing way in the process of living and resolving the experiential field. These process activities are not separate temporal stages but dynamic elements of a unitary process that is experimental by nature, each part continuously informed and redirected by all the others, and by the structuring effect of perceptions/beliefs, feelings/values, and environmental feedback. The unitary action or strategy which is the result of this holistic process is what we have been calling "creative adjustment," or "contact" -- the solving of what is at hand, and the using of that solution as the ground or learning for future and ongoing contact. At times these creative acts can amount to the construction of a whole new adaptation or contact style which integrates as much as we can and as well as we can both the "inner world" of desires, beliefs, memories and fears, -- and the "outer world" of perceived resources, problems, risks, gains, and other subjective selves, in a whole new way (but always remembering that that key word "perceived" means that this inner-outer distinction is a fluid experiential boundary, not an immovable marker of two rigidly separated "places" in the experiential field).

These adaptations, which are always originally in the service of survival and growth, may then open the way for new experience and new learning -- or they may themselves become rigid and constrictive, in one life area or many different areas, leaving us to repeat stereotypic moves and self-fulfilling prophecies based on old, untested assumptions and beliefs, generalized now to new situations. This kind of repetitive self-limitation can then be self-reinforcing, in the way of any phobic pattern, where the avoidance of the feared situation seems to confirm the perceived danger, validating and strengthening the old beliefs and projections those fears were based on, screening out other resources and possible new strategies in the present field. In a real sense, this is what psychotherapy is then all about, under any school or approach: the deconstruction of old integrated wholes of feeling/action/belief/perception, in support of a new experience and a new experimental gesture.

At times this can be quite threatening. Especially when we learn these old styles and moves in childhood, under relatively helpless and unsupportive conditions, they may be very cohesively organized, deeply embedded in our habitual self-process and our lives, and thus very resistant to change.

We saw the beginnings of these repetitive loops and fixed patterns in some cases in Chapter Three, as particular dyadic patterns or "systems" began to organize (without anybody's directly "choosing" them) around particular, complementary projective interpretations, seemingly poised to repeat (and confirm) old beliefs and fears, leading toward new versions of old scripts and vicious circles. And again in Chapter Four, we heard other people (and maybe ourselves) speaking of the difficulty of going beyond old solutions and fixed styles, applied uncritically now to new situations, screening out the potential for new contact and growth. Again, the more those old styles and solutions were created under unsupportive, even traumatic conditions in the long dependent time of our childhood, the more we may cling to and rely on those styles and assumptions now, continually fueled as they are by the force of our own projective interpretations and careful avoidances in the present -- which is to say, continually reinforced by the integrative action of our own constructive self-process and nature.

Thus it would almost seem that we can never change -- or not at any rate in any area that was difficult or traumatic for us long ago, where we made a strong adjustment and relied on it to thrive, perhaps even just to survive. And yet we know we do grow and change. At times we even make a "breakthrough" -- the kind of radically new connection and behavioral experiment that take us beyond our old interpretation of the field and ripple out into a whole new self-organizing pattern, which is to say a new self. For that matter the old, now-rigid self-pattern was itself once a breakthrough of this kind, a new connection and creative solution to an old life problem.

How can that happen? How did we do that then, and then how on earth might we "undo" it now, in the service of a new solution, a new organization of self? What goes into important new creative constructions in living; what are their components, and how do we find them and put them together in new ways? By the same token, what inhibits and constricts them -- why don't we construct an "even better" solution than we do? And then once self-process is inhibited or constrained in some deeply habitual way, what do we need, to open it and ourselves up again to new possibilities in the field? What does it take to repair a wounded self -- in therapy, or in our own personal and relational lives?

Questions like these will take us in this section of the book into a triad of familiar themes or issues in life, support, shame, and intimacy -- each of them seen now in a significantly new perspective, by the light of the new approach to self-process and self-experience we are exploring and articulating here. More than that, each of these terms, charged and complex in themselves as they are, will turn out here to be in dynamic reciprocal relationship with each of the others. Shame, which in this new model will turn out to be the opposite of field support, inhibits intimacy; support is the enabling condition for intimacy which is itself the particular kind of support required for full self-development; and intimacy in turn repairs shame and restores the self. To see how each of these is true in this new perspective, let us turn now in Chapter Five to support itself, which we will find taking on new meanings, against a new paradigmatic ground.

Chapter Five: Support and Development -- The Self in the Field

What is *support*? What do we mean when we have recourse to this familiar notion, yet another of those terms which seem obvious and innocuous on the surface, but which turn out to be a minefield of rich and surprising associations as we dig a bit deeper, some of them positive but many others strangely and unexpectedly negative? Why should this be the case? What is it about the frame of our received paradigm of individualism that makes this seemingly neutral term so charged, and the process of negotiating support so often fraught with emotional backfire and relational breakdown? And then how does our new paradigmatic view of self as the active constructor/integrator of experience transform our understanding of the dynamics of support, and open up new possibilities for growth and change in the shared field of self and other people?

We have said again and again here that the self we are discovering and constructing here is a *strong integrator*, an active constructor of coherent wholes of feeling, perception, action, and belief, which serve to solve something in the moment, and may also persist across time and situation. Even perceptions themselves, we maintain, are not passive events but are themselves a kind of "contact" or interpretive construction, never completely separable from belief, prediction, evaluation, and the perceived possibilities for action in a subjective field. Given all this, how does change happen? How does a new "strong integration of the field" come about -- and then once strongly formed and held, how can it ever change? The answer, we will find, is inseparable from an exploration of support in a new way, in the kind of field view we are constructing together here.

Once again, we start by turning back to our group, to continue our exploration of self-process in a more hands-on way, more at the level of the felt experience which has the promise of destructuring old assumptions and unexamined beliefs, even as those beliefs color that experience itself. Here as elsewhere the reader is invited to add her/his own experience and reflections, by way of testing out these terms and concepts in the real "lab" of real stakes and lived experience.

The Experience of Support

What do we find as we begin to "unpack" the word *support*? What feelings, attitudes and beliefs do we carry, both aware and unaware, around this familiar concept and term? To get beyond the purely theoretical and beneath the level of our conventional or expected responses, we ask our group to "free associate" to the term -- just throw it out there, and let it evoke whatever it evokes, without any correction or intent to be logical or analytic, in as free and spontaneous a way as we can. Of course, given the picture of perception and self-process we are constructing here, where every percept is understood as a dynamic interaction of prior expectation and new conditions in the field, we have to note that the term "free association" is really a Freudian misnomer. Our associations, under this model (or for that matter Freud's model), can never be "free" of prior valuation and meaning; indeed, they would be meaningless if they were. Rather, it is to surface just these partly hidden beliefs and assumptions that we do the exercise in the first place.

When we do this, typically what we get first is a rush of terms in response that are warm, "fuzzy," and comfortable (often these three words themselves will figure on the list). Words like:

warm	at home	welcoming
soft	cozy	comfortable
fuzzy	understood	generous
relaxed	friends	comforting
deep breath	ease	feminine
understood	need	comfortable
massage	nice	unnecessary
holding	undemanding	unexpected
water in the desert		a nice warm bath

and so on. These samples are taken from repsonses provided by past groups; as before, space is left here for adding the reader's own responses, which may echo and/or differ from these.

In other words, a lot of inviting terms, perhaps with a bit of a question mark around that word "need," which carries a good deal of ambivalent charge in our society, especially as a euphemism for "poverty," or when we meet it in its adjective form, "needy." ("It's okay to want things, but not to *need* them," more than one participant has offered. Then when challenged by other participants, this may be emended to, "Well maybe it's okay to need things, but not to *be needy*, that's definitely not okay.") As for the gender typing represented in that word "feminine," which often appears on lists like this in association with support, this too is striking, and will be taken up more directly in Chapter Eight.

At the same time, what is interesting by its absence on these lists, in many groups, is any word association like "strength," "energy," or "achievement," -- as if support, while nice as a feeling, maybe even necessary at times (that troublesome idea of need again), doesn't actually empower us or make us stronger. This is odd if we think about it, and certainly contradicts much of life experience as many or most of us know and live it, at least a good part of the time. And yet the reasons for this absence begin to become more clear as we stay with it, and wait for more associations.

Oftentimes after a first rush of words with this kind of "soft" feel to them, as people keep going other terms begin to emerge, usually more slowly, which are still quite positive, but a bit "harder" in feeling. This may be a distinct stage of the process, or these terms may begin to be mixed in, in alternation with the original, more cozy tone. Words like:

challenge	difference	learning
new idea	feedback	wake-up call
obstacle	competition	stimulation
clarification	information	directions

and so forth, plus any others the reader may want to add, in this vein or any other vein. By way of explanation the group members may begin to report, as they think and feel more about it, that confrontation, even unfriendly confrontation or "negative" feedback may actually have a supportive effect --at least in retrospect, some time after the possibly painful shock of the moment. These unexpected differences can sharpen our direction, alerting us to possibilities or perspectives we're overlooking and need to take into account if we're going to reach our own goals, or at least spurring us on to make more effort. In this sense any information, any environmental signal or reaction, whether "positive" or "negative," might be a kind of support for whatever it is we're trying to do at the moment (and we're always "trying to do" something, at least potentially; again, this is what our evolutionary self-nature is all about). Some participants will term these things "tough supports" -- or "unwelcome supports," as one participant put it, -- things that may seem to go counter to your wishes or feelings at the time, but still serve you in the end, as in the popular parenting term "tough love." This is in distinction to the "soft supports" above, which may seem more purely welcome and reassuring, in an uncomplicated way.

But are they, and is support ever so uncomplicated? Are "soft supports" really so purely reassuring and welcome, and nothing else? As we let the exercise go on, yet another flavor may begin to emerge (or again it may have already been sprinkled in here and there, as an ongoing counterpoint), responses that strike a different, much less comfortable chord. Listening further, we may begin to get words like:

embarrassed	vulnerable	not up to the challenge
exposed	dependent	avoid it if I can
needy	clingy	small
inferior	helpless	baby

or even --

desperate	hate it	ashamed
weak	pitiful	take advantage

These are strong words, and deeply difficult feelings for most of us. At the same time it's not at all hard to see how they could start to come up, given the terms of our culture's dominant individualistic ethos about self and relationships, which seems to rest on an ideal state of complete autonomy, with a corresponding devaluing of field connection as something dangerous or inferior, something that compromises the real self (see for example the discussion of Freud and Sartre in Chapter One). If "self-reliance" is the ideal, then support will easily be tinged with associations of weakness or even failure -- the failure to do it completely alone, which is held to be somehow better, somehow more worthy. If you "needed help," participants will explain, your accomplishment is diminished. As one put it, "You're supposed to be able to do it all yourself, that's the goal." "If you need support, you lose points," said another. When asked points for what exactly, group members may have a hard time giving a clear analytical answer -- but no one, not even those who wanted to dissent vigorously from this system of values, ever yet claimed not to know full well what kind of "points" were meant, not to recognize the scale. Some have recourse to metaphor: "It's like a giant scorecard, like those lifetime stats they put up in lights at a game, when a player comes to bat. There it is, exactly how you did, for everybody to see. It's your ranking, it's just you at the bat, nobody else. If you had help, that would be cheating." "That's right," another man agreed, "that's why baseball is the national sport. Football is war, and soccer is wimpy. In baseball it's one man at a time, it's all up to you." Again, some bridle at the characterization of the rough-and-tumble, strength-and-endurance game of soccer as "wimpy" -- but even those who disagree still recognize the attitudes described. "That's crazy, just because you play as a whole team it's 'wimpy?'" one indignant member protested -- yet still adding, "But you're right it's *seen* that way, in this society."

It's probably no accident that this colorful metaphor comes from the competitive world of male sports. After all, in our culture the cult of hyperautonomy, which on the one hand is the logical consequence of the old paradigm, is at the same time deeply gendered, more punitive and rigid in certain ways for males than for females -- as we will be looking at in much greater detail later on. Participants who want to dissent from this whole value system -- and many do, including many men, -- may appeal to arguments from some of the newer feminist revisionist views, or from the ecological movement, or they may take support for their position from an "Eastern" or spiritual perspective (which is to say, an entirely different self-paradigm). This stands to reason: as we discussed in the Peface, it is next to impossible to critique the basic assumptions of the individualist paradigm, or the direct implications of those assumptions, from entirely within that cultural self-paradigm itself. In the kind of view we commonly think of (in the West, that is) as Eastern, by contrast, which doesn't necessarily start with the positing of a fixed and definitive individual self-boundary as the most fundamental level of reality in the first place, that critique becomes easier to ground and support.

These then are some of the contradictory and ambivalent associations we carry (and the field carries, around us and in and through us) to the term and concept of support, which both underlie the word and also necessarily color the *experience* of supportive relationship, in that unitary way in which thought and feeling are inseparable, in this new view of self. In this paradigmatic *climate*, support is at best a kind of necessary evil, and at worst an outright weakness or failure of self, a shameful admission that I can't live up to the demands of the individualistic ethos and ideal.

Turning now to the different kind of self-model that is suggested, at least, by Goodman's proposals for a Gestalt field perspective discussed in Chapter Two, and which we have been elaborating and building up all through the chapters since, we get quite a different picture. In this newer view, if self-process means the *imaginative integration of the whole field*, based on an interpretive evaluation of conditions around us and in us as we subjectively perceive them, then self can never be separated in that categorical/individualistic way from the whole field in the first place. Rather, self is comprised of "elements" of the field -- where those elements themselves are constructed understandings ("figures," in Gestalt language) of some part and relationship in the field as we experience it. In other words, the conditions of the field are not merely the *setting* for the self, but *are the dynamic elements and parameters of self process itself.* And these conditions would have to be understood as including the supportive or non-supportive elements and dynamics of that field, both inside and outside the individual self-boundary.

What does all this mean, in "real life" and "real relationships?" To explore this more concretely, before going on with a more abstract theoretical discussion here, let us turn back to our group, taking up the exercise material again from the previous chapter now, and adding the dimension that will take our ideas about process even further, out of the isolated individual and into the whole relational field.

From Support to Creativity

Here are the instructions for the next step in our group exploration:

> You've been looking back on your own life and development, with a particular kind of lens. You went back into a life problem, a time of some difficulty and challenge, where you weren't sure of your own capacity and power, in relation to the needs and demands of the field around you, as you saw it at the time.
>
> We've taken a look together at your own creative resolution of that problem, and then at some of the ways that solution became a *style*, which may serve or disserve you -- or both -- in your life today. In the process some people have had new understandings about each other, and some have had new insights into their own lives and development, looking at old familiar feelings and events with this new lens.
>
> Now take a look at that solution again. Where exactly did it *come from*? How did you come up with it, so creatively, at such a difficult time? Be specific: what *supports* did you have around, for finding and making that particular solution, that particular style, in your field at

the time? Where did you find them, and then how did you weave them together, in such an effective way?

Remember that "field" here means both your inner world *and* your outer world at the time. That's your inner resources and capacities, plus all the conditions around as you saw them and understood them at the time. Some of these supports will be obvious, others you may not have thought of in this way before, or may not have looked on as supports. What were these inner and outer conditions, and how did they enter into your solution to the life dilemmas you found yourself in back at that time?

Some of the same participants' responses are given here, at some length because the question often seems to give people pause, and requires some time to think about in this new way. Again, space is left for the reader's own thoughts and feelings:

Jake: Well, let me see, it just sort of happened, I don't think I was aware of doing it really -- I was just scrambling for something, you know, anything. I guess I was pretty desperate, back then, more than I really admitted to myself at the time. But if I think about it, I mean obviously I was smart, I don't know if that was just inborn or was more an environmental thing, but school and symbols and math and reading and all that -- that was never a problem, that was just there. So I mean naturally I went with that, because that's what I had in stock.

And then my family valued that -- they were all high achievers that way, that was just a given in the family. As for psyching people out, getting them to sort of depend on me for insight and understanding and all that, well, I guess I was already too sensitive, so the ability to read feelings like that was in me, if anything I couldn't get away from it. You know, what they call emotional intelligence now. Back then they just called it being a total wuss, or maybe a girl.

What I did, I think I just took that hypersensitivity and used it to see into other people. I could see things they didn't even know they were feeling -- I did have to learn to be careful on that, because it freaks people out. And then the job of family caretaker -- that was open, that was definitely going begging. So I became everybody's confidante, and that way I covered up my own stuff. So I guess you could say the whole thing was supported by the family in that way -- I mean, they were glad to see me shape up that way, they really needed me, without knowing it --

Kathy: hmm, let's see. of course I was always physical, always too active, too aggressive for a girl, that was my whole problem -- well, my mother's problem really, I see that now, but back then I felt it as my problem. Too angry all the time, my mother said, but I'm not sure I really was angry so much as just too *restrained* all the time -- I needed to get out and run, you know, hit things. So I hit my sister. "You'll never get a boy that way," that's what my mother always said. Understand, I'm about seven at the time, getting a boy is the remotest thing from my mind, but I do know it's something bad about me.

The funny thing was, tennis was okay with them, it was whacking the hell out of this ball and competing and sweating, but you had these pretty little white pleated skirts -- no shorts back then! -- and that worked for them. And then we played at the country club, which for my parents was definitely a step up -- of course we weren't members or anything, but the school didn't even have courts. So everybody was happy.

I never really looked at it this way, but I guess you could say it was supported all over the map, I just went the only way that looked open, and milked it for all it was worth, which was a lot, as it turned out. Tennis got me my friends, a college scholarship, and through that a lot of the people in my life today. But I never thought about it at the time, I just did it. In retrospect I can see how supported it was. It certainly didn't come out of nowhere.

Sam: Talk about negative support, unwanted support -- believe me, I'd have done anything to get out of sitting there feeling stupid all the time. I think maybe it was feeling so outside of things that gave me that funny slant on everything, and once I realized that worked for people there was no holding me. But seriously, I almost think I could have ended up as one of those kids who come in and shoot up the lunchroom -- I could see how that's supported in a way too, you could say that, because everything else is blocked, just for lack of anything else you can do.

And then I could tease anybody -- anybody, because first of all I was strong, and then I had this savior reputation, I protected all the kids that were picked on, so I think everybody knew I didn't mean it in a mean way. So that gave me two things I could do that got me into a better place, even if I couldn't read -- I'd even make jokes about that. So yeah, I guess I'd say I was pretty directly steered by the environment, into anything they'd accept and value, that I could actually do. Because believe me, I'd have done anything in the world -- anything I was capable of. That's how bad it was.

The table below shows a brief summary of the responses of all the participants we have been tracking since Chapter Four, organized here in terms of "outer" or environmental supports, and then "inner" supports, all those talents and capacities that we somehow found ourselves able to develop and capitialize on:

table 4: supports for the creative solution

problem/solution/ problematic aspect of solution/style now	outer supports for creative solution	inner supports for creative solution
Jake: too sensitive -- academic star, learned to "psych people out," mediator, now too masked	family valued academics, had need/role for caretaker/listener	academic intelligence, sensitive, emotionally attuned, "desperate"
Eleanor: too verbal "took the show on the road;" gifted teacher but "can't write"	mother had music/drama background, school had strong performing arts program, teacher-mentor nurtured talent, understood shyness	verbal intelligence, musical talent inborn? "secretly loved to show off"
Barbara: afraid to leave mother, became caretaker; "codependent," difficulty with intimacy	"the job was open" -- family rewarded the role, church group rewarded the role	sensitive, could sense distress easily, "organized planner type"
Kathy: "too aggressive" became sports star	parents did support sports; school rewards; sports gave her a "high"	naturally athletic, "aggressive"
Ricardo: afraid of people, especially men; career as artist/designer, converted shame into superiority, fear of men, intimacy	both parents "artistic," artist identity offered "relief of shame," new identity group	natural design talent, humor, charm, intense "relationship desire"
Jane: terribly shy, learned find other shy friends, "wait in the shadows"	"oblivious" parents did offer some support for music	piano ability, patience "talent for accepting help when it comes"
Sam: "stupid" ("ADD"); became clown, also protector role; uncomfortable with intimacy, defensive	family and peers loved his humor, protector role valued; even teachers could be seduced/distracted	quick and verbally intelligent; size/strength "goodheartedness"

Here once more we can see how what matters in creating a solution to a problem in life and development is not just the personal capacity alone, and not just the environment alone, but the *match* we can make or find between the two realms, the *integration and synthesis of field conditions* which is our own particular creative act. In other words, the whole unit of "contact," or self-process in our sense here is the inner *and* outer worlds in some moment or mode of integration, where each is brought somehow to meet and fit with the other in some way. Where the talent is there but the two realms don't come together very well, as in Jane's story above (in somewhat more detail in the previous chapter), the solution itself is less robust and flexible, less able to serve as a base for launching new experiments, new styles, new growth and learning. In other words, it is the *absence* of outer support, not the presence of it, that weakens or inhibits robust self-process and vigorous, flexible self growth.

Again, this illustrates too how the two subjective realms of the experiential field, which we label inner and outer, cannot really be separated from each other in any meaningful way. Rather, an "inner resource" only becomes a "resource" when it is *good for doing something* -- which is to say, when it matches up with some imaginable reception or possibility in the outer world. Otherwise it remains a theoretical potential which may be irrelevant, unnourishing, or just completely unknown. Likewise, the environmental support that doesn't connect with a real inner potential or reality, can't serve the needs of the developing self (Ricardo's father may have had a lot to offer to a son who was talented in sports, as he himself had been; Sam's parents had academic careers, interest and availability for enrichment on those dimensions, and a house full of books which he couldn't read).

And then the same thing is true in the other direction, of potential problems that never develop because the environment didn't favor them. The person who may be genetically or experientially predisposed to some substance addiction may never have to confront that challenge, in a culure or sub-culture where those substances simply aren't commonly used or available. Thus a prohibition too may serve as an environmental support (but this is two-edged, because a strong prohibition is also an attention-getter, and attention, as we discussed in Chapter Two, is a chief organizing dynamnic of self-process). Kathy's borderline dyslexia didn't particularly hold her back in a working class family without college aspirations and a school district that didn't place great emphasis on academics (her condition wasn't diagnosed and overcome till college, where her state tennis championship had gotten her admitted despite her mediocre test scores and grades).

Meanwhile, as the longer vignettes above also indicate, looking back on the time when they were originally struggling with these things, many people report a sense that they would have tried just "anything in the world," as Sam put it, to escape from the desperate feelings of their life problem at some painful point. The process may strike them as somewhat mystical as they recount it now: "somehow" they emerged, after some period of struggle and more or less despairing feelings, with a fairly workable sense of identity and set of life skills -- as well as some persistent life problems or issues today that they may feel they've had "since forever." Oftentimes what they found so surprising and gratifying in all this, in the course of the original exercise back in Chapter Four, was that new sense of agency and empowerment they felt as they began to take in the depth and extent of their own active role and creativity in solving what may have been quite desperate life problems in childhood. They simply hadn't thought of themselves as such active, creative agents in their own lives -- much less as people whose relational or life struggles and growing edges today were in some ways deeply intertwined with their greatest strengths and most creative life adaptations back then, perhaps now too rigidly employed. Both their strengths and their struggles today are no accident, a number of participants report, with the relief that a new perspective can bring. Both these things follow in some way from a creative solution back then, that they may hardly have been aware of making at the time.

But how did they make that creative act? What went into it, and what came out? At this stage of the exercise what people report may be more a sense of surprise as they begin to see how the solution itself didn't "come out of nowhere after all," as Kathy put it -- and as the tables above suggest. Rather, it was actually a creative amalgam of elements that were *already there*, perhaps potential or unnoticed, somewhere in the field. Many people do report that they were already aware, if they think about it now, of some inner resources, at least potentially, that went into their adaptation -- things like "being good in school" for certain kinds of success, or general athletic ability as a precursor and ground for learning specific sports skills at a high level. This stands to reason, after all. An adaptation or "defense" (which would be the older psychoanalytic/individualist term for a creative solution to an important life dilemma and tension) is always something we naturally construct on a strength, not on a "low spot" in our own makeup. And thus it is not so surprising either, once people take in the idea, that their "strong suit" and their "defensive" areas in life very often turn out to be flip sides of the very same trait, the same adaptation, in the way we have been tracing here.

By contrast, what often surprises people more at this point, as they look back with this particular focus, is the degree of *outer support* that may also have been available for the particular path or style they created or chose (or perhaps simply "woke up and found myself in," as one group member put it). Indeed, where this outer resonance and validation are weak, as we have said, the solution itself may seem less vigorous, less able to take us into new worlds with new energy. As Jane reported, "Well, I guess I was good at piano -- *am* good at piano. But really, that didn't seem to mean all that much to other people. It was useful, that's about all." And of the participants we've been tracking here, Jane is the one who still feels most hesitant and stuck, with "one string to her bow," to take a phrase from Sam, who felt that much of his own flexibility in living came to him through having "two strings to his bow," the clever comedian and the warm rescuer/protector, which had the effect of making each role, each style, less rigid, less tightly clung to.

Of course, there may be many reasons for Jane's hesitancy and general holding back in living; but lack of vigorous environmental response and support, leading to a lack of a good "inner-outer" match in living, will also contribute to that flat or "stuck" feeling, a lack of robustness and flexibility in the solution or style, and a diminished confidence in making new experiments that would help that style go on growing and evolving. (Sam too, along with others, was dealing with the "dark side" of his own strong adaptations, as he struggled to co-create a new intimate relationship not based on "saving" a dependent partner -- or on the use of humor to distance from vulnerable intimacy. The difference was that he felt able and supported to make this experiment, and to continue the struggle to make intimate contact in a more expanded register).

In other words, while a given capacity itself (or at least the potential to develop that capacity) may be in some sense "internal," the *quality and energy of the solution and style themselves are very much related to the "outer" field of reception and response.* A moment's reflection about ourselves bears this out, as does observation of children (or for that matter adults) at work or play. Certainly we like to do what we're good at, but even more than this, we also feel an additional access of energy for things we do that are *well-received and validated in the outer field.* By the same token, we often have to wrestle with a sinking or deadening feeling in areas where we are criticized, rejected, not wanted. We may well be able to deal with it, of course: the point here is that it is always something to be dealt with. The one feeling is of being "on top of the world," a sense of rising or being literally, at times physically "uplifted;" the other is "downcast," "behind the eight-ball" -- ultimately "depressed," in the root sense of pressed downward or sinking.

Of course, this is not to say that the reception has to be right around us, as it mostly needs to be for children. For adults a distant reference group, even an imagined community may serve, as in the case of lonely and courageous dissidents who draw comfort from the inspiration of a religious tradition or community of values and beliefs, even at times one long ago or far away, or from long-dead writers and other fighters for their cause. Nor does it mean that we are never motivated by solitary anger or lonely obsession: we certainly can be, but the argument here is that the quality and feel of that motivational energy, the subjective experience of that person is much more stressful and brittle -- as opposed to Kathy, for example, who practiced tennis for "hours and hours and hours a day," for the sheer joy of it, just as many other young people may work at their music, their art, their writing or math or science or sport -- or relationships (again, a gender-typed activity, in a cultural field which often responds more to relational focus and practice in girls than in boys). In all these cases, the discovery of an inner potential or talent may well carry us for quite awhile; but eventually we need to find that resonance in the social field, or the sense and source of energy for that activity, that self-exploration, begins to fade. And all of us, in isolated or undersupported areas in our lives, know the feeling of thrill and energy surge that come when we unexpectedly find some person or community who respond to us in an area where we thought we were alone.

We often tend, under our dominant paradigm, to celebrate the lonely artist and obsessive genius, but this celebration is probably just a paradigmatic assumption, little justified by the evidence. Most creativity undoubtedly comes from people who are well-connected with a supportive, receptive community (however small, and however much that community may differ from the "mainstream"). And indeed, most of the people we celebrate as "lonely heroes" or "lone geniuses" were in fact well-supported in just these ways. In the end, most lonely obsession remains what the term suggests: "obsessive," which is to say unnaturally driven "from the inside," rigid and inflexible, without enough meaningful energetic connection in the outer field, leaving the activity and the person alike both stereotypic in behavior, and ultimately exhausted and drained.

Again, it is the "match" between inner and outer which energizes, and sustains the energy, and serves to promote that fluid and flexible kind of adaptation which itself becomes the ground for further adaptation, further flexibility and growth. And this brings us back to the question of support, and back to our exercise.

Energizing Creativity: Making the Solution More Flexible

To continue our exploration of support now in this broader, more dynamic sense, and of change processes in general in a field-paradigm view, we go back to our group with one more question:

> The adaptation or solution you made or found back then was a creative act, your best self finding the best creative solution you could, in the field you had at the time. Probably that solution has served you well over the years since, and had some role in some way in getting you where you are today. At the same time, you may find places and situations where that adaptation hasn't served you very well at all, or has outlived its usefulness in some area. We've said that when support in the field is lacking -- inner and outer, -- then the creative solution becomes more rigid, less energized, harder to build on and expand to new situations, new challenges -- and most of us have found places in our lives where this might be true.

Here's our next question: if more support makes the creative solution more alive, less rigid and limiting, then what *additional supports* would have made a difference to you back then? You might have made the same creative adaptation, the same general approach or style -- after all, your solution didn't come out of nowhere: it was based on a strength. But you might have made it more flexibly, with more suppleness and variation in it, if you'd had more support back then. What was most missing, in your field at that age? What would have helped?

Take a minute to write this down in your journal, and then dialogue it with your partner. Don't forget to note the feelings and body sensations that come up as you think about it. What additonal support would you wish for now, to give to your child-self, back then? What would have helped keep you more experimental, more open to new possibilities in the field?

Pay particular attention to the outer field -- not just the inner world of talents and capacities. Imagine adding something there, in the outer field, that would support your growth and opening up, back then and maybe ever since, so that the *contact style* you created then would serve you even better, then and now.

We ask specifically for "outer" supports here because of the general individualist bias of the culture itself -- the same bias that gave so much troubled or negative charge to the idea of "support" when we first brought it up for focus, at the outset of this chapter. If we simply ask people what they think they need to add, to accomplish some important personal or professional goal (intimacy, relationships with family or kids, managing anger or depression or the like, health or diet or exercise, new job or job project, writing up their work, and on and on), then very often the answer will be more or less entirely in internal terms. "I have to try harder." "Get up at six every day and write/run/meditate/ study, just force myself to do it, it's the only way." "Just control my anger, don't lose my temper no matter what." And so on -- work harder or longer, eat or drink or sleep less, produce and perform more, the list can be endless, often trailing off in a familiar spiral of renewed inadequacy and shame.

If the goal has something to do with a habitual relational style or reaction to the world, then this may be only all the more true. "It's me doing it, right? -- it's all up to me," spoke up one participant, with a commendable desire not to evade self-responsibility -- if (as we're arguing here) a somewhat narrow view of self and the world. And even those people who can see the flaw in that for others, may turn right around and apply the same ideology of self-sufficiency (and often the same shaming) to themselves. "I just have to get out there and try harder, be braver, take more risks," offered Jane, bravely, in response to a question about how her shy and fearful approach to the world might ever change. "I mean, I have changed, over the years -- some. A little. And so I ought to be able to do more. The trouble is, I'm such a chicken."

Is Jane a "chicken?" That's one way to look at it -- the individualistic way. Perhaps she can do more, even without any additional outer support. Indeed, the experience of articulating all that and then affirming it in the group may itself serve as enough social support to make a difference, energizing her and making the task at least somewhat less daunting (much social research has long confirmed the beneficial effect of stating intentions publicly in the presence of a group, as opposed to making private resolutions; Lewin, 1951). The point here is not that "trying harder" or "taking a risk" has no meaning or benefit. "Inner" supports and resolutions are a crucial part of the experiential field -- *but they are not the whole field.* And as the rueful or dismissive popular phrase "New Year's resolutions" suggests, they are not by themselves a very good recipe or predictor for change. To facilitate and support important, lasting changes, *we need support from the whole field*, outer/social as well as inner/private. To see more what we mean by this, take a look at some of the responses to this question, as participants imagine changing or adding new outer supports back at the time of the original problem. (As always, the reader is invited to add her/his own experiences, in the space below):

Jake (academics, "psyching people out;" high achiever now, yet finds it hard to take a stand; perceived as aloof or superior; lonely): What would have helped back then? I guess I wouldn't really wish to have been less sensitive -- not now I wouldn't, anyway. Parents more available, I guess, more able to see what was going on with me. Or no -- just anybody. If I'd had *anybody* who really knew me, I might have been less lonely, less afraid of losing everybody. And I think I might have an easier time sticking up for myself, instead of always trying to figure everybody else out. And maybe not so much need to be so *smart* -- I know that keeps people at a distance, at times. Not "being smart" -- but being so stuck in it, I can't just drop it, and relax (long pause)... it's like this -- you know what would have made all the difference back then? Somebody who just said to me, Jake, look, *I see what you're going through*, I just want you to know that the sensitive feelings that feel like a curse to you now, will be your greatest asset someday, way more than that brain of yours you're so proud of. That's all. Just somebody that saw me, somebody who *knew*. Then I wouldn't have been so alone, and I wouldn't be so tight-wound now.

Eleanor (valued teacher, presenter; can't write up her work): Well the thing is, I'm so unsure of my voice. People think I'm such a great teacher, and it's true, *if* the students are right there and I can see their response, that's one thing, that's fine. But the minute I sit down by myself, all the old fears come up -- nobody's interested, the way I talk is stupid, really terrible things. Music got me over the hump, I loved the way I felt when I was performing. But I needed something else too. I needed somebody to really listen to me back then, to tell me I was okay, and bright, and my feelings were normal -- *and my words made sense*. My grandmother did that -- she talked too much too, we were just alike. She made me feel understood -- I lost her too early. There's what I needed -- my grandmother, longer. I honestly think that would have made all the difference -- well, a lot of difference anyway. My husband tries now, my students even try, but it's not the same. *I needed it back then*. Then I think I wouldn't be so alone with the blank page, when I sit down to write. I'm just too anxious, I panic, I can't handle it --

Barbara (caretaker, well-connected; but afraid of intimacy, drained): I don't really want to give up being the way I am. I don't want to be hard, or uncaring like some people. But sometimes I get burned out, which doesn't help anybody. And I can't stick up for my point of view when that really would be good for other people too -- like my kids for instance. If my mother had been different -- or my father, I can see that now, I've always sort of blamed her, or blamed myself, but he was in there too, I can see that now. Then I don't think I would have been so afraid. Or anybody. I got so many strokes for being so nice, and so kind, which was fine, I like being nice and kind. But nobody ever looked inside me, and said you're losing yourself, you need to be firm sometimes, and it's not necessarily unkind. That's what I needed -- somebody to do that. just somebody, it wouldn't have to be my mother, she couldn't do it. And then I could handle the rest, my parents and all -- I mean I did handle it anyway. But I paid a price, I can see that...

Ricardo (artistic; still afraid of men, afraid to take a stand): Of course, my basic problem wasn't me, it was my dad. When my brother came along, now *he* was the son my dad was made for. It's not their fault -- they were made for each other, they were born that way. You know, all boy, all sports, always with the banged-up knee or in some fight. The only fights I was ever in was when I was bullied, and then I was mostly trying to get out of there -- that distressed my dad too, he so wanted me to toughen up. The truth is, I didn't mind about my brother -- it took the pressure off me. I loved my dad, I think I knew then that he couldn't help the way he was. What really would have helped if I think about it,? -- just to know *any man in the world* who was like me, who could understand. He wouldn't have had to be gay, I wasn't thinking about that then. Just an artist, somebody different, anything. Later on, in high school, there was one, a music teacher. But I wasn't a musician, so our paths didn't really cross that much. I did feel like he would have understood me though. In grade school there wasn't *one single man teacher* -- and if there had been, it probably wouldn't have helped. I only related to women, and I knew there was something wrong with that. I like women -- but I still feel like there's something wrong with me when I'm around men. Not just straight men -- all men.

One thing that can seem surprising, at this stage in people's responses, is how they oftentimes don't seem to say what you might logically expect about their own childhoods. That is, given the opportunity here they often don't seem to wish for what might seem the simplest and most radical way to solve the problem, in fantasy anyway (e.g., entirely different parents, a perfect family and background, wholly different abilities and natural talents and so on). It's not that people never think thoughts of this kind. Kathy remembered her family's working class background, and wished for an environment where the images of girls and women "were just a little less rigid." Sam did say he sometimes wondered what life would have been like without ADD; but having wondered, he couldn't imagine it, and moved on. Barbara regretted that her parents weren't able to deal with their own problems back then, instead of decades later, and Jane, only half-facetiously, wished for a "fairy godmother who would have touched me with a wand and just totally changed everything." But having formed these thoughts or wishes, people don't often seem to stay with them, and quickly pass on to other images, other imagined changes that are less drastic and wholesale. (Exceptions tend to be in cases of extreme abuse, illness, or devastating loss).

Of course, one reason for this might be that it's just too painful to go there, or at any rate to stay there. "That's just too much of a downer, to wish for entirely different parents," said one participant. "You can't look at things that way, it's too pointless and depressing," echoed another. At the same time, the people in our groups are generally what we call "high-functioning," at least in some important areas of life. It may be that on the whole their lives as they know them -- now, at least -- do contain enough important sources of satisfaction and esteem (again, both of them intimately linked to the idea of connections in the field) that they don't need to go into such wholesale change fantasies -- or at least don't have to, or at least can get back out of them when they do.

If so, this may not be just a matter of "defending" against painful feelings, but rather takes us back to the nature of attention and the self-organizational processes we discussed in Chapter Two in particular, and then have been referring to all through this book. Remember that our self-process functions as a "recursive whole" -- scan/focus/interpret/evaluate/feel/act in a back-and-forth way, -- and that the whole point, in an evolutionary psychology sense, is to *understand predictively*, so as to cope with the environment and solve problems. Looking at it in this light, we could say that we just aren't "wired" to invest a lot of energy and attention in things that seem hopeless or unimaginable. Indeed, when people do spend a good portion of their life energy and attention on "impossible fantasies," or "obsessive regrets," we tend to think of this as problematic, perhaps a "Walter Mitty syndrome" (after the James Thurber character), an interruption or dysfunction in living self-process. Our self nature is never separable from the idea of mobilizing for action in the field. Where action seems too hopeless in the outer field, our subjective energy goes out of it -- again, the concrete idea of the feeling of "depression" or "discouragement" (literally "losing heart"). This is another way of stating what we've been saying above about field support: without some possible responsiveness in the outer field, our action idea "loses energy;" attention is reinvested elsewhere. Again, "heart" or rising (as opposed to downward) energy is always related to connecting up effectively somehow (or at least trying to) with the field around us.

Beyond all this, another and more sweeping reason for not simply wishing for a different life altogether may well lie in what

Sam said, and a number of other participants have echoed: that he "just wouldn't know himself" without the particular challenges and adaptations he had faced and made. Again, this follows from the notion of the active, constructivist self we are deriving and elaborating here. After all, in our view here, we don't just live "in" a field, but rather are constituted *out of that field*. Those early conditions are not just the setting for our child self: they *are an integral part of that self*. If our "inner self" is not some given substance or pre-known essence, but rather is built up out of the activity of living self-process itself, the ongoing "field integrations" of subjective experience, then it makes sense that we know who we are, and feel and experience ourselves, in and through the fields and challenges we have lived in, and the adaptations and creative solutions we have actively made and found. In a real sense we are those fields: to wish them away entirely is to wish not to be oneself -- a possible wish, of course, but an extreme one, probably formed only at times of desperate discouragement (literally "non-heartedness," the absence of responsive energy from the outer field). Our adaptive creations are more than just compensations or "defenses." Rather, they are the operation of the self, the realization of our own nature. The more hard-won the solution, the more we are likely to feel it belongs to us and comes to define us, to ourselves as to others (with mixed results, as we have seen).

Imagining an Additional Support

What do people tend to project backwards into their lives at that difficult time, if not a quick and imaginary solution to everything? Often it seems that what they picture is the same basic defining challenge -- only now resolved in a new way, with less stress, more panache, or perhaps more outer recognition. Instinctively people seem to know this means the addition of new supports -- both inner and (despite the cultural aversion) outer.

Of course we may express a longing for "inner" supports like more nerve, more style, more athleticism or charm. But when people stop and consider the question more reflectively, as they do in this exercise, then very often they will voice something like what these participants offered. That is, in one way or another, the support they identify as missing, the element that might have made their resolution and their style even more serviceable and supple than it was, is *another person in the picture who could see them, know their world from the inside, and thus understand what it was they were dealing with and going through.*

Just that. Not necessarily a helper or rescuer; often this imagined person (or real person, like Eleanor's grandmother) does nothing at all, beyond the act of seeing. And yet that act is felt as crucial. Apparently this need to be *known and understood from the inside by another person* is a crucial dynamic element of selfhood in the experiential field -- for reasons which will become clearer in the chapters ahead, especially Chapter Seven, The Restoration of Self, where we will call this the *intimate witness*, and identify it as an essential developmental condition. For now we will just note that without this person somewhere in the living field, the creative solutions we make and find tend to be less adaptive, more constrictive, less serviceable as the platform for future flexibilty and growth.

This makes sense when we think back to the terms of the original exercise question, in Chapter Four: something that was "wrong with you," something about you that you needed to fix, and weren't at all sure you could. In other words, we're now in the territory of shame, all those feelings of personal inadequacy in the field, which will be the particular subject matter of the next chapter. Almost invariably when they think back on this kind of question, people come up with experiences they report feeling *too alone* with. Indeed, in the field model we are developing here we will try to show, in the next two chapters, how and why it is that the experiences we are "too alone" with, and the things in our life that "stay stuck," are generally the same things. Here too we can begin to see why it is that people so often wish for the "intimate witness," with experiences that were hard to integrate at the time, and/or that remain hard to recover from now. Again, in the following chapter we will develop the argument that once we take a field perspective on self process, "shame" and "too alone" are both ways of characterizing a particular kind of lack of field support, and amount to the same thing.

Self and Support in a Field Model

Meanwhile, all of this prepares us for a new and broader definition of support, based on the field terms of our new model of self-process and experience, growing out of the ground of this new paradigmatic view of human nature. Support in this perspective is *all those field conditions, "inner" and "outer," which favor certain outcomes, certain types of field effects, and disfavor or inhibit others*, in a particular field at a particular time. If everything that happens is a field event or field effect, then nothing can happen without support in this sense, by definition. That is, whatever happens was by definition supported somewhere in the field -- whether in my "inner field" of beliefs, desires, and that mobilization and focusing of energy we call will power or determination -- or in the rest of my field somewhere, or both.

This then means, as we have said, that the meaningful question is never "do you need support," for some particular action or desired outcome: we always need support, and support is always there -- for certain outcomes, at least, if not for others. The meaningful question then becomes, what supports are available, in a given field, for a particular kind of effect; or conversely, what outcomes are supported, and which ones disfavored, under some particular field conditions at a particular time? Or in the same vein, what supports will you draw on, in your subjective field, inner and outer, to move toward certain outcomes and away from others? If we take the whole field of living experience as our starting point (as opposed to starting with a given, preexistent individual self), then we have to say, again, that anything and everything that can happen (including the emergence of individual selves, with coherence, awareness, integrated action) happens out of that field, out of everything that is, and is in that sense a field effect. The conditions under which that effect can happen *are the supports for it.* To repeat, what happens is what is supported to happen, and nothing happens without the requisite support. Put this way, all these statements sound like truisms or tautologies, but they are quite different truisms and tautologies from the ones that stood out under the older, individualistic paradigm (like "where there's a will there's a way;" or the proposition that individuals are autonomous beings, and autonomous beings are mature individuals, and so forth), which generally make no mention at all of support or the social surround.

Toward a New Model of How Change Happens

As a corollary to everything we have developed so far in our exploration of our human nature and self-process, we can phrase all of the above discussion in this way: if anything we do requires support, from somewhere in the field, then any *change*, anything new we want to do, *will require a new support* -- again, from somewhere in the whole field of experience, inner and outer. For there to be a significant change in the field, there must be a *corresponding change in the organized conditions of support in that field.* By that we mean that the field conditions that existed before were those that supported the outcome before; for there to be a new outcome, a new pattern or change in the field now, the support conditions that would favor that new outcome, inner or outer, have to be in place. This is an observation with clear and important implications for the theory and practice of interventions for change, including of course psychotherapy, consultation, and management, which will be discussed further below.

A number of other implications for work and theory also follow from this way of understanding and formulating support. For example, to analyze a situation, or "diagnose a person" with a view to some intervention for change, has to mean analyzing or "mapping" the relevant field, inner and outer, in terms of what supportive conditions are there, or potentially there, for which particular outcomes. (And here it is well to remember what we observed in Chapter Two: that the relevant social system that really operates on a given person is the one that person believes to be the case -- the subjective, not the "objective" map). Again, *to envision a change entails envisioning a new arrangement of supports in the field.* Put this way, the point seems obvious; but if it is, that doesn't stop it from contradicting the terms of our dominant self-paradigm, nor from being often neglected in interventions and models of change -- and no doubt neglected for that very reason. Things that clash with the dominant paradigms of a given culture oftentimes are simply invisible to view, no matter how "obvious" they may be.

These considerations then also radically alter our notions of causation, under the new field model. In the older, individualistic model of persons and things who existed in isolation (at least until they bumped up against each other), causation was basically a linear model: A leads to B; or a little more complexly, A + x + y + ... = B. Of course, "everybody knew" the picture was more complex than that, that A only led to B *given certain other factors*, just as "everybody knows" that an individualistic description of self is incomplete, to say the least. Still, the basic linear model of causation prevails, because it expresses the dominant paradigm that underlies the thinking and language of the culture. One result of this fiction is the kind of pointless either-or debate we see about whether, for example, intelligence is nature or nurture, or whether poverty does or does not cause crime, or media violence does or does not cause violence in the "real" world. (Intelligence is both nature and nurture, and poverty does cause crime, and media violence causes real violence

-- *given certain field conditions*, and not under others). In place of that linear model, in a field/supports model we find a discourse of context and conditions, favoring or disfavoring some particular action or result: A will lead (probabilistically) to B, given certain other field conditions -- conditions which are the field supports for B to occur (with A as one of those conditions, perhaps a necessary one).

And finally (for now), we can note that people who make and lead changes successfully and ongoingly in the field of real living, *are those people who are skilled at mobilizing support in the whole relevant field* -- by which we mean the outer, social world of other people most specifically, and not only the inner world of will power, imagination, desire, resolve, and effort. The mobilization of both these realms will be required, for changes that are significant, lasting, and can provide the ground for further change and growth in the field.

To see what this notion of support then means in our own lives and development now, how it plays out on an experiential level and not just in these abstract terms, let us turn back now to our exercise from the last chapter, for one more look at how support in this different sense continues to operate in real life and development with particular people, and how that exploration then advances our understanding of self in a new paradigm. Here are the instructions for this last additional segment of the exercise:

> We started by taking a look back at a bind we were in long ago, what that felt like and then how we managed to solve it, and go on. We've seen the ways that those old solutions become strong adaptations in life, that serve us well and then can also limit us later on, getting in the way of new creative adaptation in the future.
>
> Next we looked at what all went into those creative solutions, where we found the conditions and the supports -- in ourselves and in the environment -- for solving or managing important problems in our lives, and moving

on. We looked too at what additional supports we might have needed and used, to make those old solutions more flexible and adaptable, more open to new challenges and new growth.

Our next step now is this: What is it you want to develop or change in your life *now*? What goals or problems feel important to you now? What would you want to be able to handle, manage, or create differently from here, at this point in life? And then what supports are you imagining and drawing on now, to make those new changes and reach those new goals.

Pay especial attention to some goal or problem or desire in your life that's been on your mind and in your life for some time now -- something that somehow seems to stay stuck, never getting really achieved or resolved. A habit, a longing, a relationship that stays difficult -- or maybe a relationship you'd like to have, or have more fully. Something problematic in your life now, or maybe something missing, maybe something we've tried to work on before, without real success.

Once you've got it, stay with it for a few moments. Make some notes about it, the thoughts and feelings and body sensations that come up. Is this something that's often on your mind? Or is it something hard to focus on, something you'd rather not think about, maybe because it feels painful or hopeless?

Once you've noted these feelings, make a shift and let your mind's eye go to the *whole field of the problem.* Here's the new question:

Where in your field now are you looking, for *support* in reaching your goal, or solving or managing this issue? What supports do you find, what do you try to draw on, to make this change? We've said that an important new move has to be based on some *new support in the field.* Where are you looking for that support here? On the "inside" -- your own energy efforts, habits, good resolutions? Or on the "outside" -- new energy, support, perspective from and with other people?

Remember, whatever it is, it's not going to happen without support. Where are you finding the support for the change you're imagining? Are you even looking? Is it all in one part of the field -- only on the inside, or only in the outer world? Be concrete, name specific resources or names. What feelings come up now?

> Now, imagine locating and adding a new support, specifically from the "outer field," -- the world of energy, new perspectives, and other resources you find in other people.

As we begin this exercise, once again the energy in the room changes. The atmosphere shifts, from feelings of power and celebration (albeit rueful, at times) as we stop to admire and take in past achievements, old creative solutions to painful challenge -- to the new focus on places and problems in life that seem to stay stuck in our worlds today. If we took a mood reading at this point, no doubt once again we'd find a good many words to express feeling small, down, stuck, hopeless, resigned, flat, and so on. These are the affective colors of "depression," in the literal, physical or energetic sense of being pressed down, deflated --*all those tones and feelings we're coming to associate here with the experience of being cut off from support and resonant energy in the outer field, the world of other selves*. These feelings are the opposite, as we saw before, of the quite physical sense of uplift, fullness, and energy we get when we're in touch with strong resonant response in the social field.

Thus it's no surprise, really, to find that people having these feelings are also feeling cut off in some way from support in the outer field. Indeed, so habitual is this sense of being isolated and alone with our own troubles that we often aren't even aware of it till someone points it out to us, as we're doing for (or to) the participants here. A kind of deep, habitual resignation settles over us at these junctures, so that we don't even notice that *the problem or goal or relationship that stays stuck is the problem or goal or relationship we're too alone with*, the one we just assume we have to carry "by ourselves," in isolation from the wider field.

Indeed, when we're asked to imagine or identify a possible new support in the outer field for the change we have in mind, our first response may be to feel that the question itself doesn't make sense -- as indeed it doesn't, out of the premises and inside the blinders of the individualist paradigm and culture. To see more of how this plays out in practice, let's return now to the responses of our group:

> Jake: ah me -- what I want to change in my life now? Simple -- I want a real relationship, one that doesn't look just like all the ones I've already screwed up so far. Not that I did that all by myself!... In another way, I did sort of do it by myself. I mean, I did try to do those relationships differently, and be different, but I for sure tried *that* all by myself. I know I can get tight, and intellectual, and defended -- and then I cave in too, it's sort of paradoxical. I can seem so rigid, but really I cave. The thing is, when you're in a relationship, and you're in trouble, then you're really alone, because the person you're depending on *is the one you're having the trouble with....* but then that sort of answers the question, doesn't it? It seems hopeless, so you go into therapy, and you learn all kinds of things, but you still get stuck.
>
> I mean, what I need is a relationship coach. I know, that's what a therapist does, but I mean somebody I can call up anytime, and get coaching from. Like a sponsor, like they have in AA, and you can call them at any hour -- that's what I need. Somebody you ring up in the middle of a fight, and they say, "well look, Jake, you know when you get tight it's because you're scared. So what you need to do is go back in there and tell her that, just tell her you're scared, and then stick with it." Like that. That's what they do for you in AA -- they do it for each other. Does a person have to be an alcoholic to get support around here? -- because I'm ready to try anything!

> Eleanor -- are you kidding? how do you get help with writing? You can't. I mean, you can take a class and all, but when you sit down with that page you're totally alone. What can you do? I would need somebody who would call me every morning, and say, "Ellie, are you at your desk yet? Remember Ellie, it doesn't have to be perfect. All that matters is you just get three or four pages cranked out -- they don't have to be good ones. And call me back at 11:00, before you go off to work to tell me you did it, and how it went, and all."
>
> But that doesn't really exist, you can't ask anybody

for something like that, can you? Well, can you? I mean, if I say it like that, it actually doesn't sound that totally impossible, does it? You could do that for each other, so it would be fair, and they wouldn't hate you or look down on you... I have to rethink this --

Barbara -- well, yes, a coach -- that's it exactly. I've had therapists, and they helped me understand the whole thing, why I can't say no, why I can't assert myself. That was all very helpful, it got me started. But it doesn't really change. The only thing is, I think I would need the coach to be there *all the time*. Every time I have a meeting with my ex-husband, or my boss -- even my teenagers. Especially my teenagers. Or a date with a new guy -- now that would be something, if somebody could coach me on that one! Or maybe not coach me exactly. Just be there. Somebody else to *look at*. I want them to be physically there. Because the minute anybody looks distressed, because I'm not going to do something they want, or fix everything for them, then I'm gone. And as for relationships -- forget it! The men I get involved with -- well, no matter how it starts, it ends up with them being basket cases, and I can't get them to move out of my house. It's hopeless -- I'm hopeless! What should I do -- make a contract with some friend, every single time I have any significant conversation whatsoever, and then check in with them before and after? Can you actually do that? Isn't it too much to ask?

Ricardo -- Well, I guess nobody here can take a stand, can we? Except Kathy, and she can't stop! And maybe Sam, I'm not sure about Sam, he stands up for other people, but that's not the same thing, is it? Me, I'm just like Barbara -- only she's that way because she's so nice, she's genuinely soft-hearted. Maybe I'm soft-hearted too, but the real reason I can't take a stand is because I'm terrified. And it's not that I was beaten or anything as a child -- I just can't face the *disapproval*. As long as I stick to an arty world, and it's on an arty question, I'm fine. Well, pretty fine. But I would like to be able to just function in the regular world, without a keeper. I mean, I can't deal with the *landlord*, he just petrifies me. I know he's judging me all the time, so I just give him more money, and then he thinks I'm a sucker, as well as a wimp -- and I am! I know -- I need a manager. You know, like, "well, I'll have to get back to you on that, because I'll have to take it up with my manager." He could be made up! Or just some friend -- there you go, I just need a deal with some friend, maybe somebody as bad as I am, that no matter what anybody says, we just look, you know, judicious, and I stroke my chin, and say, you know, very basso, very macho (clears throat), "Well, I'll have to get back to you on that, because that's up to my manager, harumpf, goodbye now." It sounds important, doesn't it -- *manager*. By myself, I can't do it-- and then, I'm just so disorganized -- I call it creative-- that I have to have a staff for all those details. I mean, I do! -- have a staff, I mean. But I never thought of using them this way. Or my friends. But why not? OK, I got what I needed, I'm outta here --

We're not going to discuss these particular responses at much more length here -- not because everybody's problems are now solved at this point, like Ricardo's, but because the vignettes make the point: once we pose the question of what *outer, social support* could be added in some long-stuck situation, generally an answer begins to suggest itself, in dialogue, with almost surprising ease. Even Barbara, having proclaimed her own "hopelessness," seems well on the way to imagining a new support, at least. The first problem is, we don't generally pose the question. It's a simple question: what external support would you need to accomplish or change what you want to accomplish or change -- and most often, we don't ask it. Much or most of the time we are so deeply caught in the cultural habit of extreme autonomy that it just doesn't occur to us that there might be more support out there, that we are simply blind to. And yet -- and yet, we would argue that as we look around, and identify the people we work with and know who we would say are living well, organizing their lives creatively, with heartfelt connections and meaningful activity, people who have important satisfactions and productivity in their own terms -- we regularly find that these are people who are skilled at mobilizing their whole fields, inner resources *and* the world of other people, in a way that is meaningfully nourishing and supportive of their own needs, goals, and relationships.

This is not to say that to live well, you have to be surrounded and immersed in scores of active connections. It is the quality and nature of the real connections that count, not the number. Nor is it to say that important parts of any creative activity don't have to be thought over and oftentimes enacted alone; nor that nothing worthwhile or significant was ever contributed by a too-lonely person (though that person may not have been doing anything we would call "living well"). All these things do happen and are real and important. But to repeat: the supposedly lonely creative genius generally turns out to have been quite well supported, in this "outer" sense, or at least to have been profoundly dependent on those connections she/he did have (even that loneliest of archetypal lonely geniuses, the artist Van Gogh, was actually immensely, touchingly attached to and dependent on his brother Theo, who was not just his best friend but also his only customer). And to the extent that all of us need a protected space at times for creative productivity (whatever that productive activity may be, from art or science to healing or teaching or business or childraising), most often the relationship with the person doing the co-protecting of that space is as important to the activity as the space itself. If there is no such person -- the overburdened single parent, the undersupported healer, even the lone artist or entrepreneur, -- the result is typically not vigorous autonomy but rather constriction of energy, a drained feeling, and the somaticization of stress. We simply aren't evolved to live that way, without a meaningful fabric of intersubjective support. It isn't our nature, and it isn't the nature of the self.

A second kind of problem, beyond complete inattention to the question in the first place, arises when it comes time to move beyond imagination, and actually negotiate supports of this kind in the real field of relationships and other selves. At this point, between the conceiving and the doing, in Eliot's phrase, "falls a shadow." What that shadow is, as a number of participants' responses begin to suggest, is all those feelings and apprehensions that came up at the very beginning of this discussion, in the associative wordplay to the term "support" itself. Once we imagine an actual support that could conceivably come from the outer field, that may feel like "too much to ask of anybody." Feelings of dependency and exposure may arise. The other person may resent the imposition, or look down on us in some way, or both.

Thus it is not surprising that bids and offers and transactions around support seldom get *fully explored and negotiated.* Rather, they may tend to come -- when they come at all -- in the form of a single request, and often an indirect or hidden one at that. This then redoubles the charged and problematic characteristics that actual bids and offers for support may often take on in the living field: first we aren't in the habit of even thinking about what we might need from the outer field (because that would violate deeply paradigmatic cultural values), and then if we ever do make such a bid, it may well be so hidden and glancing that others misinterpret or fail even to notice it -- which only seems to confirm the phobic feelings and beliefs we held around support issues in the first place. Or if a clear request is ever actually spoken and received (or somehow heard through our own muffling), we may know so little about our real needs in this area that the request was not quite on target in the first place -- or else the nature of what needs to be communicated and transacted is just too richly nuanced and complex to be understood and negotiated in a one-shot message. And yet, as most of us know, the only thing more difficult and awkward than making a clear bid for support, oftentimes, is to *stay with that bid and that communication* until it has been fully understood, corrected and enriched in dialogue, adjusted and revised in a negotiated process, and moved to the kind of concrete level that holds some real promise for being actualized in the real field of living.

Thus our notions and experiences of support may become further clouded with feelings of hopelessness and failure. And as we know, we are predisposed to invest most of our energy in those directions, those "figures" that actually seem to hold out the promise of some satisfying and viable integration in the whole field. The need or desire that chronically leads nowhere, other than to failure and disappointment, tends to be invested with less and less energy and more and more resignation or inattention, as we follow our natural field-integrative nature in the direction of other more achievable goals, at however great a cost to our real longings and needs.

Support and Shame

What holds such difficult and ultimately dysfunctional patterns in place in the social and personal field? If all this is true, why don't we just see it for what it is, "snap out of it," and manage the whole issue -- and our own relational lives -- much better than we often do? What is the force or field condition that inhibits easier recovery and growth in this troublesome area of living, constricting new relationships and growth, holding us to old patterns we think we've long since outgrown, and have long been meaning to change? The answer to that kind of question takes us into the territory of the next chapter, all those sensations and field dynamics we know as feelings of shame, the sense that there is *something wrong with me*, at least in relation to the field I find myself in at the time. This means we've come in a sense full circle, since our first retrospective exercise question, back in Chapter Four. To see what we mean by shame in this new perspective -- and what we can do about it, -- we will turn now to Chapter Six, Shame and Inhibition: The Self in the Broken Field.

To prepare the way for that, and to close this discussion for now, we might sum up our exploration of support thus far in the following way: when we step back and look at our own lives now, or those of our clients and others we know, we might identify several kinds of problem areas, and then categorize them along the following lines (which are not meant to be exclusive or exhaustive, but rather to shed light of a certain kind on any problematic area):

> 1) "unfinished business:" old painful issues or relationships in our lives that somehow don't seem to get worked out, but just stay unsatisfying and unresolved over time. We may feel resigned about some of these things, and just try not to think about them; but when we do, we may feel the same old level of frustration and pain;
>
> 2) difficulties and frustrations in life that we feel "too alone with;" things that are somehow "all up to me;" and
>
> 3) goals and projects in our lives that don't seem to move ahead, things we have on our "to do" list for a long time, often many years, that we just never seem to find the energy and time for, even though they may be very important, even our heart's desire. Here too we may reach a point where we try not to think about these things -- and still they keep showing up, perhaps painfully, on our wishlist or our New Year's Resolutions, year after year.

Our point for reflection here is that with startling regularity, these three categories turn out to be *one and the same list*. Even when the lists are not exactly coextensive, they will almost always overlap considerably, and even those specific items that aren't exactly identical will still be closely connected, from one of these categories to another. Simply put, again, the things that stay stuck in our lives, the important goals we don't seem to get to, the painful relationships and issues that don't get repaired, and the places in our lives where we are too alone -- are all the same things. It is *support from the whole field that energizes us and makes change possible*; and it is the *absence or constrictiion of new support that makes an old pattern, an old organization of the field, persist and resist change.*

To put the same idea more positively: the areas that move well in our lives, areas where we do feel we are productive, and growing, and meaningfully connected with ourselves and our best capacities, will almost always turn out to be those areas that are well-peopled (again, it's not numbers that count) -- areas where we have the supportive contribution of some important others, who receive, challenge, exchange, dialogue, respond, perhaps even protect and admire us and what we are trying to do. By the same token, areas that are underpopulated, or not peopled at all -- all those things in life that we are carrying totally or nearly totally alone -- generally turn out to be areas of stress, frustration, disappointment, stuckness, undernourishment -- *and shame.*

To begin to see more about why this is so, how this follows from the picture of self-process and our self-nature that we are articulating here, and then how those insights feed into and extend that picture, we will turn in the next chapter to that most misunderstood of all the human emotions: shame. Again we will need the support of concrete, felt experience, to understand shame in a new way in Chapter Six just ahead -- and then to use that understanding to deepen our ideas about intimacy, growth, self-repair, narrative, gender, and healthy process in a healthy field, in the chapters that follow.

Chapter Six: Shame and Inhibition -- The Self in the Broken Field

What is shame? Why do shame and acts of shaming have such an intense, peculiar effect on us at times -- and then again not at other times? What accounts for the vulnerability to shame we can all carry at some moments at least, the difficulty we can sometimes have in recovering from shame and shaming experiences? We have said that the self we are living and seeking here is exquisitely wired by nature to *construct a functional understanding of the field*, one that we can use to assess and manage everything we have to deal with, and to make and integrate the meanings that will help us keep on doing this in the future. In academic terms this is evolutionary psychology, translated concretely here into perceptual self-theory. In more everyday language we simply say that we are born to perceive and interpret our own subjective worlds, inner and outer, making the practical connections and meanings we need as we go. And that as we do this, we are continually assessing and predicting what *support* is available in the field, and thus what gestures, what overtures are likely or unlikely to meet with success and satisfaction, and even how to tailor and edit those impulses and gestures in line with the reactions we project and expect.

All these things are the nature of our amazing and largely inborn capacity for *awareness* -- and its evolutionary purpose as well. After all, we are not born like most species with a usable, ready-made map and set of instinctual behavioral sequences for navigating the particular niche of the field we are equipped to live in and deal with. Rather, what we are born with is the capacity to make such maps and consruct such strategies, in and out of a field that is constantly shifting, and to go on adapting and modifying those pictures flexibly and meaningfully all through our lives.

Where does the experience of shame fit into this picture of integrated functioning and self-process? If anything, shame in extreme forms seems to paralyze this process, leaving us less able, not more, to deal with everything that comes to us, and make the ever more complex and articulated meanings that integrate more and more of our inner and outer worlds -- the process we call *growth.* Even in milder forms shame seems to get in the way of that process, which most of us experience most of the time as an organic and naturally unfolding part of our lives and being. How can this be? Evolutionary psychology, as we will see below, suggests that all of our strong, basic categories of emotion rest at least on some inborn patterning, and serve an organizing, orienting function. What is the function of shame, which if anything seems to disorient and disorganize us. Why all these seeming contradictions?

Shame in the Individualist Paradigm

To begin our exploration of these questions and topics, let us first take a look at the meaning of shame in the individualist paradigm, and how that meaning relates to the premises and implications of the individualist model of self, relationship, and experience.

In the individualist or separate-self model, as we explored it in some detail in the first chapter of this book, we saw that the most fundamental premise of the paradigm was the essential and absolute separateness of the individual self from the field around. Of course, biological needs require some physical exchange with that environment, in a transactional sense, and part of the assumed physical nature of the individualist self is the drive to maximize those exchanges in some way, to the benefit of the individual agent. As long as a divine Creator remains as part of the picture of the individualist self, some beneficent presence or goal may still be considered to be at work in this sharply competitive picture -- even as this physical, "selfish" drive for individual satisfactions may be held as alien or evil, perhaps the work of the devil (himself a fallen angel, in the Judeo-Christian-Muslim tradition, whose natural individual self-assertiveness crossed the line and turned against God). Later on, in a materialistic age, these same drives for dominance and power become, as we saw in the closely parallel thinking of Nietzsche and in a certain sense Freud, the two great intellectual mentors of the 20th Century in the West, the complete and essential nature of the self, without any social softening or divine limitations at all.

What stayed the same through these cultural shifts was the paradigm itself: the assumption that each individual self was essentially or ontologically separate and completely distinct; and that the ideal of the system is the maximizing of each separate individual's potential for self-expression (whether that be the progress of the individual pilgrim soul toward God, or just the untrammeled expression of individual aggression and dominance, as in Nietzsche, or the more circumspect version of the same thing in Freud). Autonomy and separateness from the outer field are thus the ideal of self-development under the individualist regime. Connection, relationship, and field-dependency will then all tend to be associated with risks to that autonomy from the rest of the field, and the compromise or failure of the self.

Now shame, in this system or any system, is the *affective sense of being seen, judged, and found wanting* -- in other words, the affect of *belongingness and dependency in and on the field.* But under the individualist model we are supposed to be free of this dependency, if not from birth then at least as the goal of individual development. As we have seen, in Freud (1999) relationship and connections with others (beyond the purely exploitative) belong to the realm of "secondary process," the domain of the strategic ego -- but not to the predatory world of "primary process," which is our actual self-nature. Again, real connectedness in and with the field represents a *failure of self*, and goes against our true self-nature, which is to be independent of the field.

A theoretical problem of these individualist premises is of course the fact that in real life we aren't born independent at all; rather we are born totally dependent on the field, and condemned to undergo the longest state of immature dependency of any mammal, perhaps any living creature. This contradiction Freud resolved with the elaboration of the Oedipal crisis, that period of childhood when the growing self-assertion and predatory drives of the (male) child come into inevitable conflict with the dominance and possessive claims of the (male) parent, with death or castration as the presumed threat. Now however much we might doubt the likely viability of a species that really was programmed to destroy its own caretakers and its own young in this way, to Freud all these things were literally, concretely true: the four-year-old boy really was seeking "primal murder" of the hated father, and actual phallic "possession" of his mother, while the murderous father really was inclined by his nature to commit genetic suicide by eliminating his own issue.

As we have said, this was surely the high point of individualistic psychology in its most savage, Nietzschean form; and many a psychoanalytic practitioner, from Jung on, was excommunicated for suggesting that any of this might be no more than a metaphor for competition dynamics in family relationships, and not a literal, biological event. Such suggestions (like Spinoza's challenge to individualism in a different era), clearly cut to the heart of the extreme individualist position, and thus threatened the paradigm, which by now was the cornerstone (buttressed by the somewhat distorted reading of Darwin discussed above) of European politics at the height of the age of North Atlantic imperialism, a century or so ago.

This brief review is important for our discussion of shame because of the theoretical links between the Oedipal crisis and the dynamics of shame in the classic psychoanalytic system. The resolution of that developmental crisis, of course, comes with the small boy's deferral to the overwhelming threat of paternal aggression. In the process, the child neatly salvages a kind of compensation for this defeat by means of *identification with the aggressor*, in effect "becoming" the father, and internalizing his (and society's) values, while denying the threat, hatred, and fear and his own desire and rage). At the same time, he necessarily breaks the infantile fusion with the mother's field, and joins the father in the world of (more or less) completely autonomous individual selves. Thus the boy, at least, achieves his ideal nature by an act of forcible rupture with his relational world. Autonomy replaces field-dependency, and by the same act internalized, self-enforcing standards of right and wrong (i.e., guilt) replace the old, infantile sensitivity to the judgments and reactions of the social surround, or shame. (Never mind that this could be seen merely as substituting one set of introjected values from the environment for another; the point for the model is the independence from interpersonal reactions and feelings in the immediate social surround -- i.e., the world of lived and felt relationships).

Thus the Oedipal crisis, in the classical system, is the linchpin of development, the key to breaking infantile fusion and dependency. *The boy becomes a man through an act of rupture and separation from the relational field.* After that, any sign of a reemergence of that dependency and connectedness is therefore also a sign of immaturity, developmental failure, infantile regression, moral weakness (because field independence and capacity for guilt are the same thing here) -- *and failure as a man.*

Importantly, the case for the girl is far less clear. Because of lower aggressive drive, lower degree of threat from the less aggressive mother as she bids to retain possession of the father, and the fact that she has seemingly "already lost" her external genitals, in this system the girl never undergoes a full-blown, life-

and progeny-threatening Oedipal drama. For that reason, it seems that girls and women can never be fully mature selves in this sense -- just as women lacked a fully developed soul in some Christian traditions, until quite modern times. And as immature selves, women remain morally immature as well, and thus unfitted for occupations that depend on the abstractions of right and wrong over relational attachments in the field -- such as judge, policeman, military office, or the administration of colonial empire (for an influential critique of these moral implications of Oedipal theory, guilt, shame and attachment, see Gilligan, 1982).

Second-order Shame: Shame as a Shameful Feeling

But note too that this means that *shame itself is shameful*, under a purely individualist model. Shame, remember, is the affect of field dependency *par excellence*: if we really don't care how a particular person or group reacts, then we are impervious to their shaming. If we aren't impervious -- if we do still register and feel a wince, at least in some arenas, -- then that means we *haven't achieved the full autonomy, the complete break with infantile field dependency* demanded and idealized by the system. Thus a particular hallmark of shame feelings in this culture is that we feel that *just having the feelings is itself a sign of inferiority, and a reason to hide*. First we feel inadequate or inferior about something, and then we feel inadequate and inferior about *that*. Small wonder then if shame has been among the most difficult feelings to explore and develop a discourse for in this culture -- and the most neglected clinically (along perhaps with intuitions of a spiritual or cosmic nature, for much the same reasons), in the dominant models of psychotherapy which have tended to derive from the terms of the dominant cultural paradigm. Thus shame becomes entrenched, hidden, and "toxic," while parts of the inner self experienced as shameful (i.e., those which have been deeply shamed in some essential social field) also remain hidden from view, often hidden from ourselves, and unavailable for full articulation, development, and growth.

Individuals and groups can then be ranked, on the basis of how shame-sensitive they are, into the familiar hierarchy of dominance patterns in Western society, at least a century ago and to a considerable degree still today. At the "top" are adult males of the dominant European cultural strain, those who have presumably attained full autonomous selfhood (and are thus by definition immune to shame; if they aren't immune, then they haven't achieved that adult autonomy imagined and prized by the system). Next come adult women, also of the dominant group, followed by their children and then all the various subgroups of society, other "races," colors, classes, who are taken to be closer to a fused or "tribal" self-structure, farther from the field-independence that is the hallmark of paradigmatic value. The farther you and your group are from the top of the heap, the more it is reasonable, indeed necessary in this ideology, for you to be dominated, exploited, and generally regarded as chattel, our "little brown brothers," in the catchphrase of a century ago, legitimizing both existing class structure at home and imperialism abroad.

In other words, shame sensitivity is taken to be a measure of degree of individuality. In this way cultures too can then be ranked by their sensitivity or supposed imperviousness to shame. A culture and a meaning system which do not rest on the individualist paradigm are declared by definition "primitive," meaning unevolved, fused, childlike, more like a herd than a society of full human selves. Such cultures, seen to be based on a paradigm of "fusion" such as the community or the "world-soul," must then rightly bow to the superior evolution of the West, since they are too immature to govern themselves, without the help and dominance of Western culture (a proposition which strikes us as quaint today at best, after the horrors and internecine slaughter all across this past century in Europe, which still continue today). Thus "objective science" is invoked to justify the political values of conquest.

Shame in a Field Model of Self

All those are just some of the far-reaching, real-world implications and consequences of the individualist paradigm, for our understanding and experience of shame and the dynamics of shaming. Before turning now to an exercise and our own experience, what does all this look like in the model of self-experience and human nature that we have been developing all through these pages?

We begin with the basic premise of the field model, which is the living constructive activity we know by the name of "self," the ongoing integration of the whole field, inner and outer, into wholes of meaning and action that represent the best creative resolution we can make, in a given field with the available supports as we know them, for surviving, growing, and "living well" in the field. It is this process, this creative organization of the shared field, which yields the phenomenon and the experience of self and selves in this model, rather than the other way around.

This is a recursive process which is imaginative and interpretative, affective and evaluative, meaningful, experimental, and intersubjective, all by its and our very nature. Those are the defining hallmarks of self, the things, once again, that we cannot not do, by virtue of existing as distinct (not separate) beings in the living field. All these things are at one and the same time experiential truths, empirical givens, and evolutionary necessities for a species with our field conditions and challenges, environmental and organismic supports, and awareness-based nature and process. Making use of the available supports from the whole field, we resolve our inner and outer worlds of experience in terms of each other, into some new creative synthesis, a new organization in and of the field, more complexly articulated and thus more satisfying than what went before. This is growth, development, and the ongoing operation of self.

So far so good. But what if those "available supports" are absent, or inadequate to the desires and demands of our inner reality? What if all this isn't working out very well, or is even completely blocked in some important area or areas of living? What happens when there is no receptive field available, for some important gesture or dimension of our inner world of potential "figures" of experience and action -- no realistic-feeling expectation that I'm going to be *able* to integrate the whole field of living in this way -- which we are saying is the very nature and operation of my natural self-process? What if what I need and who I feel myself to be doesn't look like it can ever be matched up, in some kind of workable way, with the "real world" of possibilities for action and reception in the world of other people? What do we do, and what do we experience, when the field as we know it, inner and outer, *resists integration*?

Even worse, what if our relevant social field, in childhood or later in life, is actively hostile or punitive -- or else just completely indifferent and unresponsive, to important aspects and dimensions of our "inner selves," our desires and feelings and needs as we know them? What happens to those needs and aspects of the self, in development? Can we even come to know these potential needs and feelings very fully -- our "true nature" -- without some receptive field of this kind? So long as we viewed self in the old way, as something purely internal and essentially there before contact and social interchange, in the way of our inherited individualistic paradigm, then we were able to see needs and desires as wholly inner states (as Freud did), which would exert their pressure without regard to reception in the outer field. If the needs were both basic and thwarted, then they would by definition just grow stronger over time -- again along the lines of the steam compression and escape valve metaphor we talked about in Chapter One.

Here all this, like so many things, looks quite different. Once we conceive of self as an agency that in some way encompasses the whole field, then we have to see the reception and resonance of the outer field as a crucial part of our construction and understanding of our own complex needs and states -- and thus of our development and constructive knowing of ourselves, through resonant interchange and intersubjective articulation. Thus our whole-field, process-oriented model once more clarifies a point that "everybody knows," but which the older model had difficulty accounting for: namely, how is it that *field conditions of receptivity, resonance, and support* are so crucial to self-development, especially in childhood? Exactly what kind of support is developmentally essential is a question we will take up in Chapter Seven: The Restoration of Self: Intimacy, Intersubjectivity, and Dialogue. For now, we will leave the topic here with this question: can importantly unreceived parts of ourselves go on developing "underground," even in the absence of an integrative field of living which we've been saying is the dynamic domain and the constructive material of our living selves? And if so, in what way, and at what cost? In Chapter Five we spoke of that sense of "rising energy," an expansive self-enhancement we feel when the outer field answers and resonates to our unfolding inner world. What would be the opposite of that feeling here, as the outer field recedes or actively pushes us away? What feelings are we then left with when this happens?

All this is the territory of shame, the shrinking,"too-small," or even broken self, my sense that the natural process of integrating my inner and outer worlds is just not going to be possible. If the shame is chronic and severe, then I will come to feel that the world I live in is "not my world," I wasn't born for and of it, it isn't made for me, and there's no real place there for a person whose inner world and experience are like mine. A disjuncture or break opens up, between "me" and "the world; I'm in some sense "on the outside," looking in.

But as we have said, that outer world *is the domain of self-process and field integration*, just as much as is my inner world (which was the only domain of self under the old paradigm).

Neither "inner" nor "outer" can make any sense or have any real meaning, experientially or evolutionarily, except in terms of the other (and these two terms themselves, experientially and evolutionarily, must ultimately in some sense be the same thing). In other words, a break in the whole field such as we are describing and experiencing here *is a break in self-process* and in the sense of coherent self. Of course I may react, or try to, by disdaining that outer world, denying any need or connection in it. But such a reaction doesn't mean that the threat to self-cohesion and self-process isn't real or wasn't felt: on the contrary, the particular emotional coloring of disdain indicates that it was. The consequences for self and self-growth will inevitably involve at least some brittleness, some loss of growthful flexibilty and energy, some compromise in the ongoing development of self.

All these questions and issues, we have said, were difficult or impossible to explore fully under the old paradigm -- because of the way shame itself was shameful under that model. But this also means, steeped and shaped as we are by that model, that there are felt limits on how far we can go with an abstract discussion of this kind in this area, before we come to a point of diminishing returns. Therefore we'll turn back now to our group, for a more hands-on exploration of this charged and challenging part of our lives in and from our shared field.

The Experience of Shame

At the same time, as we do this, and particularly as we take up exercise material and personal experience, we'll do well to keep in mind how inherently difficult these feelings can be, particularly when we experience them in isolation. To put it briefly -- and the point is crucial for our work with others, in therapy or any other setting, -- *we cannot talk about shame at all without evoking shame*, stirring old feelings that may at times have been among the most difficult and unresolved of our lives. This is what Gestalt shame theorist Robert Lee calls the "contagious" aspect of shame (1996). How well we can tolerate that stirring and that contagion then depends entirely on our own relational history of "metabolizing" or integrating shame states with others in the past, and in our interpersonal support for processing strong feelings now. What is important for the reader to bear in mind here is that: 1) all the feelings and reactions we are going to be exploring and discussing here are universal, necessary human emotions, and 2) getting close to them is universally, humanly stirring to us in one way or another (and hopefully not just one more occasion for further shame, about being stirred by these feelings in the first place. If that happens, then it is important to remember that that too is a consequence of our cultural paradigm, and practically universal in this culture).

For ourselves and for the people we work with, our developmental concern is not just for people who experience and react to shame (though they may need extra support, if they have been too alone with these feelings in their own history and development), but rather, and even more seriously, for those people whose defenses against shame feelings are "airtight," in the sense of not registering any felt reaction at all when they think deeply about their own history of shame and shaming. In other words, our stance and our perspective here are the exact opposite of the ones found in the classical psychoanalytic, classically individualistic position, which were that shame was an infantile emotion, something to be outgrown and resolved in the oedipal crisis (and therefore something to be ashamed of) -- and then thereafter replaced by its "mature" elaboration, which is guilt. Rather, what we are insisting here is that *shame and susceptibility to shame are the marks of humanity and the human condition*, deeply and inseparably part of our basic human equipment and functioning -- inseparable, finally, from our integral connection in and with a more or less resonant field. Again, to see why we say this, and how both the old and new perspectives are clarified by the approach to self and self-process we are constructing here, let us turn to personal experience itself, in exercise material and in our own lives and development.

Now in one sense we don't need an new exercise to locate the experience of shame in our own self-process, past and present. All we have to do, really, is to look back to column one from our table of responses to the exercise from Chapter Four, our own memories from a time in life when we experienced ourselves as too much, too little, not right, or in some other way just not up to the demands of the field, with the resources of the self we knew and could draw on at the time. Experiences of this kind are what we mean by shame -- that sense of being inadequate to the demands of the field, in some essential and unescapable area. As we have seen, our response to those challenges of development almost always represents both a compromise of the self (a partial or severely limited expression of some part of the known or needed inner world) and also a creative expansion of self-capacity and self-integration in the field (some new adaptation to circumstances, both using and expanding the capacities I already knew or somehow found -- oftentimes with more productive and creative result than we may have been giving ourselves credit for all these years).

At the same time, returning to these feelings now, as we explore the role of shame in self-organization process, we may contact once again the same feeling tone we read in the group when we did the original exercise itself. Typical feelings reported by groups at that point in the exercise responses included sadness, isolation, a sense of being small, helplessness, even hopelessness, some degree of depression or desperation, feelings that are close to a kind of despair. Shame too will often be named specifically, which is not surprising in view of the way the exercise instructions were phrased: "something wrong with me," a way that I am too much, too little, or otherwise ill-equipped to meet the demands of life and the world around -- feelings that are definitional of shame itself. Again, even just re-contacting feelings this difficult can be stressful, or leave traces of a bleak mood space -- a stress which is very much mitigated in the exercise by the presence and processing of the rest of the group (an effect which is well-known but not always well explained under an individualist paradigm of self).

For the reader, who may be going through these exercises and memories in relative isolation, again it is well to remember that this kind of mood effect is not uncommon -- and that it is often relieved or transformed by sharing it with another person, or even thinking of another person we can remember or imagine as receiving and resonating with feelings like these. If you are working through this exercises on your own as you read the material here, this may be one you will find most useful to do with a partner, someone you feel could understand and receive this kind of feeling. (If you can't easily think of such a person in your life, then the material of Chapter Seven on intimacy may be particularly useful and timely. If you do work through this exercise on your own -- or any other exercise in the book, -- and then find yourself troubled by material or stressful feelings you can't readily think of a good person to process with, you're always more than welcome to contact me about it directly, by fax or mail, for suggestions of where to seek that kind of contact. I can be reached through the publisher's address given at the end of the acknowledgements to this book).

Or we might approach feelings like these in another way, more indirectly, by going to some more recent life experience, again in the register of something I somehow haven't been able to accomplish or resolve in my current life, or in my adult history. Here are the instructions for the first part of an exercise in this key:

> Once again close your eyes for a moment and let your mind go to something in your life now, or anytime in the past, *that somehow hasn't gotten dealt with or resolved*. Something that *nags* at you, maybe a difficult or unfinished relationship, a project or a person or group you left

> in some problematic way, or were left by. Something you've tried or wished to work out, to finish it or bring it to a better place, but somehow that just doesn't seem to happen. Maybe you don't think about this very often, but then when you do, it still bothers you, you can't seem to work it out, and yet you don't entirely put it behind you either.
>
> When you're ready, open your eyes and write a few sentences about this situation, enough to sketch what's involved, and what the problem was and is. Be sure to include the feelings you're left with now, thinking back on this, including body sensations, longings, and other memories or images that come up.

Again, the first thing that is striking about this invitation is how utterly universal experiences of this kind are. As with the initial exercise question itself from Chapter Four, so far in the course of exploring these questions with students and training groups and others, we've never once come across a person who said she/he just couldn't come up with any feelings or memories of this type, or that there was really nothing in his/her current life and feelings or adult memories that corresponded to this kind of state. This is not to say that there are not or could not be any such people, who are not carrying any difficult or unfinished situations around with them that still bother them at times; but if there are, apparently such people are extremely rare, and not much to be found even among even among the kind of population where you might expect to find them: generally non-clinical, high-achieving, professional, apparently well-functioning and pretty well-adapted people such as graduate students, managers and administrators, teachers, and other young and mid-life professionals who are basically successful in a variety of demanding fields, such as the participants in these groups. Rather, what we find are responses like the following:

> Jake: Well, of course the first thing I think of is my divorce -- the way I felt so blamed, for things that weren't really my fault, or weren't only my fault. We let each

other down, and somehow I was desperate for her to say that too, only of course she never would. I still don't know why -- I guess she just can't. Even just thinking about it now, I'm sort of right back in it -- the same hurt, the same defensiveness. Why is everything always all my fault? It's funny -- I don't think of it all that often anymore, not at all. But then when I do, it's right back almost the same as ever. I guess I don't really know why that is --

Eleanor: Oh easy, whoever was the last student who criticized one of my presentations. I go over and over those things, I obsess, I really do. They don't even happen that often! And the thing is, nobody knows it -- I cover it all up, everybody thinks I'm so open, so undefensive, but that's an act. I don't want anybody to know how much it gets to me, really. Not criticism -- it's not that really. It's when anybody says it was boring, not lively, not interesting. That's what I can't take -- and then I can't shake it either.

Barbara: Oh you know, any one of the men who have ever rejected me. At least that's the way it feels. Which is funny in a way, because usually it's me who breaks it off. But I break it off because I already feel rejected -- I don't know, maybe it's a self-fulfilling prophecy, I can't get to the bottom of it. But I know I wake up nights thinking about it, about how now I'll always be alone, because nobody wants me, I'm cursed. I wake up in a sweat sometimes, literally, I really do.

Kathy: It's anytime anybody breathes a hint that I'm not a good mother. My younger daughter -- she's just like me, always battling something. So of course she's the one who gets to me. Anytime she says I'm not really there for her, anything like that. I blow up at her, but then afterwards I can't shake it off, for the longest time. Because I think it's true? I don't know...

Ricardo: You know, relationships -- well, one in particular. Maybe the only time I've ever really been in love, so naturally it had to be the full catastrophe. I'm so confident in my work, I frighten people -- and then the minute I'm in, you know, an intimate situation, it's just gone, I'm a jellyfish. Not sexually -- that part's okay, but I mean emotionally. I'm a bottomless pit, and then, well, he left. I mean who wouldn't? And I just obsessively go over it and over it, how I could have been different, confident, in control, a little masterful, a little distant even -- like him! I could even fake it -- well, let's face it, I'd have to fake it. But it would work -- this time it would work, he wouldn't leave. Only I can't do it over. I blew it, and that's what I can't get over --

Jane: Everything. All the ways I didn't count today, I go over them every night when I get home. I've never told anybody this -- people have no idea. I mean, that I'm sensitive, insecure, shy, sure -- but not how I go over every slight, every snub, and over and over. Half the time I think I'm imagining these things -- but then I'm not so sure. Inside, I'm still that little girl in fourth grade, looking at the confident girls and wondering how in hell do they do it. Like I made a comment a minute ago, and you (to another participant) spoke right over it. Well, I'll go to bed with that tonight -- that and a few other things. There, now I've said it. Now I'm afraid to look at anybody, nobody will want to speak to me ever again, because I'm sitting here keeping score, you're all in my book -- *I can't believe I'm saying this...*

Sam: Oh. Well, the old "stupid" stuff of course -- but that's not really there so much anymore, I think that really has been laid to rest, so that's not what you're asking for. You know what it is that gets me -- I'm embarrassed to say it, it's so trite, and nobody else is saying it. It's my mother. She has this way of just totally ignoring whatever you say. I mean, you can say I hate blue, and the next day she gives you a blue shirt. And anything personal, anything emotional -- forget it. That's what I love about Sally -- she doesn't do that, she remembers everything. There, you see, that's what I do -- I drop it and switch immediately to something happy. I can't stay with any bad feeling, that's what Sally tells me, and she's right, I can't. But there it is. Such a little question, but lord, look at what it brings up. Just look at us -- we're sweating, over some little damned thing that isn't even here ... (pause).... But then that's what I do too, Sally's right again. I switch it to other people, or else I trivialize it, -- or both. It's not trivial, what people are saying. You're not trivial. I'm sorry.

But trivial or not, as Sam says, that makes a lot of material, and a great many difficult feelings, stirred up by a seemingly small question. If we ask specifically for the feeling tone in the room at this point, we tend to get words like these (with a space as always for filling in or imagining the reader's own):

frustrated	discouraged	defeated
resigned	sadness	pissed
hopeless	powerless	insignificant
impotent	small	misunderstood
can't understand it		

Again, these are all quite close to the feelings people reported back in Chapter Four, when we asked about a time in childhood when they felt too much, or too little, or otherwise unable to deal with the demands they were feeling from the world around them. Of course this is not surprising: in both cases we're asking about something the person is not able to do, or stop doing, or somehow work out. With this in mind, we go back to the exercise now with an additional step, to deepen it and see if we can find out more, about why we all seem to carry things like this around with us, and why it is that they seem to nag so long, or at times cut so deeply:

> Now go back again and take another look at all these memories, images, and feelings. Our question now is this: in what way might you say that the difficult, nagging experience you've been thinking about here was and is an experience of shame. How might shame feelings enter into this experience -- for you, or possibly for the other person? If this idea is not how you're used to thinking of this experience, just stay with it, and see where it goes, without forcing it. Can you locate dimensions or feelings you would call shame, as you think back on this situation? If you can find shame feelings now that we're talking about it, but you weren't aware of them before, then where were they, up to this time? How have you been holding them and managing them out of awareness up to now? And what did you do, if anything, to keep the shame feelings themselves from coming to the surface?

Of course, it's no mystery that if we begin thinking about something that nags at us, something we can't seem to resolve (as the instructions asked us to do), then difficult feelings of frustration, even powerlessness may well come up. What is less clear is why those feelings should be so strongly associated with shame. The answer from our new perspective lies in the fact that shame, as affect theorist Robert Lee points out, (1995), is always associated in some way with *desire*. That is, where an important need or longing of the inner world of experience cannot find and achieve any satisfying resolution or resonance in the outer field -- then we feel shame. Thus we feel shame at times in situations where we are left, or discounted, or "downweighted" (in the language of attributional psychologist Fritz Heider [1983]), that have nothing directly to do with individual inadequacy or inferiority. Shame, that is, under this model, is not so much just the sense of personal failure (though it includes that sense, to be sure), as it *the affect and the sign of a field that resists integration.*

We've spoken already of that sinking feeling that some part of my inner self just can't find resonance or meeting in the outer field -- and of that shrinking sense of self as definitional of the feelings we call shame, under a field model. This follows from our idea of a self which is constituted out of integrations of the whole field, inner and outer in some kind of liveable, workable congruence. When this can't happen -- when a given "inner state," trait, or need of mine can't find resonance and resolution in this way, -- then in a very real sense my experienced self really *is smaller*, and my potential for new exploration and expression really is inhibited, to that degree. It is for this reason that we speak of shame as an *inhibition of self-process*, under this new model.

But then of course that's exactly the kind of situation people are describing in this exercise -- that problem that nags and drags at us, but we just can't resolve it, can't get the other person to see us or trust us or deal with us, can't get understood, or met, or dealt fairly with in some way. In other words, as we said above, a place that matters, where our natural self-process, of integrating the inner and outer worlds, *can't achieve resolution*, because the *outer field pulls away*, leaving us with the feeling that our inner need or state is unwanted, unacceptable, and exposed. This is different from feeling that the rupture is our fault, or even that it has to do with incapacity to do something on our part, as the old model had it. Likewise, this is different from opposition, which may at times energize us, alerting us to the need to increase our efforts or adjust our approach. Rather, shame in this sense goes more to our core sense of *worth*, when an important part of the field just isn't available to me in this area, no matter how hard I try -- except perhaps at the sacrifice of some real, felt part of my inner world.

This is a subtle but radical shift in our understanding of the dynamics and definition of shame, one which clarifies a number of points which were mysterious under the old model. If our very self nature, the capacity and activity that make us ourselves, *is this process of integration*, and if that integration is blocked in some important place, in a way that matters to us, then some of the mysterious power shame can have over us, and the devastating effects of shame we can feel at times -- together with the lengths we may go to to avoid shame, even at a milder level -- all begin to be understandable in a new way. Gershon Kaufman (1980), writing about shame from an affect theory perspective, calls shame an "entrance to the self" -- a reference to its penetrating, cut-to-the-bone quality, which is quite inexplicable under an individualist model. With the kind of field perspective on self that we are developing here, this notion of shame's intimate access to our sense of core being becomes clearer in a new way.

The key to all of this is in the phrase "matters to us." Shame will be experienced, in this phenomenological or subjective perspective, not in proportion to how great our "failure" is, how far we fall short of this or that standard in an objective sense -- but rather in proportion to *how much the relationship in question, the particular field resonance and integration we are trying to achieve, matters to us.* To see more of how this plays out, let us now take a look at just a few of the answers given by our participants (and ourselves) to this last question, of how the nagging situation we can't quite resolve or let go of is inevitably tied up with feelings of shame at a deep level:

> Jake: You're kidding -- right? I mean it's too obvious. The only odd part is that I never put that word on it before -- shame. I mean, I got from the judgments and the blame to my own anger, and then from there to my hurt, underneath the anger. Sure, it hurt like hell, for a time anyway -- maybe still does, being treated so badly, just singled out for blaming -- being hated really. Okay, it still hurts. But shame -- there it is. It's all that old fear, that we talked about before -- bottom line is, there's just something wrong with me, there must be, I'm too sensitive, and at the same time I'm born to have my feelings hurt, to be misunderstood. It's not anything I can do anything about -- it's just something I am, sort of like a curse. I'm not going to get seen, considered, handled carefully -- I'm just not.
>
> In another way I know that's not true, that's not me, my life is entirely different now -- and at the same time I

still carry that inside somewhere. It's still there. It's the thing that's wrong with me, the flaw, that's underneath the hurt, that's underneath the anger, that's underneath my distance and my judgments. No wonder people say I wear a mask. No wonder I couldn't leave that marriage -- and no wonder I still can't completely let go of it now --

Eleanor: Whoa, the minute you put that word on it, something happens. It goes to another place, a more hopeless place, someplace I'm not sure I want to go. It's not any different from what I was saying before, really -- I can't take it if anybody says I'm not interesting. They can fight, they can challenge me, they can say I'm full of bull -- all that is okay. But if they say I'm not interesting I'm up at night thinking about it. So that's it, that's why I can teach, but I can't write. It's all shame, you're right, I give up (laughs).

No, I mean it, there's a flaw at the core, the shame thing is, my worst fears are true. It's my mother, she's right, I talk too much, and I have nothing to say that's interesting. My brother maybe -- now he's interesting -- whoa, where did that come from? Actually, he doesn't talk or write. But if he did, everybody would be interested, they're all just waiting and hoping he'll say something, anything. And there I am talking my head off, and it's too much. Okay, so it's all shame, I can't shake these things because secretly I know they're right. Only what's the point, it's a dead end, there's nothing you can do about it. Now I understand it all the way down to the ground, so now I know it's me, and it's hopeless. I'm hopeless. If I think about it, I'm actually mad at you, for taking me there --

Kathy: That's it -- a curse. I'm not a real woman -- that's my secret shame. That's why I go ballistic when my younger daughter hits me with that inadequate mother stuff. I think I hear my own mother telling me I'm not feminine enough, not like a girl. I've trained her to get me, by having such a drama when she touches that point. Like maybe a hysterical reaction would finally prove I'm okay, because women get hysterical, men and tomboys don't! It's crazy, isn't it -- I mean, I'm a grown-up person, and I hardly ever have those thoughts anymore, much less the feelings. And yeah, obviously, it's like Jake said -- it's not something you're doing. It's just something you are, so there's nothing you can do about it.

Ricardo: my shame? I'll tell you my shame. I bet you think it's being gay, don't you -- well you're wrong, it's not, that's not it. It's way simpler than that. It's that I'm not a man. And don't tell me internalized homophobia, it's not that either. It's internalized all right, but it's not homophobia. I *like* gay men -- gay men are real men, Todd was a real man. You know, cool, sexy, able to take care of himself, believes in himself. Well actually, maybe I just believed in him, but that's another story. But it's nothing to do with straight or gay -- *it's just me*. *Other* gay men are real men -- some of them. I'm not a real man.

And straight men -- you want to know what I really think of straight men? You don't, actually -- but I'll tell you anyway. Basically I look down on them. It's like women think of them -- they're sort of pitiful, and sort of boring, but basically they can't help it -- did you guys know that's what women think? Trust me, they won't tell you, but they tell me. So there it is -- I'm not a man, I never will be a man, that's why I'll never have a man, because deep down I have nothing to offer. That's it -- that's the shame that's behind everything. And now nobody in this group will ever speak to me again anyway (laughs). So yeah, sign me up for that mad-at-the-leaders club. Because why take us here, when that's it, there's nothing we can do about it.

Sam: Oh forget it, I don't even want to go there. Next thing I'll be blaming my mother for my ADD. Man, that way lies madness. But then what if they did have something to do with it? I mean sure, I was born with more distractibility than other people, I know that. I couldn't pay attention. But then look at all the things they gave me not to pay attention to. Just the way they looked at me --it was so, I don't know, sort of withering. Hell, ADD was a solution. *I couldn't stay with that look*. That's probably how I got to be such a savior too -- saving other kids from that feeling. From the look. So now what do we do?

Responses like these help show us how it is that strong shame feelings are hard to go with and stay with, and why it takes extra support, extra resonance to do that (all of which will be the material of the next chapter, on intimacy, intersubjectivity, and dialogue). When it comes to shame, we all may tend to cultivate an attention deficit, as Sam suggests. Those of us that are born with at least a borderline tendency to attentional difficulties may then suffer from the doubling up of the load, if our environment is particularly shaming, spiraling into a vicious circle that seriously interferes with development.

And note, when we do stay with it, how quickly shame goes to a self-statement, from something I do to something I "just am," in Jake's and Kathy's words -- increasing the sense of hopelessness, making the feelings all the harder to stay with. Inevitably, the fundamental self-statement it goes to, the ultimate shame that underlies other, more momentary shame experiences is, again, *this is not my world, I was not born to it and of it, there's no place in it for me, my feelings, my experiences and needs.*

It hardly seems necessary to ask for a report of feelings and body sensations in the group at this point, but if we do, what we find may read like a replay of the same terms from the read-out a short while ago, only now with each term exaggerated along the same dimension. As several participants suggested, frustration may go to anger or even a kind of rage, sadness and discouragement to depression or despair, defeated to completely crushed, "can't understand it" to "can't possibly do anything about it," and insignificant or misunderstood to utter aloneness and paralyzing shame. These may often be the effects of introducing the word shame into the conversation: a kind of opening up of an empty place, underneath our usual defenses and distancing strategies, which as Jake suggested may include judgment, anger, and even hurt feelings themselves. Again, as several people also suggested, this effect may constitute a good reason for "not going there" in the first place -- for avoiding the shame topic altogether, in our cultural models and in our lives.

The truth is, under an individualist perspective there really isn't anyplace to "go with it." Under the persective we are offering here, by contrast, there just may be. We can see this if we ask for a read-out now of what it's like, right at this moment, to be telling all this to the group, to hear others' experiences, and perhaps feel and be heard. Here the mood shifts considerably, as people "shift figure" to focus not on the past memory, but on their present experience. "It feels shitty," joked Ricardo at first, "because now everybody will hate me twice -- once for being such a wuss, and twice for saying what I really think." And then in a lower, quieter voice, "no seriously, I feel less alone, because everybody else is copping to the same thing, we're all in the same boat. Actually I probably feel more accepting of myself, saying it all right out like that, than I ever have...." When asked if his humor was covering a real fear, of new rejection in the present group, Ricardo grew even more reflective. "Well probably -- no wait, no, I mean really, I don't think so. Tell you the truth I think it's more a habit... just a reflex, turn it all into a joke *just in case*, before I really have any idea what I actually feel right now, with these actual people." When pressed further about what he imagined the effect of this kind of reflex might be on his relationships with other people, his eyes teared up. "Well isn't it obvious?" Ricardo spoke barely audibly now, "It drives them away. I guess I'd rather drive them away, almost, than have them see what's really wrong with me, that can't be fixed." More than anything it is that word "almost" that carries so poignantly the longing of the self to reach out, connect where connection failed in the past, take the old painful risk and make the old painful gesture, however awkwardly, to be seen, known, and met in a resonant field.

Others echoed parts of Ricardo's experience, specifically that just *being heard*, in the company of other people who at least might be feeling some of the same things, took away from the isolation that normally seemed like the necessary accompaniment to that much feeling of shame. That is, the assumption many people seem to carry -- which after all is implied in the individualist self-model itself -- is that when it comes to feeling shame, we're all utterly alone. Small wonder then if we don't want to go there! As long as shame is synonymous with purely internal inferiority, then the idea of sharing it seems likely to make it worse -- since we shouldn't really be feeling it anymore anyway, under the maturity ideal of the autonomy model.

The fact that actually sharing it, with others who offer not just "sympathy" but real, felt resonance, actual field integration for the experience of shame feelings themselves (with or without joining in the particular issue or shame content for that particular person), then changes that experience and *changes how we are impacted by our own shame.* All this is the accumulation of material that begins to deconstruct that individualist self-model itself, in favor of something closer to our lived and felt experience. Once we make the present contact salient, the participants' anger and their feelings of "why take us there if there's nothing we can do about it" seem no longer to be the point.

Repairing Shame -- toward a Restoration of Self-Process

In other words, we can do something about deep shame -- which is to share it, but share it *in a particular kind of setting, with particular supports and under particular conditions.* Specifically, those supportive conditions need to include a process of meeting shame with shame (as opposed to shaming), rather than with reassurance, "fixing," or any of many other ways the listener might have to distance her or himself from the evocation of shame material. Remember, if shame is "up" in the field, it's going to be "up" all over the field: we can't talk about it, or hear it, without experiencing our own shame, to some extent at least.

The new step, which may feel counter-intuitive under an individualistic tradition which taught us to hide when we feel shame, is then more than just a palliative ("misery loves company"), and more than a mysterious "fix." Rather, it is the *reversal of the field conditions that caused or actually were the shame feelings in the first place* -- because when we meet shame with our own shame, and join the other person's experience (as opposed to sympathizing or fixing from outside that experience), then we are offering the kind of connectable field that was missing in the problematic life situation, and whose absence, again, either caused or actually was the experience of shame in the first place.

An implication of this view is that shame experiences are by definition hard to shake, and that shame cycles or episodes will inevitably tend to repeat. This is because of our irrepressible self-nature in action, which is always the attempt to knit up the field into a meaningful, workable whole. Note that the available "whole," or field understanding, that is based on the conclusion that there's just something basically, irredeemably wrong with me is meaningful all right -- but not workable. That is, it does not serve me for further self process, further integration in the field, that thing I cannot not do, by my very nature. If we keep coming back the same painful shameful memory or relationship, that's not because we're "neurotic," "masochistic," or in the grip of a "repetition compulsion." Rather, it's because we *can't not keep on* making that gesture, of trying again and again to resolve the whole field of experience in a more liveable way. To offer a different interpersonal field, where the present experience of the past shaming experience can be met and integrated in both my inner and my outer domains, then interrupts that old cycle, satisfies the demands of self-process at another level, and thus frees me to resume growthful living.

In other words, the key to something new in old shame cycles and feelings is always to be *less alone with them*, to engage in a sharing which is beyond mere reporting-and-listening, to arrive at an active exchange of the shame material, or the shame feelings at least, that each of us carries someplace within, in that place where a significant part of ourselves was importantly unmet or shunned, by important others in our lives. Significantly, psychotherapy under traditional models -- models in which the therapist, as "objective expert," is admonished that her/his own experience has no open place in the therapeutic process -- does not satisfy these conditions. In the end, this may be why the topic of shame has often been so little addressed, both by those theories and under therapy models which derive from them.

Not all of us carry the same degree of shame, and certainly not about the same particular content. It's not in the realm of content to content that this matching or resonance needs to occur, to support the transformation of shame, but feeling to feeling, experience to experience. In this regard, perhaps the final word on this different way of holding shame experiences was offered by Sam, talking about his own experiences of learning disabilities, and the quite different history and material of others in the group. "The thing I'm seeing here," Sam reflected, "is that ultimately all shame is the same. It doesn't matter if you're dyslexic, or too wimpy, or too masculine, or too sensitive, or too whatever your content is. The shame is the same. In the end, it's that feeling that something about the way I am, something really true about me, part of who I am, is just not acceptable to other people -- you know, people who matter. That's my real shame -- that I'm not okay, basically, deep down, just being me. And there's nothing I can do about it. And damned if every one of us doesn't have a piece of that. It's all different, and it's all the same."

Managing Shame -- Strategies and Costs

But what happens if we don't have this kind of special space -- meaning that intersubjectively supportive field, in this sense -- for experiencing and processing these difficult feelings? The feelings by definition, under our model here, have to do with *too much aloneness*, with parts of the self that (like all parts of the self) seek to be *met in the field*, and to use that field and that meeting for the organization of new self-experience, which is the growth of self. And note that by "met" we do not mean agreed with or acceded to -- which would be to restrict *engagement* to a win-lose or dominance dimension (which is never far from the surface, under an individualist model, where the power dynamics of encounter are always prepotently present). Rather, we mean seen, known, engaged with in some way, which may well include differentiation or open opposition.

Here too we can see how the exercise above was a "loaded question" for shame responses, under our model. Something that doesn't resolve, that nags at us in spite of our best efforts and desires to solve it or let it go, will almost always turn out to be something we are too alone with in this way -- because it is that lack of support, in the sense developed in the previous chapter, that blocks the emergence of some new creative resolution in the field. But then this sense of being too alone with our own experience, of lacking a resonant field, is also definitional of shame, in our new perspective here. Over and over we find, in our groups and in our lives, that these three kinds of feelings -- painfully "stuck," too alone with our own experience, and states of shame -- *are one and the same thing*. This is another one of those insights with powerful implications for relationship and for working with people, that never could have been derived from the individualist self-model, where this same sense of aloneness was a mark of maturity and a badge of existential courage (if anything, under that model it was the *sensitivity* to aloneness that was held to be shameful and unnatural, for the fully-formed individual).

But then what happens when these shame feelings are "up" and we remain stuck there -- when shame can *only* be held in too alone a way itself? Under these field conditions we have to expect basically one of two things: the one suggested by the participants' responses here, and the other having to do with the longer-term effects, not of shame *per se*, but of *shame held without support*, in the special sense of the word "support" that we developed in the last chapter, meaning, again, not agreement but seeing and receiving, *support for the integration of experience itself.*

First, there are all the things we do to stay out of the shame space, experientially, which may simply feel unbearable to be in alone. Again, the reason for this, we would argue here, is not that we are "weak," or "too immature" to face these feelings bravely, even heroically, even in the absence of support. The reason is simply that it is not in our nature to do so. Our nature is to move to integrate the whole field, in as coherent and serviceable a way as we can, all the time. If the field simply cannot be integrated in some particular place, in some important way -- then we simply don't stay there. If we somehow cannot get away -- and at the same time cannot imagine or find that intersubjective support that would make a difference -- then the results can be disastrous. In the extreme, unalleviated, unavoidable, sustained feelings of intense shame are probably at the root of most suicides (see discussion in Wheeler, 1996b). The natural self-process of each person, frustrated without any respite or escape, becomes unsustainable; in the unrelieved extreme, shame literally brings the self to a full halt. Again, the rupture in the important field is a rupture in self-experience, the integration of the self.

Short of this, shame can have the effect of disorganizing experience and behavior, in a whole range of ways. This is just another way of saying that shame interrupts and thus disorganizes self-process, in all the ways we've seen above. As affect theorists from Darwin (1873) to Tomkins (1962), Kaufman (1980), and Lee (1996) have pointed out, this makes extreme shame structurally different from the other "basic affects," which generally function to organize and target our response in the field (though each of them might have a disorganizing extreme, as in the move from anger to rage, sadness to depression, interest and excitement to a manic level, and so forth, which we will touch on below).

Shame may rather operate, again in the extreme, to interrupt that response-making process altogether. Short of that extreme, the milder shame states we know as shyness, uncertain reception, opposition, anger, disappointment, loss, frustration, outright rejection and so forth -- all of these may serve at times to organize our behavior and experience, by signalling us to pull back, reassess, build more ground for the figure of our action or desire, seek supports, wait for a better day, and so on. All of this can be understood as the functional aspect of our human capacity for shame feelings -- a point much emphasized by Darwin, his heirs in modern affect theory, and the newer tradition of evolutionary psychology as well (see Wheeler, in press): the use of shame is to serve as a signal and a corrective, telling us when to pull back and regroup when our desire or need can't be met at the moment. This is shame-as-field-information, a line of thinking much developed by Lee and Wheeler (1996), which will be discussed at somewhat more length below.

But if these same bumps in the road flip us into a deep side-ditch of developmental shame, a place where we were desperately imprisoned at a vulnerable time (as for example in some of the exercise material from Chapters Four and Five), then they can disorganize us as well -- in the sense of blocking the new integration, the incorporation of the present experience and field into new self-experience and self-capacity. This is the shift which affect theorist Gershon Kaufman (1980), as well as some other popular writers on shame, term the shift from shame as a feeling (or "shame as affect," in Kaufman's terminology), to internalized shame (e.g., Bradshaw, 1994). "Internalized shame," which is the kind we've been talking about through much of this discussion, as opposed to just shyness or embarrassment of the moment, disorganizes self-experience, and distorts behavior, at times in dangerous or ugly directions.

Thus anger, which mobilizes and organizes our energy for important action, when combined with deep shame becomes rage, which mobilizes without organizing. And indeed, in states of rage people lash out irrationally, hurting themselves or damaging the relationships they depend on most -- at times damaging those people as well. Physical strength and mobilization, under those conditions, may become destructive violence -- again in ways that make no rational sense, and don't serve even the most narrow and immediate goals of the self, other than the desperate, momentary alleviation of an unbearable accumulation of tension energy (of the kind which Freud, theorizing at the apogee of the individualist tradition, imagined to be the wellspring and driving force of the whole personality. Thus again, the individualist model in general, and the classic psychodynamic model in particular, *are shame models by definition*, and thus particularly ill-adapted for understanding and transforming or healing shame).

By the same token, sadness, frustration, and even resignation may organize our energy, our behavior and our experience. Combined with deep shame ("I lost her/him because I am born to be left, I carry a flaw at the core that can't be met or healed"), the experience may tend toward the chronic self-disorganization we know as deep depression, a hopeless state in which the self doesn't strike us as able to mobilize or inspire any satisfying meeting in the world at all. In a classic model, based on tension discharge and individualist assumptions, depression was thought of as "aggression turned against the self" -- which makes sense, in the terms of that model. Similarly in a behaviorist model, depression is the absence of any satisfying stimuli or gratifying operant, cause-effect sequences in the environment. Again, that makes sense in the terms of that model, and is not basically different from our picture here. What is different is our understanding of the *self who is the subject of the depression* -- and in our model the constructor or architect of it as well (by our terms here, we would say that depression, even extreme, paralyzing depression, is still the self's attempt to find and construct a field small enough, and flat enough, and unstressful enough, to admit of some kind of integration).

In each case the disorganizing extreme of a particular emotion is activated by combining that feeling with feelings of deep shame. That is to say, the extreme has to do with the *field conditions* for the emotion. Thus just as anger may go to rage, action to violence, and sadness to deep depression, so fear may go to violent panic, erotic excitement may go to sexual frenzy or compulsion, interest to obsession, discouragement to despair, even joy itself, again, to a kind of manic state. In each case the hallmark of the extreme state is the way it is *cut off from the field*, of inner feelings and other people as well -- and the way the natural process of self-evolution and learning, the emergence of new patterns of self-organization, is stereotyped and constricted, repeating the same pattern over and over. This constriction, again by definition, is the sign and the effect of shame, under this new perspective. (None of this of course is to say that shame is the *only* dynamic factor in moving from, say, anger to violence, or erotic adventure to sexual compulsion: only that shame is probably always a necessary dynamic factor in this movement to extremes, and in both the recurrent and the stuck nature of these moves).

Along these same lines, in less extreme cases and states we can see how shame plays a role in what was called, under an older model, "character" or "armoring." Character, under a classic model, was understood to be a kind of basic and rigid defensive self-adaptation, which was so deeply integrated into the personality structure as to be highly resistant to change, by psychotherapy or just by the processes of living (see e.g., Freud, 1999; Reich, 1970; Klein ,1932). In other words character, in our terms here, belongs to those early "strong adaptations" we met in Chapter Four, which we were calling contact styles, and which as strong self-integrations made under more or less aversive conditions, are then afterward very resistant to change. But those aversive conditions which we explored in Chapters Four and Five, of non-support for some parts of the self, *were the field conditions of shame*, under our terms and definitions here. We said then that the less supportive the self-conditions at the time, the more rigid and resistant to new growth the old self-adaptation or contact style will be now. But this is exactly equivalent to saying that the more the old conditions were field conditions of shame, the more the adaptation becomes "character," in the old, rigid sense of the word.

In other words, shame and support are *dynamically reciprocal field conditions*, when viewed under our perspective here. This in turn enables us to restate the ideas from affect theory mentioned above, about the functional and even necessary aspects of shame, as a component of our human "affect kit," our survival equipment as social beings. Shame, in this new view, emerges as our *essential affective field-scan*, our affective instrument for sensing and measuring support in the field. Of course this measurement is always subjective and may under- (or over-) estimate the potential for support that is "really there." But then the remedy for this would necessarily be some kind of checking, the possibility of dialogue about support and shame conditions, with the important present players in the relevant present field. If that dialogue is blocked -- say for instance by a belief system that tells us that concern about support and shame both is infantile, regressive, shameful, and weak (not to forget "feminine" -- to be discussed in Chapter Eight), -- then the result will be a field in which each person bears his/her private shame alone, or rather manages and avoids his/her shame alone, through extreme or less extreme measures. In other words, exactly the field we do live in, under the *regime* (to use Foucault's deconstructionist term) *of the individualistic paradigm*.

And what are some of these less extreme character adaptations, constructed partly as styles to avoid unbearable shame? A number of them are suggested by the participants' responses above, including many familiar traits and habits we recognize in ourselves, and recognize too as destructive, when they are chronic and serve to cover other, more difficult, less supported feeling states. These will include criticism, judgmentalism, blaming, avoiding relationship altogether, masking, breaking off contact (because of the rejection to come, as several people put it), and even hurt itself (which may feel shameful or "weak," as Jake put it above, but still considerably less shameful, and less hopeless, than unrelieved shame itself, if it has to be borne alone). To this we can add not just the violent antisocial acts above, destructiveness toward others and toward the self, but also the whole range of addictive behaviors, which serve to manage shame, keep it at bay, even translate it for a moment into grandiosity, the seemingly triumphant "false field integration" of the moment, which is captured in the experience of being "high," of conquest sexual or otherwise, or the gambler's winnings, where for one fleeting moment she/he is the favored child of the universe after all, the one born under a lucky star, and not the dark star of shame. (The field integration is false precisely because it does not and cannot include the whole relevant realm of important parts of the inner self -- including fears and feeling of shame themselves).

Again, none of this is meant to suggest that there's "nothing but shame" going on in our lives and process, or that shame is the only dynamic component of all these behaviors, defenses, and/or adaptations and styles. Rather, what we draw from the newer paradigmatic view of a field-integrative self is the notion that everything that is chronically stuck in self-process, every adaptation achieved under aversive, non-supportive conditions (as is often the case in childhood), every rigid character structure or contact style which resists growth and change -- as well as everything we hold in too-alone a way, everything that keeps mysteriously and painfully recurring in our lives and relationships, everything that nags at us maddeningly, that we can't get over or beyond -- all these things probably have an element of buried shame feelings in their dynamic structure, that contributes to maintaining them and keeping them more or less rigid in present process. And that our exploration and understanding of everything problematic in self-process -- and our interventions to change all that -- will remain hampered and incomplete, *unless and until we build in an analysis and transformation of shame*, in this sense.

These then are some of the ways we defend against or avoid shame. But what of other long-term effects? What happens to parts of the self that are shamed, in this sense of just not being met in the important social environment, for interaction, influence, integration and further growth? Under an individualist model we imagine that development goes on primarily internally, and thus that if expression is blocked in some area, then somehow it will just go on "underground," and come out then in full expression when the time is right. Therapy under this model might then look something like assertiveness training, where the goal is the expression of something that is already there, but hasn't been given permission and support to come out fully.

The clinical and folk wisdom of therapeutic work with addictive problems offers quite a different model, one more in tune with our notions of self-expression and our newer view here. A clinical axiom of addiction treatment is that the addict, once sober, *returns to the developmental point at which active addiction began* -- because the addiction interrupted self-development at that juncture. That is, if active abuse of some substance began chronically at age, say, fourteen, and sobriety was achieved and fairly well stablized at age, say, 38 -- then in some real sense what you are dealing with at that point is a sober fourteen-year-old, in terms of emotional and relational development -- in the body and perhaps with the career and relational commitments of a person in mid-life, and thus perhaps primed now for an "adolescent identity crisis" and a "mid-life crisis" all rolled into one. Not an easy picture to work with, or to live in or with either for that matter.

From our perspective here we would take that even further. Since addiction represents a vast reduction and oversimplification of the experiential and contact field, we can assume that we were dealing with a self-field and self-process that were *already severely compromised and impaired in some important ways to start with*, long before the age when the active addiction began. That is, we assume we were dealing with an experiential field constricted and conditioned by considerable shame -- since it is shame that reduces the available field, and constricts self-process. Thus we would say that therapeutically, to establish a transformational field, we need to go back to the original field conditions of reduced support and heightened shame, to restore enough full, flexible, robust self-process to permit a resumption of growth and full living (for related discussion, see Clemmens, 1997).

In more general terms, we could say that the structure of an addiction -- a fairly rigid structure or style for reducing an overwhelming and unsupported contact field down to a few repeating gestures and moves -- is the structure of any important self-adaptation or creative adjustment we make, under seriously undersupported conditions. We saw these patterns and structures over and over in Chapters Three and Four -- and we know them in our clients, patients, and partners, and in our own lives. Again, under each rigid adaptation, each self-organizational pattern which repeats and repeats when circumstances change (like always assuming and projecting judgment from the other person, say, no matter what the signals and behavior), there is a history of *adaptation without enough support*, as we saw in Chapters Four and Five. And under each undersupported adaptation we find a field condition of shame. Again, shame and support are two aspects, two poles of the same field dimension, the same quality of greater or lesser "tissue strength" in the field, that quality of coming to meet whatever we offer, as opposed to a rent in the cloth, a split or pulling away in the contact field.

That "coming to meet," which is basic support, is not necessarily the same as our ordinary notions of support as "soft support." Rather, it is the opposite not of softness but of absence. People who report a childhood in which they were argued with and opposed all the time, for instance, may well turn out to be pretty robust personalities, if perhaps a bit rough or "hard-hitting," but not mean, in their style. By and large they may be in better shape -- in the sense of more available for new growth and new creative adaptation in living -- than people who were faced with a pulling away, a disapproving or simply non-responsive lack of contact with regard to important parts of themselves. It's no accident that traditional or cohesive cultures have always known that "shunning" is the ultimate punishment, and the ultimate social threat. Under an individualist model, this threat would have no meaning or power, except insofar as we conceived the members of that culture as by definition immature, or "primitive" (which is to say, insufficientily individuated). Under our perspective here, we understand rather that the withdrawal or absence of the intersubjective field is always the ultimate threat, and the ultimate damage to the self.

In a pluralistic culture such as ours we may see this "shunning" less clearly (though the shunned groups, religious, ethnic, or sexual minorities, or women or men who display parts of the self which depart from gender/shame strictures, see it clearly enough); but it is still there, perhaps more subtly in the cultural field, but all the more vividly for that in the family field, which replaces and carries the sociocultural field in a pluralistic culture).

Developmentally, what happens under conditions of heavy shame, or a significant splitting in the experiential field, is then not that the unmet parts of the self go on developing fully (how could they, under this model?), but rather that the compromised integration itself goes on, as best it can. In other words, the split in the field itself is integrated, and becomes experienced as a split in the self. If it is sexuality, or perhaps my particular style of sexuality, that is split away from, then sexuality will both remain underdeveloped in some way in my self-process, unable to interact and integrate fully with either the outer field or other parts of the inner field -- and it will remain split off, a part of myself that is not fully "owned," and again does not really interact with other dynamics and needs of my inner world. Thus the shamed sexuality integrates poorly with the rest of my emotional life and world, with my social relations, with my family life, with my body experience as a whole, and so forth. By the same token, all the rest of my world, inner and outer, will then be in some way *erotically impoverished*, not easily and fully energized with the play of erotic energy spilling richly and healthily into non-sexual relationships, aesthetic and emotional life, and my personal investments in the world (as is generally the case, again, as we look around us in the world of our culture, with its exploitative, non-loving, and abusive attitude toward "out-groups" and toward the natural world). Developmentally, we could say that the structure of the interactive field in childhood, *becomes the structure of the person's inner world*. The split in the inner-outer field cannot be overcome, by the child self anyway, but rather becomes integrated into ongoing self-development and self-process *as a split in the inner world*. (And here compare the parallel insight from adolescent developmentalist Mark McConville, speaking in the metaphors of a different model: "The structure of the family field becomes the unconscious structure of the child;" personal communication; see also McConville, 1995).

On the far side of that split, somewhere "within" the person, those needs and feelings which were more or less split off still remain more or less alive, still subject to our basic integrative instinct and process, yet still compromised, still "thin" in some way, by virtue of being cut off from a full flow and cross-infusion of the rest of my "inner life" -- and perhaps most of all, cut off from the easy play of transactive experiment, that way in which every contact with the "outer world" is a trial and a hypothesis, continually infused and informed by ongoing feedback, modulation, and the exchange of energy with and from the outer field. This exchange, and this experiment and feedback, after all, are what learning and development are, under this model (and as far as learning *per se* is concerned, under any model, since perhaps Plato's).

Thus each of us carries some part of ourselves that has lagged behind the main thrust of our self-development, and may likely emerge startlingly or even devastatingly under conditions that reevoke or replicate the kind of family field where those dimensions of the self were unreceived and "went underground" long ago. These situations may be an intimate relationship, parenthood (or the sudden arrival of an aging, perhaps dependent parent on the scene), some other new personal or professional relationship that echoes a shaming frame from the past -- or simply the entry into a new group, job, living situation, and so forth. Depending on the extent and the severity of the non-reception or shaming -- and most importantly, depending on the presence of other, compensating supports in the developmental field, -- we may then be more or less disorganized, more or less distressed by the new eruption of the old themes and dynamics, as we saw in the exercise material above.

That distress and disorganization will then likely be more serious, the less we recognize the old sources and resonances of the troubling feelings -- because recognizing those old sources opens the possiblity of a reintegration, the resolution in the field that permits and actually is new growth and movement, the opposite of self-disorganization and anxious self-inhibition or paralysis. Again, the difference now is in the supports, or lack of supports now. As we have said, these supports have to be of a quite specific kind, for healing and transformation of shame to begin to take place. Let us turn now to how we go about doing that kind of healing work with shame issues, as we live and work with people beyond the individualist model.

Working with Shame

We have said that working with shame in a healing way -- or even just being with shame, in our own lives and relationships, in a way that doesn't merely replicate the old wound and resolidify the old defensive reactions -- means *meeting shame with (our own) shame in some way, either implicitly or openly*, and not with "fixing" or other strategies for putting a distance between ourselves and any direct experience of shame. What are these moves and strategies -- for healing or distancing either one? How do they work, and how it is they can so easily go wrong?

First of all, this is where we need to remember again, whether in a therapeutic setting, in couple or family relationships, with coworkers, students or supervisees or friends, that we *cannot be part of a field in which shame is evoked with awareness for another person, without testing and being thrown back on our own capacity to process and bear our own experiences of shame.* It may be that in this way shame is not really so different from other affect states and experiences, in that all affect, all strong emotion, is contagious. This too is part of our evolutionary self-nature as deeply social beings -- and just another way that our evolved, experiential nature violates the terms of our inherited individualistic ideology. Pain, joy, grief, depression, sexual excitement, anger -- all strongly energized feeling states represent *strong organizations of energy* in the shared field, and as such, all of them have strong field effects on the people around us. This is what we have emotions for, as Darwin pointed out long ago (1873) – to organize the field, from the locus of a particular point of view or desire, -- and why we are such an emotional species, whose social and affective nature are completely interpenetrating.

This is why, for instance, a culture that has lost meaning and thus fears death will segregate and avoid the old, the grieving, and the dying -- as indeed our culture does: because grief itself is contagious, and like other intense states of feeling, too strong to bear in a purely individualistic way. By the same token, a culture that fears and constricts (and is thus obsessed with) sexuality will isolate and distance from anything homoerotic -- not just because homophobic people are "repressed gay" necessarily (though in a repressive culture, nearly everyone may tend to repress a normal range of homoerotic energy), but also because the reminder of any erotic energy at all, especially outside prescribed social bounds, will likewise be contagious, and hard for people to understand and bear in themselves (the trouble with gay sexuality is not that it's gay but that it's sexuality, and being "deviant," is harder to ignore or deny: thus "don't ask/don't tell.") Or a culture such as our own, that fears and avoids shame, will also fear and avoid all those people who are shamed and "defective" in a mainstream perspective -- and especially all those most conspicuous "failures" of competitive individualism (which is to say, the poor). Thus as Goodman wrote (1997), there can no longer be such a thing as "decent poverty" in our society -- because the more the society becomes connected only through the unstable bonds of competitive capitalism, the more anybody who "loses" under that system is in a shame state, *and we cannot bear to be in the contagious presence of so much shame.*

This inherently contagious nature of strong affect is of course mysterious and/or pathological under an individualist model, yet understandable and self-evident in a field model of self. It becomes more problematic when the affect in question is shame, only because shame itself is shameful under the old model, and thus we are even less skilled and experienced in holding it and processing it in relationship than we may be with other feelings (though in general, holding affect in relationship may always tend to be somewhat unnatural, as long as we stay within an individualist model). But what do we mean, "holding affect in relationship," and then how might we do this, or block it, with shame in particular?

In general, to hold feelings in relationship (as opposed to holding them more individualistically, more alone) means to meet awares feeling with awares feeling -- in the same way as we said "meet experience with experience" and "meet shame with shame" above, but now in a more general sense. Note that this does not mean we have to meet a feeling with the same content feeling -- any more than we have to meet a thought with the same thought, for a conversation to take place. If I say that talking about shame tends to evoke past or present feelings or apprehensions of shame in everybody, you may say that you don't think that's necessarily the case, or you do, or some other thoughtful response, and we will go on from there. If your reply is that you're not sure about that, but you are aware that putting it that way is making you anxious, then you are meeting a feeling with feeling material, at least inviting a fuller, deeper conversation, one in which the full dimensionality of cognition (feelings as well as thoughts) is available for exchange. Ultimately, to meet in an intersubjective dialogue is to recognize the subjectivity -- the constructive/evaluative, meaningful field-organization -- of both people, which necessarily includes both perceptions/conclusions and feelings/evaluations. When those processes themselves can be shared in the field, then their construction itself becomes subject to this same kind of constructive/deconstructive, hypothesis-feedback attention -- which means self-growth, by definition in terms of our understanding of the nature of self in this new perspective.

All this is the material of the next Chapter, Intimacy and Intersubjectivity. What particularly concerns us here is what happens to these general principles and processes when the particular feeling material in question is experienced as shameful. Ordinarily, for intersubjective process to be supported, it is enough to meet the full range of self-organization with the reciprocally full range from the other person -- feelings, thoughts, evaluations, perceptions, and at times the shift to the meta-level of considering how all these constructs are themselves created, the experiential process itself. Again, the fact that I am talking about anger, say, does not necesarily mean that you have to reassure me that you too feel and know anger, for me to feel that the field is safe enough to continue. The feeling is common enough and accepted enough in the culture for me to trust that you do know what anger feels like, and what that experience involves.

If, on the other hand, anger is exactly the area where my own developmental field shrank away, the place where my own inner range was never met safely and receptively in the outer field, then I may need more, if I'm going to be supported to learn and grow in a new way. This can become a dilemma at times in individual therapy, places where "unconditional positive reception," let alone the "blank screen" of the analytic method, may become intersubjectively problematic. Remember that in an important situation or relationship, we *cannot not project*, we *cannot not* interpret the meaning of relevant field, so as to be able to cope in a predictive way. Indeed, for all the shaming that projection itself comes in for under an individualist perspective, this insight, that we will fill in the blank screen with our own imaginative assessment, is actually of the essence in the psychoanalytic approach (where the projection onto the therapist is the source of the "transferential relationship," the one supposedly based entirely on projective imagining). If we are silent in the face of material that is shameful to the client, then our silence *will be interpreted* -- either in the light of the relationship we've already established, or in light of other, past, presumably less affirming relationships in the client's own history. (The same thing applies of course to our speech, which is also always being interpreted for its motivation and meaning, by the other person. If we are reassuring, does that mean sincerity? superiority? pity? lack of confidence? a trick of some kind? a kind of induction into agreeing that the therapist is "right" about something? everything? and so on).

Here we can see why "establishment of trust" or "relationship building" is such an essential precondition for therapeutic learning -- a point which all schools recognize, but other, non-constructivist models have difficulty explaining. The reason is simply that we *have to decode the other person*, decide where he/she "is really coming from" -- always, in every significant communication, at every moment. No given act of speech automatically "means" anything: the listener has to *interpret* a meaning, ascribe a motive and a relationship, imagine a predictive value to what the person is saying, and the fact that she/he is saying it now. This is self-process -- we don't have any choice about it. When we are "building trust," we are building up an interpretive relational ground -- what we call "getting to know a person" -- which can then serve us in making future communications stable and usable, so that we can attend to the content, and not just to the conditions and safety of the exchange itself.

Where the material is extremely shameful to that person or in that culture -- whether the topic is shame itself, or anger, or sexuality, or grief, or depression, or any other content, -- we thus may be faced with a therapeutic dilemma. On the one hand we risk leaving the client too alone with the same material he/she was too alone with before (an unintended and unnecessary recapitulation of a shaming interpretation); and on the other hand we risk intruding on the therapeutic space the client needs to focus on her/his own process, by bringing in something of our own. One support for resolving this dilemma is the use of group therapy, where the question of how other people process difficult moments, charged material, generally becomes part of the subject matter for learning. Another one is for the therapist to make some reference to the supports he/she needs and uses, to process this kind of material (a question the client may sometimes pose directly, as long as the therapist has not subtly or directly conveyed that this kind of inquiry is not appropriate -- i.e., is itself shameful): for example, "I've always found that it's impossible to stay with feelings like that without someone else to be there with me, at least part of the time;" or "No, I don't have much trouble with anger (say), because that's not the area I was shamed in -- but when I do get to a shamed area, then sure, I need support to stay there.") Or alternatively, the therapist always has the support of intersubjective inquiry: "What are you making of my own reaction to what you're telling me? How do you imagine I'm holding it, and holding you, right now? Am I feeling empathy? sympathy? allied? superior? do I know those feelings myself?" And then potentially, "What would you like to know about that? Would you like to check it out? Is there anything you want to ask me?"

Our particular point here is that under the regime of individualism, shame itself will virtually always be held by the client as prime among this shameful material -- and that intersubjective process in therapy, which is self-growth, will be to some degree blocked, *unless and until shame itself can be addressed and "held" in the relationship*. To repeat and review, we hold this to be theoretically, necessarily true because: 1) the client brings material to therapy which she/he is too alone with, is holding in too individualistic a way; 2) this material is blocked or frozen in self-process by virtue of being "not in play," being held in this too-alone way (with cause and effect going in both directions here, in the way of our field-conditions perspective on causation discussed above); 3) the "too-alone" material by definition involves shameful parts of the inner world, again by our definitional understanding of shame here; and 4) therapeutic process inherently involves confronting, holding and processing/transforming feelings of shame. Shame interrupts self-process, and deforms or constricts it in cerain particular ways. Therapy involves the restoration of that full, flexible self-process, which is also inherently the process of self-development and growth of self.

What can the therapist do -- or any of us do -- if we are not supported enough to stay with shame material ourselves, and need to distance from the feelings the client is having, or is threatened by? Obviously, advice-giving, which all of us slip into at times and which may at times be wanted and needed, will carry a strong risk of boomeranging where shame material is involved -- if only because of the inherently "one-up," unexposed position of the advice-giver. Given an enormous amount of relational trust, the advice may be taken up without new shame, but the risk is probably not necessary, and can be avoided by the same kind of intersubjective inquiry outlined above: "I'm aware of feeling like I have some helpful advice to suggest here, but I'm wondering how you may experience that, right at this moment, in the midst of all these difficult feelings. It could feel like I'm above the kind of feelings you're talking about, that I want to get away from them. It could even feel like I want to get away from you, when you're having a difficult time like this."

Beyond advice-giving is the whole realm of "fixing" the situation -- including interventions based on trying to talk the client out of her/his feeling ("Oh no, you shouldn't feel that way at all. Nobody is judging you, you shouldn't take it like that"). Often "fixing" amounts to a subtle changing of the focus, on the part of the therapist or other intervenor, from the experience of the feelings themselves to anything else in the world -- solving the problem, framing it differently, persuasion of the non-necessity of feelings like those, abstractions and generalities, and so forth. In a still larger frame, all these interventions are ways the therapist (or any conversational partner) may have of distancing from shame -- including, of course, of the therapist him/ or herself.

At times these moves may have the effect of "transferring" the therapist's shame, or shame apprehension, onto and in a real sense "into" the client (remember, the self-fields of any two dialogue or contact partners interpenetrate in a sense, since each is mapping and making meaning of a field that includes the inner world of the other). An example from the group can serve to illustrate this sequence. As the training group went on and people shared more and became more involved with each other, Jane's shyness and feelings of inadequacy inside and outside the group had become a part of the life and attentional investment of the group members. Thus when Jane began to talk about how discouraged she felt in the group, how she felt everybody else was getting more out of it than she was, and that once again she was lagging behind, various group members moved to reassure her that she was doing well, that she was forgetting real experiments and steps she really had taken and made right there in the group itself, and that at a number of sensitive points different members had told her they liked her, she was doing well, they admired and affirmed the creative steps she'd made in her life under difficult conditions, etc etc. As the group expressed these things, Jane looked more and more shrunken into herself, more and more crestfallen. When the trainers inquired about her experience, she reported that she was doing her "usual number," "beating up on herself" for first failing, and now letting it bother her, probably turning success into failure in her head, just as the group was telling her she was doing. Worst of all, she "ought to be able to take in everybody being so nice;" the fact that she couldn't seem to was just one more reason to feel inferiority and shame.

This was indeed Jane's "number," as she had explained and to an extent demonstrated before -- perhaps a way of keeping herself small and still enough to survive and connect in an early family field, with parents who were themselves shy and depressed, and deeply uncomfortable with "big" feelings, as Jane painted them. From an individualist point of view, this would then be the whole relevant story, including the inappropriate "transference" to the present situation: something Jane "did to herself," on many if not all occasions.

But when the inquiry was turned to the group, a richer,

more complex picture of field organization in the present began to emerge. What were group members feeling, as they moved to be so reassuring (and from such a safe position, as one group member observed after a bit, with no one joining in the kind of feelings Jane was constructing and experiencing at the moment)? Concern, to be sure, but what else? Some irritation, a couple of members admitted -- Jane was "unwilling to use" the good feelings people had offered her. Hurt feelings, said several others: she was seeming to forget or discard important, intimate, and affirming exchanges they had shared, in and out of the group, over meals or in the corridor. And finally -- "inadequacy," offered Sam, "because, you know, I'm Hector Protector, and I can't seem to save you. I've tried this and I've tried that, but nothing helps you. So I feel sort of irritated, and under that sort of hurt -- but bottom line is, I feel inadequate, like I'm failing, I'm just not up to it. You don't like my brand of protecting, I'm not the right protector guy for you. And hey, that's an important part of me, I protect people from people being mean to them -- in this case you, being mean to yourself. Only I can't do it. So I'm stupid after all, you might say I'm emotionally dyslexic, I can't read you. And that's shame -- right?" At which point several other group members agreed that Jane's feeling made them feel inadequate -- but (and this is the important point) that they hadn't been in touch with that, till Sam began speaking of his own shame.

At this late point Eleanor, who had been quiet for all this processing time (though active before that, in trying to persuade Jane not to be hard on herself), spoke at length of her own feelings of shame at her own self-punitiveness, a place where she identified strongly with Jane's feelings now. She too was ashamed that she couldn't seem to "just get over it," couldn't seem to take in all the positive feedback from her students and others, and use it to maintain a steady feeling of "okayness" and confidence in her life -- and perhaps especially in her writing. She apologized to Jane now for not sharing this up to this point, for "letting you hang out there" like that -- "not intentionally, but just because I literally sat here and went blank, I actually didn't know I was feeling all this, till Sam then some other people began to talk."

Thus even in a training group of this kind, which is explicitly not a "therapy group," important self-articulation and growth can and will occur, to the extent that supportive intersubjective field conditions are established -- because our inborn self-nature is to *begin to resume self-process and self-growth in any area where those conditions begin to exist*. That is, as soon as the favorable field conditions are there for renewed and expanded self-integration, the self begins again to work on integrating the whole relevant field. Once again, self-growth is not a special activity, apart from ordinary living and learning, but is the normal constructive/deconstructive, hypothesis/experiment/feedback/new-integration process of our self-nature, when that self-nature and process are not constricted and inhibited by unsafe and unsupportive field conditions. And among the primary field conditions for unsafety and self-rigidity is the felt, present interpersonal field condition of shame.

To review the construction and deconstruction of this sequence, it went like this: an access of shame in one dialogue member (Jane), shared with a sense of despair (and possibly as a plea for help, an angry protest, perhaps an element of irrational punishment of those who seemed to be doing well and leaving her behind, etc) -- elicited distancing in the form of reassurances and talking-her-out-of-it from group members, who were the other partners in the dialogue. This was as opposed to joining Jane in the particular feelings she was having -- feelings that she "ought to be doing better," "ought not to be bothered" by what actually was bothering her, feelings which after all, virtually everyone knows and might potentially join in on (for example by sharing times and topics where they felt that themselves, talking about what in their own lives they "shouldn't even be feeling," etc). What accounted for moving away (and possibly "up," to an "above it" position)? The answer is unspoken feelings on the part of the group members -- including variously irritation, hurt, rejection, anxiety, inadequacy -- and shame.

The general intersubjective rule is then: feelings which are denied in a powerfully significant other person, may tend to be held shamefully by the subject her/himself. And as a corollary, if those denied feelings are inadequacy and shame themselves, then the same feelings of the other person may be heightened. This is not to say that the group members were "causing" Jane's shame. Rather, in the language of field conditions rather than linear cause-and-effect, we would say that the denial of feeling, and particularly denial of shame, on the part of some people, will set up favorable conditions for more aloneness with shame, and thus an intensification of shame, in some other people. If I tend to organize self-shamingly already (out of my own unsupported history), and you move to a distant, corrective, and thus safe/superior position, in effect denying felt shame of your own, then it's not surprising that I will map this distance self-shamingly, along the lines of "I shouldn't be even feeling this." First I felt bad, and then the field conditions supported (not forced or caused) me to feel even worse, about feeling bad in the first place -- when after all, "everybody is being so nice."

Conclusions

All these are the implications, perspectives, and insights we draw by taking a field-organizational, constructivist view of self process in general, and of shame processes and dynamics in particular. Our task and our nature, as actively constructivist selves, is to resolve the field meaningfully and usefully, all the time. The ways we do this, and the actions we then take based on these meaningful field resolutions, will be shaped by definition by *the supportive or unsupportive conditions of the field for that meaning and that action* -- my own inner beliefs, expectations, capacities, hopes, resources and dangers as I perceive and understand them, and then my subjective understanding of all these things and more in the "outer" field. What happens is then always and necessarily what was supported to happen, in this broadest sense of support.

In this same broad sense, *shame is the opposite of support*, for any particular field resolution of meaning or action. That is, shame conditions are part of those support conditions most broadly understood, only shame is part of the conditions making it harder to go one way -- but at the same time part of the conditions making it easier to go some other way. My shame about feeling weak and inadequate, for example, will act as an inhibitor on my getting to know that part of myself, or perhaps my capacity to be with you when you are feeling those feelings, or just to bear such feelings myself when they come up; yet the same shame about the same thing will act as an enabling support for my becoming, say, critical or distancing when the feelings do come up -- possibly even violent, addictive, or otherwise self- or other-destructive. Thus *shame modulates contact* -- the role designed "by evolution," as we say, for it to play, as long as it remains fluid, "in play," available for naming and processing and dialoguing intersubjectively, in the ongoing unfolding of hypothesis, self-experiment, feedback, adjustment, and the integration of new learning in the field.

When shame becomes "internalized," by contrast -- by which we mean, carried individualistically, and thus in a frozen way that is not available for process and dialogue, -- then *shame inhibits self*. Important parts of the self -- including both the shamed area of experience (anger, intimacy, sexuality, strong feeling in general, grief, weakness, shame itself) and the experience of the shame -- become split off from the fluid, supple process of ongoing field-integration, not subject to the new experiment and new learning of our natural, ongoing self-process. At this point, shame inhibits growth of self. The shamed area remains the same -- to the extent that, and as long as we do not have supportive intersubjective conditions for addressing the shame itself, so as to set a full range of self-experience back in motion.

The healing corrective for this stuckness is always the *restoration of that particular kind of intersubjective field that we have been discussing and referring to all through this chapter.* What does that kind of field look like? What's involved, in establishing and maintaining it -- the conditions which we've said are both the prerequisite for, and the same as, the restoration of self-growth? How does growth happen in the first place, and why are these particular conditions so essential, all through life, for full experiencing and full living? All these points have been touched on here. Now, in Chapter Seven, Intimacy, Intersubjectivity, and Dialogue, we will take them up for specific focus and intervention,

Increasingly here, in place of yet another exercise we will rely on further discussion of the material already presented, including references to the group's discussions of these themes. As always our goal will be to articulate a model of self-process and human nature than *knits up the rupture between theory and experience, our assumptions and our feelings, our discourse and our actual practice*, as we live and work with people in and out of a model that lies beyond individualism, in our experience of our work, our relational lives, and our private yet interpenetrating selves.

Chapter Seven: The Restoration of Self -- Intimacy, Intersubjectivity, and Dialogue --

What is intimacy? Once again we find ourselves confronted with one of those familiar terms -- like self, relationship, support, shame, or for that matter "perception" or "reality" -- which we use regularly, and assume we understand, but which may seem to slip out of our grasp as soon as we set about to discover or construct their meaning. The reason for this difficulty, our new perspective on self-process and human nature suggests, is that *all these terms are in a fundamental sense relational or field processes*, which we were trying in vain to freeze and capture in individualist or "thing" language, out of the assumptions of our older, inherited model.

Is intimacy then an event, a place, a process -- or somehow all three? Is it when you share your darkest secrets? Is it sex -- a common usage, as in "intimate partner" or "intimate relations?" Is it always a desirable thing? -- or is it rather a kind of Pandora's box, a sort of genie out the the bottle which needs to be hedged about with limits and precautions, as indeed it often is? Does intimacy just happen, or do we have to seek it and construct it -- and if so, how would we go about this, and what would be the goal?

In the chapter ahead we'll build on this idea that intimacy -- like self, support, shame, and a number of other terms in this discussion -- is best and most usefully viewed as a field process or event which grows out of *particular field conditions*. That is, in this view intimacy is a particular *kind of activity of self-process*, a particular way of organizing or co-regulating the field of experience, which then can become the ground condition for other, related processes of self. And like all self-activity it depends itself on certain field conditions or supports which favor (or inhibit) those processes in a given local field.

As in the other chapters, we will be discussing and exploring what these terms mean in this context, and in this new sense. But first, to move the discussion to the more immediate level of our lived and felt experience, we'll do here what we've done in previous chapters, which is to start with an exploration of experience in this area, and then use that exploration as our reference material for constructing new definitions and models. In that way, as in the previous chapters, not only is the discussion itself more grounded in felt experience, but the reader is more empowered to enter into the topic actively and use her/his own experience as a criterion for constructing those new understandings and evaluating the discussion offered here. That means, as before, first of all the experience of our sample group, some of whom we may feel we are starting to know fairly well by this time, and then moving to include the experience of the reader as a counterpoint, whenever you may choose to stop and do the exercise material along with the past participants. As always, space is provided here for reader responses to the exercise questions -- or you can use your own paper or keyboard.

The Field Conditions of Intimacy

To begin our exploration of the experience of intimacy, we'll go back once more to an experience of *shame*, such as the one from the previous chapter, continuing now in the direction of *what I might need from the other person*, what kind of interpersonal field of support, in order to feel like recounting an experience like that to another person at all, without too much apprehension of injury and reshaming. We say "not too much," because there may always still be some, but then what is it that would help keep that apprehension at a manageable level? What might I need, to be able to imagine going back into some shame-tinged experience without being completely preoccupied and constrained by the anticipated reactions of the other person (remembering here that shame itself is most often held as shameful in our culture)? Here are the exercise instructions for this next step:

> Take a moment, close your eyes, and let your mind go back again now to some experience you're carrying, some troubling memory that in some way has shame attached to it. This could be like the stuck places we explored together before in shame terms -- or you may find another experience that you're carrying now, something you feel bad about, that's hard to get over somehow, something that could feel hard to share with just anybody. Make a few notes about it, just for yourself -- how it felt then, how it feels now, what the memories feel like in your body, and then what might happen *if* you were to decide to talk about all this with another person.
>
> Stay with it a moment, letting all those thoughts, feelings, and sensations come up again now, till you can feel them in your body. When you're ready, just *imagine telling* this experience to another person. Don't tell it, for now anyway -- just imagine telling it. What feelings and sensations begin to come up now?
>
> Our question now will be this: *What would I need now from that other person*, to make me feel like actually talking about this experience now? What would I want to know, what would I need to be able to count on, for that even possibly to be a good experience? Assuming it's my option, what kind of reception would I want to feel I could expect, so that that experience now could be a real exploration, and not just another exercise in caution or hiding?
>
> Make a few notes about this too. Then when you're ready, instead of sharing the experience itself -- which can stay private or not, as you want and need, -- look back to the group and share out *those wants and needs themselves.*

How would you want and need another person to be, or not be, for you to have at least a chance of coming out of this experience feeling better, not worse? What would you want them to do or not do, so that you could stay with this painful thing, maybe even learning something useful about yourself, instead of just feeling more shame?

The list below gives some sample responses from participants, with space as always for adding your own:

no interruptions! some response at least!
somebody who's been there don't try to fix it please
it's the look in their eyes just *sit* with me
be okay with silence, don't make me talk all the time
don't let me just sit there! be okay if I cry
no judgments I'll know it in their face
know what it's like yourself just listen
don't drop me in midstream stay with me
don't push me, don't try to make me to feel a certain way
don't tell me what I should have done
sombody who isn't going to judge me
just let me know you know these feelings too
tell me your experiences, so I'm not the only one here
it's not any one thing in particular -- it's how the person is feeling about me
inside, I can't be totally sure if I don't know them, I'd just have to keep checking and see how it goes

Here too we may well be struck first of all by the sheer quantity and energy of this outpouring of responses. This is typically an area where people have a lot to say, with a great deal of feeling, and perhaps a confusing amount of contradiction as well, or apparent contradiction anyway, in some of these terms and demands. After all, how can a listener remain silent, being careful not to interrupt or push, and at the same time offer "some response?" -- "just sit there" and also "don't let me just sit there;" "just listen" and at the same time "tell me your experiences, so I'm not the only one?" Even if we can resonate with each or all of these desires in turn, how can we possibly fulfill them all? Already we begin to have the idea that the possibilities for renewed injury here are multiple and pervasive.

At the same time, as the last responses on the list indicated, the answer to this is probably not so much that the desires themselves are really contradictory, as that the whole list represents a wide-ranging series of *field experiments and tests*, to "get a feel" in a variety of ways for how safe the field really is for this kind of delicate exploration. This safety, as the group's contributions suggest, is inevitably a projective or interpretive question, like any evaluative judgment, very much of the type we explored so much in Chapter Three on orienting and relating to another person. That is, the issue here is not so much any one particular behavior as it is what the subject *interprets and imagines that behavior to signify*, about the inner state and motivations and the feelings or judgments of the listener. After all, I cannot directly see your state of mind, good or ill will, acceptance or rejection, empathic identification or judgmental shaming of me and my feelings. All I have to go on are your behavior, gestures, facial expressions, and so forth -- on the basis of which I have to make my own interpretations and construct my own meanings. Asking you your intentions directly doesn't entirely remove this interpretive step either, since whatever you say, I then still have to evaluate *that* for sincerity and reliability, interpret it for meaning and fit, map the two of us into the relationship implied by your remarks (or rather the one I imagine to be implied), assess all this for its usefulness in terms of stability and "follow-through," and so on. All this sounds overwhelmingly complicated and cumbersome in the telling, but in the new model of self we are building up here, we understand this complex field-interpretive, scan-evaluate-act process to be, for the most part, *automatic, holistic, basically inborn, and lightning-quick in real time*, the operation of our complex cognitive/affective self-nature in action, all or nearly all the time.

In an older model this kind of holistic field-assessing enterprise would have to be seen as "merely feeling-based" and "not objective," and therefore to be discounted, mistrusted, and/or dispensed with (and its importance denied). Here we would say rather that this subjectively constructed meaning-based process is *all we have to go on*, as we negotiate a challenging field, and draw on our evolved perceptual nature to interpret and process the environmental effects or "feedback" as we go along (as in any evolutionary model, adaptation, not "objective truth," is the final criterion of the "correctness" of the results). *All* perception is constructive and meaning-based in this way; thus by the terms of our evolved, problem-solving nature we are going to be doing this kind of thing all the time anyway, by necessity. And we keep right on doing it whether or not an older theory insists that this whole field-interpretive activity is in some way outgrown in childhood, or its persistence is merely infantile and regressive. (The only difference is that in a shaming model, as we saw in the previous chapter, the process goes underground and we lose the capacity to dialogue and explore it).

Meanwhile, this outpouring of conflicting demands also shows the delicacy of the task at hand, on the listener's side: being with another person who is entering a space of shame feelings. Essentially what is being asked for here are the conditions and processes we know as empathy, or "feeling into," *entering into the other person's subjective world and felt life space*, feeling some of what that person is feeling, and taking your cue from that. (This is as opposed to "sympathy," which is a resonant response to an affective state from outside that state, without the dimension of entering into that person's subjective organization of the field. In sympathy we try to imagine what the other person is aware of feeling; true empathy starts when we begin to contact feelings and needs that the other person is holding outside awareness).

What we need at these moments, when we're in touch with material that has somehow been shamed in the past, is a person who will listen and -- at least for that moment -- *know and even feel something of our world*, as we went through that experience (and as we are retelling and perhaps reliving it now) -- "from the inside," seeing, recognizing, and in a sense joining the feelings and the understandings of what all we were "up against" in that situation, and what we went through, all from our point of view. If our listener is willing and able to know our world in this way -- this piece of it anyway -- from the inside, as we knew it then, rather than just from outside, the level of our behavior and actions, then that understanding itself will be the best guide to when to speak and when to remain silent, when to reach out and when to leave the teller alone.

In the best and most growth-enhancing case, given a history of her/his own of receiving this kind of inquiry and intersubjective contact, the listener will even know when and how to move the conversation to that necessary metalevel of asking about how the present dialogue itself is going, what feelings the teller is having and what support he/she needs now, to sustain and focus this ongoing exploration of self.

But then these are exactly the descriptive and dynamic terms in which we spoke in the previous two chapters of the "*intimate witness,*" that person who so often was lacking back in those challenging times in the past -- and especially those old stuck places that are still troublingly present somehow today. The presence of such a witness, people so often find, makes or would have made "all the difference," then and now. In fact, we've already made the argument that it is precisely the absence of that essential supportive person that made that crisis seem so hopeless, and tends to insure that those events and memories are still with us in such a troubling way today, still not completely integrated into a useful and flexible sense of self and history. In other words, most often *that intimate witness was the missing support.* As we have found over and over, when the particular life challenge of that time was matched and held by an intimate witness, then that challenge can become fully integrated into the flexible lifespace and self-range of the person now, rather than lingering painfully as a stress and a limitation on subsequent creative adjustment and growth. Shame, acute and prolonged, *interrupts and distorts self-process and growth.* The intimate witness (then and/or now) *restores the resonant self-field,* for the renewed or ongoing resolution of new self-experience, new creativity, and renewed growth. Intimacy in this sense, rather than being a luxury or a leisure activity, emerges here as the *essential field condition for full creative development and growth of self.*

Here again, when we speak of shame we are not speaking of challenge, oppostion, or even outright defeat, in the hierarchical way of the old paradigm, where winning equals superiority and pride, and losing equals inferiority and shame. Rather, we mean the deeper kind of wounding experience that comes from *that sinking or sickening sense that the relevant self cannot go on integrating the whole relevant field.* Certainly opposition, setback, and defeat may be difficult and challenging experiences, in childhood or anytime; still, they do not generally enter into the lasting pattern of self-process, so long as the *experience* of challenge and difficulty is itself supported. And by supported we necessarily mean seen, known, felt with, and understood from the inside by some significant other person. Not the failure to solve the problem, but the fact of *bearing that problem and that failure too alone*, is what makes challenge into stress, frustration into shame, and setback into habitual limitation and distortion of the operation of self in and on the field.

Thus the presence of the intimate witness is transformational, in the sense of changing the *conditions and possibilities for further integrative process in the field*, These conditions now consititute a *field of intimacy*, which we see here, again, as the *essential precondition for the fullest development of self and self-expression* -- in contrast to the old model, which tends to understand self and intimacy as separable, even opposed terms. This is the dynamic interactive relationship between and among shame, support, and intimacy in this model. Shame, the affective sign of a lack of field support for full integration of the relevant self, in the extreme interrupts self-process and growth. As with any field process, whole-field support is needed to restore this integrative self-activity. The particular kind of field support needed to restore the self-field and begin healing the shame/self injury is the field process and field condition of intimacy itself, in the sense we're developing here.

How this works begins to emerge more concretely from the ongoing responses of the group. Let's go on now with the instructions for the next phase of the exercise:

> Now we're going choose a partner and move from just imagining telling this experience, to *actually telling it to another person*. Remember as you do this to pay attention to your own comfort zone and privacy boundaries. In the model we're developing here, we understand that maximum learning comes not from maximum risk and stress, but from *adequate, appropriate felt support*. If you do decide to make an experiment in this area, make it in the direction of telling less, not more -- focusing on the *feelings* that come up either way, in particular the feelings that go with choosing not to tell some incident or detail. Play with that boundary, feel it one way and then the other

way in imagination, before you make a choice. As a support, you might tell your partner when you're doing this, so that both of you can support and validate this part of the experience.

Then when you're ready, let your partner know as much as you choose to about the shame experience itself. The situation, the details, who was involved, how it felt, and what happened next. It may be something you've already thought and talked about here, or it may be something else, maybe something that feels even more uncomfortable to share with another person. As you tell it, pay attention to the deeper levels of shame, the *shame statements about the self and your possibilities in the world*, that we carry within us like stories. Fixed or stuck self-stories begin with those statements, and then may feel like they can only finish in equally fixed, predetermined ways.

As you share this experience with your partner, focus too on noting the feelings and body sensations that come up as you're telling it. How do they vary now, in the course of the telling? Specifically, how do your own feelings and sensations change, during the telling, as a function of your partner's behavior and response? What does your partner do that supports your telling your story? What gets in the way? How does that feel? Are you able to tell these things to your partner too as you go along? What happens when you do?

Once you've done this, we'll switch roles with the same partners, so that the listener becomes the teller, and the teller the listener. And then we'll share the experience of the exercise with the whole group.

As the reader will have noticed, the structure of this exercise is a little different from all the ones before, with dyads and turntaking in place of writing and then sharing with the whole group. This is because first of all, we're asking here for a direct experience of something we would call shame -- as opposed to just "stumbling onto" the shame after the fact, as it were, in the previous exercise. To plunge directly into a shame experience like this often requires extra support, which we may find in the safer, more negotiable field of one other person, before we move to the riskier level of a whole group, where my projections about all their projections may fly too thick and fast for me to manage comfortably and stay open to. (In which case I will fall back on my habitual coping strategies, probably trimming and masking a bit here and there -- the very thing we'd like enough support to try to do differently here).

Secondly, our specific goal in this exercise is to practice and experience *negotiating the field of support in an ongoing way, in real time.* Real intimacy, that feeling that my "world inside" can be safely exposed and explored and known here, requires *ongoing negotiation of the relational process in the moment*: what I need, how I feel as I'm talking, how your responses feel to me, what I imagine to be your internal state, and so on. All this is something as we've said that most of us have little skill and less experience at doing in an explicit, intentional way; in practice it often turns out to be more difficult, and more "self-revealing," than our deepest and loneliest story-secrets themselves. In fact, once I begin telling some "shameful" memory, I may tend to disengage almost completely from my partner and my own experience of the telling, with the result that afterwards all I can do is to rebury the memory and the feelings as best I can, and go on unchanged. This is why at times people may tell some terribly shameful thing over and over without any apparent change at all: because the experience itself of the telling isn't being received and supported in this way, so no new field elements are being included in the self-organization of the old experience.

All this is why real intimacy is often such a mysterious, hit-or-miss, now-you-see-it-now-you-don't kind of thing. Without it, our own exploration of our own inner world remains constricted and thin: we don't make many new connections, which means in our terms here that our growth in self-experience, the ongoing complexification of our integration of the experiential field, remains limited. With it, we learn new things about ourselves -- because we have the support for bearing the anxiety, shame about shame, and other difficult feelings that come up in the course of that exploration, in between the deconstruction of an old "defense" or coping strategy, and the integration of something new.

Thus when it comes to shame material, both our emerging theory and our experience with training groups of this kind tell us to slow down, approach these memories and feelings carefully and respectfully, and add more supports than in previous exercises with other kinds of material. Strong experiences of shame, as we've said before, are not something we can stay with for long without extra support; thus we all learn ways to dull and avoid shame, rather than going into it and staying with it. The result is that we don't know an awful lot about our own shame experiences, beyond the urgent need to get away from them as best we can. Once the idea that stuck areas of life tend to be old shame experiences is itself absorbed and integrated, we're more ready to think, as we have here, about what we might need exactly as extra support that would make a closer, more articulated encounter with shame possible. Each of these steps of slow, careful articulation is necessary, if the old shame feelings -- which are really chronic disruptions of integrative self-process -- are to come out in a new, healthier place. After all, what we are talking about now are some of the oldest, most chronically stuck issues in our lives, the kind of thing that even high-functioning people hold and carry, often for a lifetime, perhaps with a kind of frustration but also oftentimes with a sense of resignation which is itself so chronic that they may be hardly aware of it. If we skip over these careful steps here in building a supported field, we risk repeating an experience that is at best no more than a dead end, and at worst a recapitulation and deepening of the old wounds and scars that hold some particular part of living in a frozen or inhibited way.

Interestingly again, while a number of participants may decide -- quite properly -- to keep some details private (or to keep them within the dyad, but not share them with the whole group), almost nobody ends up talking only about the feelings themselves, without any recounting of the actual events and memories. This is not because the instructions were a trick, or a "paradoxical injunction," telling people not to do something just so that they will then feel free to do it. Rather, in our model here we assume that people do want and need to talk someplace, sometime about things that are held quite privately -- *if and when the necessary conditions and supports for that seem to be in place*, at least enough to begin the exploration without excessive risk. This need is universal, for reasons which we will go into at more length below. Again, this follows too from our understanding of what shame is and how it arises in the first place. Our necessary nature is to integrate the whole field meaningfully, as a basis for ongoing management and planning. Persistent shame feelings represent a place where that necessary integration broke down. The result has to be a basic, underlying pressure to go back to that place, in reality or in memory, and try again. When we don't do that, perhaps for years on end, even in conversation and memory, that has to be because we despair of finding conditions of reception any different now from what they were then -- in which case why risk the hard-won and perhaps fragile gains of our habitual strategies for getting away from the shame in the first place? Thus in place of urging people to "take more risks," we concentrate on *those conditions themselves* -- with the result, oftentimes, that people find themselves talking safely and in a learningful way about things they may never have discussed with another person before.

All of this will provide the basis for a new definition and a new understanding of intimate process and intimate relationship. But first, to get up to that point, let us take a look at responses from the group to these instructions here:

Jake: well, first of all, my partner was great. By that I mean she somehow managed to do everything on that list, all in ten minutes! No, seriously, she let me talk, about this humiliating stuff -- and then it turns out the embarrassment isn't so much the things themselves, really, as the fact that it all still *gets to me* so much, *that's* what's so embarrassing now. So I do have that sort of "shame about feeling shame" that you talked about. Like I'm supposed to be stronger than that, it shouldn't bother me so much. And you know what she said when I said that? She said, "Oh I *hate* that feeling." Just that -- "Oh I hate that feeling." And that -- okay, now here's the really embarrassing part -- that made me cry. It actually did. I don't know, I guess I expected her to say, oh you shouldn't feel that way, there's no need, it's not that embarrassing really, or else just a polite stare. Because she's a woman, maybe, and I think of this kind of embarassment about feeling too much as a guy thing -- I mean, you know, a girl thing that a guy shouldn't feel, and a guy would know that -- but then he'd probably talk you out of it, and you'd feel worse!

The thing is, none of that happened. I knew she knew what I was feeling, then and now. And what happened was -- I mean, I know this isn't therapy -- but something therapeutic happened. I had one of those real insights -- about how what gets me the most is not screwing up, or being criticized, or being resented, or even unappreciated -- I mean, I hate all that. But the real thing is, it's when I had pretty much a good intention, and I'm misjudged, for having a bad intention. That's what's really like my family. Like when I'm the one carrying the bag for the whole team at work or something, and then somebody accuses me of power tripping, wanting to control everything. When all I want is for somebody to pitch in and come through -- anybody! I could connect that with my father all right -- I really feel a lot better. Thanks, I can go now! (laughter)

Kathy: well, my partner was *pretty* good (laughter). No, really good, and I'll tell you why. Because when things got scrambled, he actually stopped and owned it, and apologized, and asked me to give him another chance. It's funny, it's like a relationship -- until you get into a difficulty, you don't know what you've got. My partner started giving me, well, you know -- advice, only I didn't think he knew he was doing it, at first anyway. I'm telling him my problem, and he's busy talking me out of the feelings. How I should solve the whole thing, and why I don't need to feel that way. You know? So I'm sitting there thinking oh great, this is hopeless, it's such a guy thing too, trying to solve it for you (sorry guys, but it's true). It's always the same, nobody every understands me, probably I'm being too much, and not feminine enough either, and he wants me to shut up, and he doesn't even know it. And then he says, "how is this going? how am I doing?" -- meaning him, how is he doing? I almost cried right there, just to be asked. It was the last thing I expected. And I said you're giving me advice -- thinking he'd, you know, talk me out of *that.* But then he says, "damn, I always do that. Please give me another chance, and if I do it again, I don't know, just kick me, okay?" And I didn't want to kick him, I wanted to kiss him! I felt so understood right there, and I hadn't even gotten to the main thing yet.

That part was funny too -- the main thing. I thought of course I'd be talking about the same thing as always, you know, not womanly enough, not a good enough mother, all that push-button stuff I've talked about before. And instead I found myself talking about some friends who I felt excluded by, and how much I didn't want them to know how much it hurt, how much it meant to me. But of course in a way it was the same stuff -- I'm not attractive enough, I'm not right somehow, that's why they excluded me. In my head, I mean. And all the rest of it checks out too -- I'm too alone with it, it nags at me, I'm always going to do something about it and I never do, etc etc. They say we only have one issue, right? Well, this is mine. And I always try to work it out entirely on my own, because I'm embarrassed about it, I feel like it shouldn't be there in the first place. And that's true of everybody here, isn't it. So we all just have one issue, and it's the same issue -- we all think we should just get over our issue all by ourselves! (laughter)

Ricardo: This was hard. And I learned something too, about myself. What I learned is that *I don't trust anybody.* To listen to me, I mean, to really listen. It's not just men -- it's everybody. And if somebody is just in a totally not-trusting space, there's no way to talk them out if it, is there? I mean, whatever you say, it could be just a trick -- or not a trick on purpose but you know, a trap, because they don't really mean it, they're just being nice, but they don't *really* want to listen to you, they're not *really* going to understand.

But then what happened was, I ended up talkin about *that*. Because, you know, that counts, I'm ashamed of that too! (laughter) I mean, I don't go around telling people I mistrust them all the time, because it's embarrassing, and then they might get offended. Or pretend to be offended -- depending on whether they were really sincere in the first place. And it was all sort of paradoxical, you know, because then he said well, do you believe me that I at least understand *this*, what you're saying right now, about being so mistrustful and all, and being embarrassed about that? And you know what? -- I did. I'm not sure why, but I actually did, it was like something you can't doubt. I actually believed he was telling the truth, for that one minute anyway. So explain that one -- you're the teacher, it's too deep for me! (laughter)

Actually we do have an answer of a kind for Ricardo, out of the terms of the new model of self and self-process we're working with here. That answer lies again in the interpersonal or field nature of shame itself, as we see it here, together with our understanding of the integrative, problem-solving nature of self-process. If I hide a part of myself from view, that after all is because I *do* expect those feelings or traits to be taken at face value by the other person if I let them be seen: this is exactly what I'm afraid of. I do expect that those parts of myself will be judged, disdained, rejected, or otherwise not met and held in the field -- which also means I don't doubt that they will be seen as really there, really parts of me. Ricardo hides his mistrust because it is embarrassing: i.e., he is sure it *will* be believed -- *and shamed.* If his listener thought it wasn't really true, there would be no shame. The same thing would apply to Kathy, say, with her fear of being seen as "too masculine" (or Jake, who feared being seen as "too sensitive" -- i.e., not masculine *enough*). If another person reassures Kathy that he doesn't consider her "too masculine," she may doubt his sincerity, suspecting him of "just being kind." But if he can move from reassurance about the content to actually receiving and supporting her *experience* -- which is to say, *hearing and acknowledging the reality and distress of her apprehensive feelings themselves,* -- then both of them step into a space where doubt about reception largely evaporates.

This subtle yet crucial difference of level and quality of discourse emerges again and again as participants struggle to negotiate these difficult domains of shame and intimacy. And again and again when people are able to make that shift in level, that in turn yields a marked difference in reception, reaction, and where the conversation can go next.

As long as the listener sticks to reassurance, participants report over and over again, little new can happen. This is because the intervention is built on the assumptions of the old model (shame equals inferiority: reassurance aims to soften or remove the inferiority threat). But the terms of that model are far from the felt terms and living dynamics of our actual experience. In our felt experience, reassurance often tends to feel like something that is offered from a more secure (i.e., superior) place -- which is to say, a standpoint which "rubs in" the feelings of inferiority, since in that model I'm not supposed to need reassurance from the outside anyway. Here we understand, again, that shame, phenomenologically and dynamically speaking, is more a matter of *isolation* than just difference or even judgment itself, of being *too alone with one's experience* and thus unable to integrate the experiential field freely and robustly. Plainly it was difficult or impossible to go very far into feelings like these under the older model, because in the individualist paradigm of self, *these feelings themselves are held as shameful.*

If on the other hand we intervene to promote field conditions which *directly support owning and feeling and voicing shame itself* -- and if the listener is supported to stop trying to "fix" the speaker and to focus instead on receiving and joining the feelings themselves, -- then the discourse shifts. In place of "nice but useless" (as one participant characterized reassurances of this kind) both partners move to an exploration of *what the experience is like* (something that most of us may never have been asked, when it comes to our experiences of shame). At this point the speaker may now believe that the listener at least believes his/her self-report, and the discourse can shift to exploring how deeply the listener can share or understand those feelings "from the inside" (surely the single most frequent phrase participants have recourse to, in an exploration of shame and intimacy of this kind). And that discourse itself -- the articulation and comparison of my inner world and yours -- *is the discourse of intimacy.*

Not that any of this is without a cost -- which is the flip side of its promise. The cost or risk is this: if I stop trying to fix your problem, stop giving you advice, stop trying (in the words of another participant) to "talk you out of your own experience" as something you "shouldn't be having," then *feelings of this same type will inevitably begin to arise in me*, to whatever degree and in whatever ways I have lived and/or avoided these feelings in the past. Really "receiving," in other words, will always include some degree of *joining*, at the feeling level. Our circumstances and histories and particular "hot buttons" will of course differ, and perhaps so as long as we stick to talking about the content details, the solutions, the outer events, some safe distance can still be maintained. But at the level of affect, those deep and broad streams of feeling and types of feeling that Darwin (1873) characterized as an inherent part of our evolutionary makeup, we are not that different. We all know joy and sadness, excitement and revulsion, fear and anger, surprise and anxiety, -- *and shame* (to include roughly the broad categories of emotion Darwin saw as evolutionarily determined). We all know them because they are part of our inborn, evolved "kit" of affective capacity, which allows us to evaluate the field from our own point of view, and our own goals and responses in it, in relation to the field conditions as we understand them. It is in this sense that emotion and value are aspects of the same self-capacity, as we discussed in Chapter Two, both of them dimensions of our evolved, evaluative self-nature. (To be sure, the content of our values and our emotional attachments will vary considerably from person to person and culture to culture, but not the inseparability of perception and interpretation from evaluation itself).

It is in this sense too that we said in the previous chapter that shame, like all strong affect, is contagious. This is because we all recognize and potentially respond to the full range of emotion we are "wired" to have, as part of our orienting, field-reading equipment (again, this is apart from the connection of particular emotions to particular situations; it is fear or laughter or grief that is always recognized, not necessarily what is being feared or laughed at or cried over, from culture to culture or person to person). How those types of affect do then become elaborated and articulated in development, in a particular person in a particular culture, into the rich and individual fabric of emotional nuance and complexity that all of us build and carry, is then the level of individual difference, or knowing and telling and hearing our own individual stories. And that is the terrain of intimacy.

Intimacy in Field Perspective

This then brings us to the point of articulating at least a beginning definition of intimacy in this new perspective, based on the field-organizing understanding of self and human nature that we are exploring and building here. Intimacy in the old paradigm was variously defined as a state, a behavior, and an event. As an event or a behavior it was by definition a time-limited thing, a particular action or transaction, a conversation or perhaps a sexual interaction we could move in and then back out of, as separate individual selves in search of some nourishment or discharge (the classical Freudian perspective, remember, was a tension-reduction model, leading in sexualized male imagery, to a predatory encounter followed by withdrawal back into the natural state of separateness). As an ongoing state, prolonged intimacy would then always involve risks of fusion, or "loss of self," a compromise of that simple autonomy that was always the ideal of the system. As for our familiar term "intimate relationship," this would then have to be seen, strictly speaking, as a dangerous illusion. Dangerous, again, in that it would threaten the autonomous self; and illusory in that all relationship is ultimately illusory, as we saw in Chapter One, under the given terms of the individualist paradigm.

Here all that looks very different indeed. Rather than seeing self as a preexistent entity distinct from the field, in the new paradigm we understand self as an integrative whole-field process from a particular point, in and of that field. This creative process, that construction of experience, which is what we mean by self, then yields an "inner world" of that self-process (what we call "self-awareness"), hidden from direct view, underlying the "outer" world of behavior in the environment. Intimacy in this model is then the process of *knowing and making known that inner world.*

This is the world of *experience,* the interrelated web of meanings we construct out of events internal and external, a deeply organized "place" of memory, habit, emotion, value, and belief, all of it learned and organized in interactional relation to our own given nature, which is prepatterned in certain ways. (For a discussion of some of those preorganized patterns of integration, see especially Chapter Two on the nature of awareness). Plainly we do need to know that world, to some useful degree at any rate, if we are to get anywhere at all with our ongoing, necessary life business of *integrating the inner world, the "inner self," with the outer world* -- the task we have been saying is the function and the meaning of the self. But how are we to accomplish that knowing? From our own experience we know that inner part of our own experiential field as a place full of mysteries and constant surprises, a lifelong voyage of discovery both worthwhile for its own sake, and necessary for living at all well -- and at times for just surviving, period. How do we go about that necessary knowing?

Now in an older individualist, positivist model it seemed to be just assumed that that inner world could be known directly to the self, by a process of "self-reflection" -- perhaps because in that model it was the "home territory" or at least the immediate neighborhood of that self, -- just as the outer world could be known directly, and objectively, to a properly trained observer at any rate. (In a traditional Western model "self-deception," all those ways in which we turn out in fact *not* to have known our own inner worlds very well at all, was often ascribed to the invasion of an outside agency, such as the devil; later, in a more atheistic age, "the unconscious" was invoked in much the same role, as the agent or territory where the self becomes masked or other to the self). Since as we have seen, this was an objectivist, right-wrong paradigm, the notion of the "expert observer" was always implicit here -- the priest, in a deistic period; the psychoanalyst, in the later Freudian age. And again this led to the most basic paradox of the individualist paradigm: the self, which is purely, objectively internal, can be known directly and objectively -- but only by some *other authority*, not by the person actually living it. The lived experience of that objective, given, individual self, again, is not taken as a reliable guide to anything.

In lived experience, by contrast, we know that we aren't born knowing our own internal world very well at all -- nor are "expert authorities" likely on their own to have a very close grasp of my world, my story as I know and live it. We have to *construct* that self-understanding, as we have to construct all understanding, a process that begins in infancy, as the infant begins to differentiate and link together inner and outer experience. Nor are we born knowing much about *how to go about* that process of knowing, beyond the simple linkage of sensation to other sensation or to outer event. That is, the human infant arrives on the scene not with fully functional adult vision, but with the inborn capacity to learn, after only a small number of trials, to integrate, say, certain visual cues with their corresponding kinesthetic/proprioceptive *and social* events. The neonate, for example, is not able at first to organize visual reactivity into the experience we call *seeing*, to integrate seeing with recognizing, and then relate that image and its associated memory to reaching, grasping, and pulling in toward the mouth. But after a brief period of cortical maturation and a certain number of trials, the diverse experiences of the arm passing through the visual field, the inner sensations of arm muscles in movement, the feel of some seen object against the skin of the hand, temperature, flexion, mouth opening, and so forth, become integrated fairly automatically into a single unified schema or flexible whole of reaching/grasping/taking/sucking, and so on. In the normal case no one has to teach the infant all this -- though even at this level, the quality and energy of the integration will differ from culture to culture, family to family, child to child (for discussion of cultural penetration of these earliest learned integrations, see Fogel, 1993).

From this early stage on, the more the infant moves on to increasingly complex levels of integrated wholes of feeling/desire/ estimation/evaluation/action, the more cultural and relational context and feedback (support and its withdrawal, which will evolve into the complex emotion of shame) will enter into, shape, and constrain this integrative process. What is okay to desire or reject, what level of energy is acceptable to mobilize in what situation, what affective signals are responded to and thus developed (and which ones begin to extinguish for lack of any response, or are more actively punished), what amount of persistence and sustained attention leads to what result, and on and on -- all this falls in the arena of relational/cultural learning, which is to say in the arena of the interpersonal world of the provision or absence of support.

As long as all this is taking place in a context of a stable environment and stable social roles and patterned interactions (i.e., what is called a "traditional" culture), then the need to develop the metaskills of attending to *how that inner world is organized*, and of *deconstructing and reevaluating those inner organizational patterns and learnings*, may be relatively low. Still, physical and social environment are never all that stable; and even in our Western, idealized image of "traditional" culture, we can imagine that the need to know and recognize inner affective states and desires remains key to the organization of particular wholes of feeling/evaluation/interpretation/action and meaning. Emotions and values in this sense are always our directional compass as we select a particular goal or path; and as we form more and more complex, multi-person, and long-range desires, we need to have access to more and more complex emotional states, as well as the skills for attending to the inner world in that way. And then all this is only all the more true, the more we turn to cultures that are themselves more open and evolving, less patterned to traditional and stable social and environmental templates. Moreover, in all cultures at all times, the ability to grow and innovate beyond our given cultural patterning is always dependent on the ability to support attention, scanning, imaginal experiment, evaluation and choice, and novel combinations in that inner world.

All this much is both abstract, and at the same time perhaps self-evident once we think about it in this way. But then where are those attentional abilities and those skills for internal scanning and experimenting to come from, if they are not themselves inborn? The answer is, *they are learned in relationship* -- specifically, in the particular kind of relational field we have been calling *intersubjective* -- which is to say, characterized by relationship among the inner experiential worlds of multiple selves. It is *through the attention and interest in our inner experiential world by some interested other person*, that we learn that that internal world is fully there as something we might focus on, that attending to it is important, and then how to go about that process. Without that intimately interested other person in this sense -- that *intimate witness,* -- our own ability to take an interest in our own inner world, sustain that attention, take those inner patterns apart and open them up to new combinations, new experimental learnings, inevitably remains primitive and underdeveloped. The self, as Winnicott remarked (1988), begins in the "eye of the mother" -- or as we would say now, in the regard of the intersubjective caretaker, the intimate witness in our sense here. This witness, this intimate partner in articulating our inner world, is our first model for how to look at and know that world -- and we know it, first, foremost, and ongoingly, by *articulating it with and to another person.* Only then, out of a ground of that dialogue, do we develop the capacities we call "self-reflection," which are the internalization of that dialogue in later life. Reflective thought, as Fogel observes (1993), is dialogic in form: in life as in theater, the introspective monologue derives from and retains the form of a conversation with an implied other.

This is a process that begins at birth -- or even before birth, as expectant parents and others "apostrophize" the yet-unborn baby: that is, they address the new being-to-be *as if he/she already had a coherent self-process in an inner "space,"* indeed as if the baby already had language and could join in the dialogue. The process is projective, in the sense of imagining the inner state and motivational organization of another person, the understanding of that term and process that we developed in Chapter Three. Once the baby is born, the parents and other caretakers will often actually carry on both parts of this dialogue out loud, projectively "lending the child a voice," speaking both their own and the child's part in the conversation, as if it were a "real exchange." As Havens remarks (1986), speaking of therapy with patients with an underdeveloped or inhibited self-process, when the self that is needed to participate in meaningful dialogue is not there, we necessarily *evoke that self*, addressing him/her and at times even supplying experimental replies, as samples of how the other person might "get there."

Now obviously, this kind of projective activity carries a risk that the projector will lose the experimental, exploratory frame and goal, and wittingly or unwittingly impose her/his own self-process and inner world, to the neglect or even destruction of the self-development and emerging reality of the other. This is the concern that fuels much modern individualistic thinking, especially that of some 20th Century existentialist thinkers: the dangers of "groupthink," -- or, in a related frame, "mom-ism," the fear of the presumably engulfing caretaker. (Ironically, some of the writers who have most emphasized these fears, and most elevated them to the status of theoretical absolutes, have also been subscribers to authoritarian ideologies themselves, as for example Sartre [1943] or in some ways Hegel [1962], as well as the followers of some of the more doctrinaire schools of psychology; see discussion in Chapter One). But it doesn't help with this problem, by our argument here, to deny the essential function of projective imagination in interpersonal contact, which can reach intersubjective depth without the ongoing use of *projective inquiry*. Our point here and all through this book is not that one pole or the other of our self-experience -- the individual "inner me" pole or the social/environmental pole -- is either unimportant or all-important. Rather, in this view either pole may be neglected or overemphasized; and both are necessary, understood not as "self-and-other" but as *dynamic dimensions of the self,* for full human functioning and self-development.

With the infant, this kind of "conversation" is indeed a real exchange, even though the child cannot yet participate in it verbally -- because of the way the caretaker is constantly shaping her/his trial verbalizations in terms of the infant's non-verbal cues. In form it may go something like this, beginning with an ordinary inquiry, but then soon moving into supplying imagined responses as well, which both interpret and (hopefully) lead the infant's internal state: "Well, my big boy is awake -- are you hungry now, is that your problem?" followed by, "Yes I am so hungry, Daddy, I am so so hungry, where is that bottle, what's taking you so long?" and then, "Here we go, just the way you like it;" and finally (again speaking for the infant), "Mmmm, that's better," and so on. Or at other times the caretaker may slip into the undifferentiated "we," to express the child's imagined feelings, as in: "Oh yes, we're so so sleepy now, we're just listening to Daddy's voice and floating off, and then we're going to sleep all night long, because we know Daddy has a big meeting in the morning," and so forth (thus the word "hopefully" -- the parent is hoping this leading will work!) (And note too here the opening provided for cultural influence and structuring by this leading, this differential response and interpretation of the child's inner states, right from the begining of life. We cannot "not relate" to the child -- and the child cannot "not respond" to that relational space. And try as we may to be attuned to the child's "real" inner self and needs, there is no relating that is free of cultural attitudes and assumptions).

By giving imagined voice to the child's ongoing experience in this way, the parent both tracks and orients him/herself to attune to the child's possible inner states and needs -- and at the same time *introduces and habituates the child to the experience of subjectivity*, through not just the words but the timing, the pause for signals and cues, the search through multiple possibilities for the right solution to the child's distress, the ongoing adjustment on the parent's part to the modulation of signs of distress or satisfaction, and so on. That is, the parent here is *modeling subjectivity in a mutual or intersubjective field, opening up an intersubjective process and inviting the child into intersubjective space*. The corresponding creative adjustment of the child, prepotently ready in its component parts both by birth and through early attachment behaviors, is to step into subjectivity, and begin all those behaviors of internal scanning, delay, choice, planning, and ultimately the languaging of all this that taken together constitute the lived experience of subjectivity, a constructed story of ourselves we understand as we live it, by telling it ongoingly as we create it, to ourselves and others.

Of course, in practice in our culture it can actually be mildly embarrassing at the least, to be overheard in this intimate intersubjective dialogue with a preverbal baby. This is because to "lend a voice" to the (projected, imagined) inner experience of the infant implies a diffusion of supposedly sharp individual self-boundaries, and as such represents a shameful violation of deep cultural values and beliefs. That is, in the terms of our dominant cultural paradigm, this kind of "babyish" activity is seen as *subverting the sharp differentiation of the preexistent self of the baby and caretaker alike*, and not (as it necessarily is) as a process of offering and modeling the intersubjective space out of which a full subjectivity, an active and robust self-process, can develop. Much less is it seen as part of the ongoing development, through this experience, of a new kind of intersubjective arena, *of the self-process of the caretaker him/herself.* And yet privately, despite this cultural load of judgment, many or most caretakers of preverbal children will go right on doing this, to some degree at least -- for the inescapable reason we explored in such detail in Chapter Three: namely, that without the support of projective capacity, so as to imagine and "aim at" what's going on "in there," "inside" the other person, *we wouldn't know how to orient and take up relationship with another self, another agent of internal experience and meaning at all.* Again, *projection is the necessary gateway tool to intersubjectivity,* that attitude and process which elevates debate into dialogue, opening the way to the possibility of something new, beyond dominance and submission played out between previously known positions.

Intersubjectivity, that is, is not just some trendy new bit of jargon in psychological discourse. Rather, it is *the necessary condition for managing our contact and relationship with other people, in a field of plural selves*. And thus intimacy -- as the *exploration of subjectivity*, is not just a luxury of the "psychological elite;" rather, it is, again, *the essential field condition for the development of vigorous and healthy subjective process and self,* which have to include a full and flexible capacity to understand, deconstruct, and modify that organization itself ongoingly in our own lives. Without intimacy in this sense, as we have seen, that necessary ongoing revision of our own inner world, which is growth itself, can never reach its full, robust potential.

This is true in infancy, where the issue is the elementary building blocks of that inner awareness and attention -- knowing and naming (and responding to) physical sensations and emotional states, first of all, so that the baby begins to differentiate hunger, say, from other discomfort or pain, partly by inner cues and consequences, but importantly also on the interactive basis of the response of the other person. And it remains true at every developmental age throughout life, *not just early childhood,* as we have seen at various points in the exercise material all through this book. That is, at each developmental stage, the deconstruction of some previous pattern and the organiztion of a new creative form of integration in the whole field are very much dependent on the active presence of that intimate support, that other person who *sees* our world from the inside, at least to some degree, and whose knowing and joining in our experience are the necessary support for opening up and staying with that inner questioning and creative flux during a necessarily anxious time of *not knowing what to do*, not having a reliable world view and coping strategy, on the way to the emergence of something new. We cannot say this too strongly or repeat it often enough -- so radically does it depart from the assumptions and implications of our inherited models of self, relationship, and development. That seeing, that knowing, *is the necessary field condition for the development of that inner realm of self,* in anything approaching a fully articulated, fully *human* sense.

This is by no means to say of course that *no* new solutions, *no* creativity at all can take place without that full support. We do what we can with what we've got. Certainly, we do solve problems and make the best new adjustments all the time anyway (or just repeat the old ones), given what's supported and avaliable in the whole field. But inevitably we will stay less long a time in creative limbo or "flux," feel the scope and safety for less exploration and experiment before fixing on the new solution. Thus those new patterns and creative resolutions, as we have seen, may tend to be rigid and inflexible, settling into new stereotyped behavior and old repetitive patterns in new situations -- all to the extent that we were missing that crucial intimate support in early development, and/or then ongoingly throughout life..

To summarize everything we've explored here so far, we can say that in our new view any new pattern, any important change in the field, *requires a new support;* that creative problem-solving, new adaptation, and growth are always significant changes in field organization in this sense, and thus always require a number of new supports; that in important new adaptations of this sort some reorganization of the inner field of self-experience, as well as the outer field of self-experience, is always required; and that the essential support for a robust and flexible reorganization of the inner world -- those new patterns of feeling, belief, expectation, interpretation, evaluation, and meaning that have to underlie important new kinds of action in the outer field -- is *intersubjective process*, the active presence of that witness who becomes for a time the *intimate partner in the growth and new complexification of our inner worlds*. Intimacy, in other worlds, is much more than just an act, a moment, or a feeling: *it is the essential field condition for articulating and knowing the inner self, and the essential support for using that articulation for creative new growth of self in the whole field.*

Shame, Support and Intimacy in Context

At this point we can use the discussion thus far to clarify how and why it is that all of us, under any model, move instinctively to draw on support, avoid shame, and, given safe enough conditions (or even oftentimes without them), seek intimacy and the intimate witness ongoingly as necessary self-functions in life. Once again, these things may seem obvious from our lived experience -- but they are not at all self-evident under the terms of the strict individualist paradigm, which would tend to view inherent needs and patterns of this kind as infantile and regressive. Our basic self-nature, as we keep saying here, is to integrate the whole field of experience, in the service of explicit or implicit present and future problem-solving in living -- the inner world and the outer, always at least potentially in terms of each other. This is how we survive, personally and as a species, and this is how we grow, adapt, and cope with a changing environment. This process is what we "cannot not do," our fundamental survival mechanism and essential human nature, the compensation for all the elaborate instinctive patterning which other species have and we lack (and which keeps them locked to a much narrower range of environments than we are, and constrains them to the glacial pace of physical evolution for major adaptations, where we rely instead on cultural evolution, which is much more pliable and infinitely faster). It is also the process we know and live as self.

But every field integration, every contact in and of the self, by virtue of being a field event, requires the appropriate field supports. Thus we scan for, move toward and draw on support by our nature, as field-integrating agents. Shame, as the affective signal of the lack of that necessary field support, then means more than a momentary bad feeling or setback. Rather, shame, as our inborn affective signal for an (anticipated) absence of support, also can threaten an interruption in self-process itself, that ongoing integration of the inner and outer worlds. And intimacy, which represents the reestablishment of that field connectedness with our inner experience, *is the experiential reparation or innoculation for recovery from debilitating shame*, and the necessary field condition for the reestablishment and maintaining of robust, fully creative self-process. All these things, scanning for support, registering and reacting to shame, and seeking and using intimacy, are then much more than regressive or early-stage activities (as in our traditional psychodynamic model), or mere behavioral side-effects (as in a strict behaviorist model): rather, they are all *essential self-processes and capacities throughout life*, basic functions and dimensions of the integrative self.

To be sure, we can become conditioned to distort these necessary self-functions. If seeking and drawing on support has itself been long and deeply shamed, we may become rigid and phobic about support itself, -- a phobic rigidity which is after all an ideal of this culture, particularly for males. If intimate process has been a trap, a source of emotional invasion or control, or perhaps just a completely unknown quantity in development, then we may have "intimacy issues" -- meaning that our inherent longing and seeking for resonance and response to our inner experience is associated with anxiety, reaction formations, and phobic avoidance. And in the extreme, if our important early relationships have been severely shaming, then we may either avoid relationship altogether later on, or else recurrently seek out relationships that are shaming now, as the only kind of interpersonal connection that "feels real" to us -- meaning the kind of field where we can exercise a self and a self-process that we know and recognize as ongoing and related to that ongoing ground of memory and belief that informs and infuses our self-integrative contact today. This last of course will be a kind of double bind, since we are then seeking integration and connectedness primarily or recurrently in a disconnective field, one where only fragmented and impaired integration is possible. The result may be the kind of jerky, contradictory, and self-defeating patterns we characterize clinically as "borderline," which are the reenactment today of an old experiential field which was itself contradictory and unpredictable in these same ways. (Again, compare here McConville's penetrating observation [1995] that the family field *is* the "unconscious" of the child --

and, we might add here, of the adult as well, unless and until corrective experiences of intimacy in later development have validated, responded to, and "breathed life into" other, neglected or shamed parts of the inner self).

What doesn't change, almost no matter the damage, is our basic self-nature, which is to construct and integrate the field of experience for survival, growth, and meaning (and note once again that in terms of both evolution and predictive management of our worlds, these three terms are functionally the same). The parts of the self that have been shamed and held back will still press for integrative expression, still -- within the limits set by past trauma -- seek for the necessary supports to achieve that integration in the field. Thus even in the face of seemingly overwhelming trauma and damage, we will still seek a witness for our point of view, still respond to the overtures of the intimate other. Painfully for most of us at times (and sometimes violently or tragically so in cases of severe past abuse and neglect), we may push that support away again as soon as it gets there, because of all the painful or shameful meanings of experiences of closeness in the past. In many relationships this becomes a sad double bind, as one or both partners become more and more reactive, just when their needs for witnessing and intersubjective joining are highest. Still, the hunger for intimate joining doesn't disappear, and the acquisition of new skills and capacities for connecting in that deeper way remains for most of us among our most important gains from therapy and related experiences, and our most essential life skills and needs.

The Tasks of Intimacy

All this then changes our view of what intimate process itself is about, and how to make it work, both in relationships in general, and in explicitly intimate fields such as couples' unions, close friendships, and family life. Intimate process is the articulation, expression, and reception of inner experience, where we are "coming from," that hidden world beyond or behind our overt behavior, which gives shape and direction to our actions in the outer field. But what has become clear through our exploration here is that *it is reception which drives or "pulls" this process*, and not just the other way around, expression leading and controlling reception, as we would expect from the terms of our inherited individualist self model. That is, both in early development and then ongoingly throughout life, the articulation of new levels of awareness and inner experience depends on the existence of a receptive field to receive that articulation. In the end, we speak and learn to speak those things for which there is an available ear.

To be sure, given a good enough history of intimate reception, we can go on exploring and expanding our inner awareness "by ourselves" at least to a certain degree, through self-reflection, journaling, reading and responding in our heads, and so on. But even there, we will tend to have new insights and make new connections, new complexifications of self-experience, most often in the same way and at the "same level," as those new connections that have been actively received by others before. This is why psychotherapy -- the intentional process of articulating that inner world -- always takes place *in relationship*, though it may of course be supplemented by reading, reflection, and the continuing realization of new insights afterwards. It is well-established, for example, that even just telling a previously untold experience into a tape or in writing does lead to some emotional relief, enhancement of the immune system, and even at times new insights (for discussion of research of this type, see for example Borysenko, 1988)). But these experimental studies always implicitly include the expectation that these transmissions are destined toward some receiver; and no one has ever maintained that the effects of doing this were anything like as powerful as when a responsive intimate listener is actually present.

Issues of intersubjectivity, or the beginnings of intimate issues in this sense, do come into play in virtually all human interactions, as we found in Chapter Three, where we saw how intersubjective projections are necessarily activated with or even before the very first moments of any interpersonal encounter. It is when we move from the level of primarily one-sided projections to the exploration and correction of those interpretations that we begin to move into intimate process per se. That is, for example we may work side by side with someone for a time, or even fairly closely over an extended time, and still say that we don't know her or him "intimately." This is not to say that we have no picture at all of his/her "inner workings:" normally we do, at least to some provisional extent, since we wouldn't know how to coordinate the work and interact with this person at all without beginning to have some idea (perhaps rough or inaccurate) of her/his disposition, sensitive points or issues, way of reacting to stress, and other issues we might call "style." Again, as we saw in Chapter Three, this is the level of necessary projection and predictive interpretation that we have to attempt to construct, right or wrong, in order to know how to orient to and deal with another person at any level at all beyond the most momentary and superficial transaction. The gathering of this data may be primarily informal and incidental to other things, but still it proceeds essentially by the same recursive process of attend/interpret/hypothesize/test/correct as all of our awareness patterns.

Or we may, as time goes by, begin to "go deeper." We may begin to know the person more "on the inside," have more of a picture of what makes him/her "tick." We may know, for instance, that she/he is sensitive to certain kinds of slights, because of coming from a deprived social background (or so we project/ hypothesize) and thus feeling at times at a disadvantage with certain other people. We may know of a loss or crisis or other absorbing event in her/his present life, that will affect the course of our work together, and perhaps of our personal contact as well. At this point we may say that we and this person are "work friends," that we know him/her "personally," though still perhaps not "intimately."

Or we may go further than this. Over lunch or a drink or a trip to the gym together, we may begin to "share our stories," letting each other in on where we are "coming from," that level of inner organization that we keep saying underlies and informs our overt behavior. Many or most relationships may show a tendency to deepen in this way over time, as the stakes and perhaps the safety of long involvement go up, and as we may become interested in doing more kinds of things together, even if that is just on a work level. The simple intervention of assigning two co-workers to a joint project will often have the effect of their "getting to know each other" in new ways, more personally, more "from the inside." All of these are ways we characterize the processes of coming to know that inner ground that gives rise, in interaction with the outer field, to the figures of overt behavior in the the social world: that is, those processes that we are defining here as intimacy.

Or something else may happen. Out of all the people we come in contact with, at work and otherwise, certain ones may "strike a spark" with us, we may feel that we are the "same kind of person" in some important way, perhaps with the "same sense of humor" (a richly complex expression which bespeaks what it is that we find surprisingly incongruous yet not threatening -- a rough definition of the construct of humor, which clearly says a lot about the organization of a person's inner experiential world). We may begin to seek each other out, and to know each other's inner worlds in a way that has *no other instrumental purpose beyond that knowing and sharing itself* -- or at least goes beyond the ways we need to know the other person's inner world in order to work productively in relationship to her/him. This then begins to be what we call "real friendship," or even an "intimate relationship," which we would define here, out of the terms of the model we are articulating now, as *a relational process where knowing and articulating the inner world is an important goal in its own right, beyond any instrumental considerations that we might have in that relationship.* That is, when we say "intimate *relationship,*" we generally mean that intimate process itself *is the main goal.* Again, the drive to create and develop such relationships, apart from any immediate instrumental goal other than intimate process itself, is familiar and universal, for all the reasons we've been exploring and outlining here (though of course it can be blocked or distorted in development, in all the ways we've discussed). And again, this is an important and, we are arguing, essential part of our self-development that we all know, yet one which is difficult to account for under the terms of our received cultural paradigm of self (for related discussion see Wheeler, 1995).

Such intimate relationships may of course be mutual and reciprocal, or they may be one-way, where the inner process of one person is explored and received, but not that of the other. Such asymmetrical relationships often arise out of a field of sharply differential personal power of the two or more participants, at least with regard to some relevant domains of living. Thus it behooves the slave to know the master or mistress (or the employees the authoritarian boss) fairly intimately, so as to be able to predict the other's actions and reactions; but the dominant partner in those interactions generally doesn't feel the same need. Similarly, the prostitute or courtesan, male or female, or the vendor of any intimate personal service, needs to know the client "intimately," at least on certain dimensions, but the client probably feels free of any such reciprocal need (indeed, the whole appeal of the transaction, to the client, may well be the relative freedom from the burdens of that responsibility -- a freedom which is purchased by the payment of the service fee).

Such assymetrical relationships may also be nurturant, not exploitative, as in the case of the parent-child relationship, at least in a relatively healthy developmental field. That is, to do his/her job of managing and structuring a safe and appropriate developmental field for the child, the parent needs to have a fairly good sense of the child's developing inner world, so as to be able to adjust supports, challenges, and safety boundaries, as well as to model and facilitate (and influence) the complexification of that inner world, which is the construction of meaning. At the same time, the child has and needs to have areas that are private -- i.e., unknown to the parent, or known only by the child's choosing, -- and certainly part of the challenge of the parental role is trying to judge the appropriate boundaries and parameters of that privacy, which will of course change over time with increasing age. All this is the largely and properly one-way intimacy of child-rearing, a sensitive and delicate business which demands a parent who already has a coherent self-process, *as well as* significant current other supports for that process, beyond the parent-child relationship itself.

But if all this is reversed -- if the child has to know the parent too much "from the inside," more "intimately" than the parent knows the child, then we begin to think of a burden and distortion in development, perhaps the kind of personality in the child that we will call "parentified," or "codependent" -- meaning *too* habituated to attention to the inner world of others, with too little attention to one's own. (For more discussion of types and asymmetries in intimacy, and their developmental consequences, see Wheeler, 1994).

The same thing applies to psychotherapy, another kind of relationship which is appropriately asymmetrical with respect to intimate process. That is, in psychotherapy both parties have the intention of getting to know more about the organization of the experiential world of just one of them. The imbalance that this creates in the relationship is then compensated by the payment of a fee. Of course, that payment itself may then be associated with various problematic feelings and meanings, all the way from the question of what it is that makes the therapist "worth more" than I am, to why I have to pay somebody to care about me and pay close attention to me, and so forth. But what the fee may also do is to tend to soften or remove the projective question of what the therapist "really wants" from me, what hidden motive might make another person suspend his/her own needs in the service of a stranger -- a question which our inherently projective, interpretive nature will naturally tend to lead us to need to know and to imagine answers for, as we construct and assign meaning to the field. This can then be liberating for the client, who may feel relieved of the burden of reciprocal caretaking. Indeed, if anything the relevant question may often then become, can or does the therapist care about me in any personal way at all, *beyond* the collection of the fee -- a rich field-interpretive question which then can be explored and exploited in the therapy itself.

This perspective then clarifies a persistent question in therapy which has always been hard to answer, under the terms of the old paradigm. That question is, how and to what extent can it be useful in therapy for the therapist to reveal her/his own personal thoughts, feelings, and meanings to the client? When and how is this facilitative in therapy, and where is it burdensome or exploitative? From a classically Freudian perspective, for the therapist to reveal his/her *experience* was never appropriate, since the business of therapy was to correct the projections, or transference, of the patient onto the therapist, and therefore the "blanker the screen," the better (noting here, of course, that under this model the therapist's own projective interpretations of the patient's inner world, which we would also regard in the new model as hypotheses or personal constructions of experience, were given the special, not-constructed status of "objective truth." At the same time, the therapist's own emotional self-experience was treated as irrelevant or problematic "counter-transference," ideally not related in any way to those "objective" interpretations. Once again, an objectivist/individualist model is inherently an authoritarian model, in the end).

Here we would rather say that the construction of interpretations, or meanings about the client's inner world, is a *collaborative or co-constructive field process*, and that the therapist's present experience, feelings, values, and beliefs, being very much part of that negotiated co-construction, are legitimately and importantly part of the therapeutic discussion. Indeed, the contrast of expectations and feelings about a particular incident or theme between therapist and client may be among the richest and most profitable field events and conditions for the articulation of new self-experience for the client. What is not generally useful or appropriate is the *exploration* of meanings, and of the process of construction of meanings, values, and beliefs, within the therapist's own inner experiential field. In terms of the model and the definitions here, that would be material for the therapist's own therapy or other more mutually intimate conversation. Again, the payment of the fee, in addition to representing a recognition of some expertise in conducting this kind of exploration, also serves to compensate this imbalance in the intimate relational field.

Finally, all this leads us to a shift in our understanding of the process tasks of intimacy themselves, and thus of the necessary processes and emphases of therapy, especially couple's and other relational therapy. Much clinical training and writing in the area of couple's therapy has tended to emphasize expression, as the key to better intimate process and couple relationships. Once we "get in touch with" our real needs and feelings, and then articulate those needs more clearly, we are in a better position to negotiate or assert those needs with our partner, this model would lead us to think -- an approach which fits well with a notion of relationship which begins with the idea of two coherent, preexistent selves, encountering each other for the expression or realization of some clear individual needs.

Here we would rather say that while all this is no doubt real and important, in an intimate relationship or indeed any dyadic process (such as a work team, or the work-team aspects of couples' lives and relationships), intimacy, as we understand it here, both offers and demands something more. Intimacy, we are arguing here, is not just the close collaboration on shared or mutually-negotiated goals: it is, again, the articulation and reception *with another person* of the organization of the inner world, both of us learning in the process how my world looks and feels *to me*. Growth of self, the articulation of new experiential connections and possibilities, begins there, in that intimate field. And as we have said, that articulation is more than the expression of connections which are already known; it is the ongoing process of organization of that world itself, in ever more complex and empowering ways (for further discussion of these and related points, see again Wheeler, 1994).

But that process of complexification, as we have seen, of making richer and more useful interconnections among feelings, values, thoughts, beliefs, perceptions, interpretations, and the outer world itself, *is dependent on a receptive field.* Intimate process, the presence of an available, attending listener for our inner world, is the necessary field condition for the organization and articulation of new levels of complexity in that inner experiential realm. And nothing happens, in our new perspective, without its necessary field conditions. Thus rather than just teaching and supporting "assertion" in relationship (though assertion is certainly crucial, and must be practiced where it is missing), under this model we are led to support first and foremost the *conditions of reception*, for the expression of feelings, thoughts, and connective possibilities that the person may well not even have constructed yet -- along the lines of the exercise in this chapter. As we find over and over again in both individual and couple's therapy, when that receptive field is there -- really there, meaning subjectively explored and felt as real by the patient, couple member, or other intimate dialogic partner, then the new articulation will come. Thus we focus most of our interventions on the construction and support of that supportive field itself, so that intimate process, the crucible for the construction of self, can develop to its full creative potential.

Conclusions

Intimacy and intimate process, then, are themselves part of the *necessary field conditions for self-development and articulation of self-experience in development,* and then for ongoing growth throughout life. By definition, intimacy, the exposure and reception of one person's inner world by another, provides that necessary connectedness in the field which enables the self to integrate more of the field, in new and more complex ways, and under conditions of difficulty or challenge. When the self attempts field-integration in some creatively new way and arena, that intimate reception is always needed again, either in real present relationship, or at least by reference and evocation of the felt memory of an energetic history of living and growing in a field of intimate reception. Without that reception, we tend to stay stuck telling and living the "same old story," as so many participants have remarked in frustration, as they first began the explorations that are drawn on all through the preceding chapters. To tell and live a new story, with new meanings and new, richer openings for new creative destinations, requires intimate support, receptive holding while we deconstruct the old story, bear the onset of feelings that were managed or held at bay by the terms of those old beliefs and expectations, and live through the anxiety that has to accompany our first steps into any new world.

But then what do we mean, in this new perspective, by that

word *story*, which has begun coming into the discussion more and more as we move to putting all these different strands and dimensions of self-process together again in this new way? Our approach all through this book has been basically deconstructive -- the taking apart of familiar processes, received traditions, old meanings and beliefs. How do we put all that together again, in analysis here or in lived process in our own relationships and living self-process? What is our experience of field-integration, as an act and as a state; how do we *hold* our inner world, our outer world, and our integrative selves, in a way that is coherent enough to be manageable, yet open and flexible enough to be useful in a changing field? To begin to answer those questions, we will turn in the next section to that word *story* itself, our narratives and self-narratives which contain our past, our present, and our future in a dynamic linkage which. This is a term, like so many familiar words and concepts we've examined in this book, that looks and feels quite different from the perspective of a new paradigm of self, beyond the terms of our culture's dominant and long-controlling legacy of individualism.

Part IV -- The Integrated Self: Narrative, Culture, and Health

In Part I of this book, we traced the origins and implications of a dominant cultural tradition which we have been calling individualism, *the doctrine that the individual self arises and stands alone, both ideally and in reality -- together with the roots and sources of alternative views of self, ranging from certain Eastern philosophies to the "postmodern" implications of the Gestalt model of awareness and human process. That dominant ideology, we argued, has had the status of a basic cultural paradigm in the West over the past three millennia: a fundamental and controlling frame which sets the limits on what can be readily thought and communicated (and even felt) within that cultural tradition. Objectivism, positivism, dualism, and what is called "patriarchy" -- all of these are inseparable, we have suggested, from the paradigm of individualism, which unites a diverse range of seemingly opposite worldviews in the history of the West, in the context of a single set of underlying beliefs and generally out-of-awareness assumptions.*

In Part II we began exploring the workings of a self that was conceived entirely differently, based on the terms of our natural human processes of perception, emotion, and essential problem-solving. The self we found is a naturally and necessarily integrative process of resolving the whole field of subjective experience -- the "inner" and "outer" worlds, -- in the service of problem-solving and growth in a difficult and changing environ-

ment. This process is composed holistically of scanning, attending, feeling, evaluating, imagining, interpreting, estimating, acting, integrating and making meaning. These stages are not sequential steps of a linear process but recursive dimensions of an integrated whole: each of them is informed and contextualized by all the others, in an ongoing way. Since the process seeks to integrate the whole experiential field, it is inherently inter-subjective: your "inner world" is a part of my experiential field, and my sense and knowing of the reality of my own inner world, and my sense and knowing of the reality of yours, arise in the same integrative interpretation of the whole field.

In Part III we took this picture of self in process and used it to explore what we might call, with a nod to Freud and Strachey, "the self and its vicissitudes." First we explored the neglected dimension of support, *which plays a crucial dynamic role in self-integration and process, one largely obscured by the terms of our inherited individualist paradigm. From there we turned to the interruption and inhibition of this natural process of self-growth, which led us to the field dynamic and emotion of* shame. *Shame too has been much neglected and misunderstood (and shamed) under the individualist model, but emerges here in clearer focus through use of a field-based lens. And then we rounded out that part of the discussion with an exploration of the conditions and dynamics of the restoration of self, and the repair of that break in the field of support which shame represents. These conditions and dynamics were the field processes we call* intimacy *-- the process of sharing of the inner experiential world. New levels of self-growth and the articulation of new self-experience, a richer and more useful inner life, we argued, are not a matter of "introspection" alone, but always depend on active conditions of intimacy in this sense. We do not first "achieve self," and then become ready to risk intimacy (which would seem to threaten that self). Rather, it is in intimacy that self grows and takes on new dimensions and empowerment -- all in direct contradiction to the* *terms and implications of our heritage in the individualist paradigm.*

With this final section we turn to the living process of the fully integrated self. What we find there first of all is that the living self is naturally narrative *by nature. That is, our natural self-process is expressed in the construction of meaningful sequences in time -- because it is these sequences that enable us to solve problems, survive, and grow. We seek and tell stories because the structure of awareness and the structure of story are the same form. Moreover, it is through nested stories that the individual self is contained and contextualized in culture. This is the material of the next chapter, Self as Story: Narrative, Culture, and Gender. From there we turn to the conclusion of this book, summarizing the journey we have taken and drawing wider implications for a new understanding of evolution, politics, and health.*

Chapter Eight -- Self as Story: Narrative, Culture and Gender

The human is the story-telling animal: to be human is to have and tell stories. Why is this? Why is it that there is no known culture without stories? Indeed, we may say that a culture is defined and held in existence by particular stories its members tell and identify with; in a real sense a culture is *the same as* its shared stories. What accounts for this, and then how does that fit into the understanding of self and human nature that we are building up here in natural, process terms? Is story just a byproduct of language, our evolved linguistic capacity running on overdrive, so to speak? Or is it rather the other way around: can we even imagine language without story? Plainly there is such a thing as narrative without language (ballet, pantomime, the dance of the bees or the specific and elaborate cries of certain animals, which give complex and sequenced instruction and information about contingencies). But language without narration seems a very limited thing indeed, no more than a series of reactions and signal cries without the dimensions of time, contingency of event, or syntax itself (which is to say, the relationships among terms beyond mere linear sequence, how one act or thing or situation *fits in* with another, the very thing we have been saying all through this discussion is what we are "wired" to construct and use, the way we resolve the field of experience by the terms of our awareness nature).

But then maybe all this is "just nurture," things we learn in the course of "socialization," with no inherent embeddedness in our natural structure and process, in the same way that an older self-model viewed relationship itself as something *added on* to a preexistent individual -- as for that matter were sense of self and other, intimacy, meaning, and whatever degree of intersubjectivity could be allowed for under an individualist model (all of them, we have been arguing here, actually inseparable from the most fundamental needs, drives, and capacities of our awareness processes and our basic evolutionary human nature). Indeed, the very word "socialization" seemed to imply, under that older model, that we are not social to start with, but must be made to be so, apart from or in contradiction to our self-nature (the basic assumption, after all, of the individualist paradigm). But then if this is true, if narrative is "just learned," then why is it that there is no human culture that has language without story, any more than there are cultures where the people have no names, no relational categories, and no meaning systems and beliefs about their origins and place in the scheme of things, all of it carried and embodied in stories?

Now obviously social learning plays an enormous role in all this. As we go from culture to culture and family to family, or from one identity group to another, we find that particular stories, particular understandings of self and other and relationship, and social and other meanings, differ enormously -- just as they will differ widely (though still generally within a shared group frame) from one individual person to another in a given culture. In each case social learning fills in the content according to the constructs and values of that culture, family, and person; this is the relativization of meanings and values pointed out by Nietzsche (1956), and then developed so extensively in our own times by the various schools and thinkers that collect under the general heading Deconstructionism. Money, murder, a maternal uncle all mean something quite different from one society to another, or from one religious or ethnic group or family to another; and the stories of that group around these and other themes will differ accordingly. Roman culture, for instance, shared a founding myth of Romulus and Remus and the she-wolf, going back to Aeneas and the Trojan War, which united the city-state and justified its conquest of Greece and appropriation of Greek culture. Later on, all of this had little meaning in the face of the tensions of a multi-national empire, and none at all to its Germanic invaders. Israeli culture at one time shared a founding story of European Zionism and the Nazi Holocaust that unified that society, stories that have little felt relevance to the new majority of later immigrants there, who are mostly from non-European countries, with resulting stress lines in Israeli society and policy today, and so on.

What doesn't differ is the fact that every culture does have such stories, which serve as an orientation and a guide to other meanings and acts in that culture, in much the same way as every person makes and carries some relational map of social expectations and of the people he/she comes in contact with and has to deal with -- *and that something about those stories is so similar, in their process structure, that a children's tale from 12th Century China is both intelligible and interesting to a five-year-old in Paris or New York City today*, without the least difficulty or struggle for understanding. Why? If story is "all culture," purely a learned thing, without an inherent structural basis in our awareness nature, then how is it that the stories of one culture are intelligible to another culture at all -- indeed, are the royal road to multi-cultural understanding? On the other hand, if narrative is a basic structural and process dynamic of our self-nature, then how does that work, and what does it say about ourselves, our work, and our relationships with people in the perspective we are building up here?

In this chapter we will offer a different view of the nature and function of narrative, one growing out of the terms of the understanding of self and self-process that we have explored down through these pages. In this view, we will understand story as another one of those terms that meant one thing in an older paradigm of self and experience, and something quite different in this new understanding of ourselves. Our argument will be that just as organized whole pictures are the basic building blocks of perception and perceptual process, so *story is the basic constructive element of self-process in the world, and of the organized personal and cultural ground we all construct and carry*, enabling us to engage meaningfully with each new situation, and with other people. *The self we know and transact and live is and has to be a story.* Self-organization and self-process rest on story, growing in and out of a field which we know as stories; and this is true whether we are talking about personal history or culture, religion or science -- because of the given terms of our awareness processes themselves.

To see how all this is so, we need first to take a look at what we mean by the term story itself, not in an abstract or literary way, but experientially and phenomenologically -- which is to say, in terms of our own awareness and experience, and how those things come to be constructed in the processes of real living. With that simple process definition in hand, we will then turn back one last time to our group, to see how all this plays out in our lives, our relationships, and the ongoing growth of self in the field.

The Elements of Story

What defines a story? What makes a particular communication into something we would call a *narrative* -- or are all communications basically narrative in form, at least potentially or implicitly? We have said that we are "wired" to scan and interpret our experiential field in *whole pictures*, organized images or "maps" that we automatically try to relate and embed in a wider context of meaning and predictability, so that the images themselves are at least potentially useful to us. These organized wholes (or "gestalts") are the beginning units of perception; this was the central insight of the Gestalt movement in psychology beginning around a century ago, in contrast to the then-dominant linear perceptual model, which tried to explain our cognitive processes by reducing them to lumens and decibels and other "objectively measurable stimuli," without reference to the crucial question of how the "booming buzzing confusion" spoken of by James (1983) gets *organized into units related to other units*, and to the pressing context of real life. (for further discussion, see Wheeler, 1991).

But a "whole" picture or even a contextual map is not yet a story. At most it is the background to a story, part of the context or field condition in and out of which a story might start. Take for instance sentences and phrases, highly organized in themselves, like:

> It was a dark and stormy night...
>
> For a long time I used to go to bed early.
>
> It was on a bitterly cold night and frosty morning, towards the end of the winter of '97, that I was awakened by a tugging at my shoulder.
>
> Rage, goddess, sing the rage of Peleus's son Achilles...
>
> Whether I shall turn out to be the hero of my own life,... these pages must show.
>
> It was the best of times, it was the worst of times...

or that classic of intersubjective irony, treasured by Jane Austen fans,

> It is a truth universally acknowledged, that a young man in possession of a good fortune must be in want of a wife.

Each of these is a well-known beginning, the first being the classic trite opener for a hack story (the comic strip character Snoopy used to begin his never-finished novel, like the blocked writer Grand in Camus's *The Plague*, by obsessively writing and tearing up and then rewriting this opening line); the others come from Marcel Proust, Arthur Conan Doyle, Homer, Charles Dickens (twice), and Jane Austen, respectively. Each is in its way highly suggestive, intriguing. If we say these lines and no more to a group of listeners (who don't "already know the story" that follows), then we'll likely get a medley of responses on the same note, things like "So?" "Well?" "And then what happened?" "So what?" or even "Who cares?" Or perhaps even more tellingly, "Why are you telling me this?" "What's the point?" -- illustrating once again the point we developed in Chapter Three, that we naturally and necessarily assume that people have some *reason* for what they do, most of the time (because we do ourselves), and that to take up contact and deal with them we generally need some working guess at least about what that reason might be. As the dialogic philosopher Mikhael Bakhtin (1986) observed, we never "just speak:" rather, we speak *to* some person or audience (at least implicitly, at least in our own minds), *for* some reason. Knowing that, the listener waits to find out that reason. Neglect that relational and narrative context, and the communication becomes meaningless, a point which will be developed more below.

Now plainly, none of these is a story -- yet. Again, if we ask a group why not, the answers will be along the lines of "because it hasn't gone anywhere yet,," "nothing is happening," -- or again, "I'm waiting to see what happens *next*." The opener is meant to be an attention-getter, and we assume (for a moment anyway, before we flip the literal or figurative channel), that if a person is trying to get our attention, there is some reason for it, and that it may somehow be worth our while to check it out.

Now as soon as we add that "next," we have the beginnings at least of a story. In the move from an observation or a situation to an action or event, we move from a static picture or simple gestalt to a living sequence in time: which is to say, out of "just description" and into the realm of felt experience -- and higher stakes. In real experience as we live it we don't just notice and register things statically or passively (as we do in what learning theory calls "incidental learning"): we take note of them *in order to deal with them*, so as to survive and thrive and deal with real situations, problems, and contingencies. Likewise in real experience we are always dealing with the way one thing "leads to another:" indeed, our whole life task and natural self-process are necessarily organized around constructing some useful understandings of *how* one thing leads to another, or is contingent on another, so that we can solve necessary problems and manage all the things we have to deal with, urgently or potentially, at every moment of our lives.

Story, in other words, begins when one thing leads to another. First you have the situation, the given conditions of a particular field at a particular time. "There was once an old woman who lived in great poverty with her only son, Jack," so begins the classic Perrault tale. "They had only one cow, and at length when her milk ran dry, the mother sent Jack to market to sell the animal, to get money for bread." Already the two elements are *in relation* to each other: not only does the second element come after the first (or punctuate the first, which was an ongoing condition contextualizing a particular event), but the second is *because of* the first. "Leads to," in other words, is more than just a simple series. Syntax, the relationship of terms, is in the move from the simple "and" to all the more complex *conjunctions of contingency*, which is to say, a relationship that serves to enhance predictability: "after," "but," "if," "because of," "in spite of," "although," "therefore," "as soon as," "until," and on and on. These are the complex connectors that tell us how one thing is contingent on another, in what circumstances and under what conditions one thing favors or inhibits another. And it is with syntax that language becomes more than signals, lists and cries, and moves to becoming a useful tool for managing the world.

And with just this much the story is off and running.

Because they are poor, she sends Jack to sell the cow. *But* Jack is a foolish dreamer. *Then* a man comes along and offers him magic beans. *So* Jack gives him the cow for the beans. *Of course* the mother is furious. *Therefore* she throws the beans out the window. *While* they are sleeping -- and so forth. The connecting words may be explicit or implicit; either way, it is the relationship among the elements in space and time and contingency that matters, and that lifts and organizes a series of isolated terms into a meaningful whole. In other words, syntax and story are very close to the same thing: the structure of language, the expression of meaningful relationships among things and terms, is narrative itself.

All these relationships, as Kant (1781) observed long ago, are what he called "categories of mind," things like causality, sequence, negation, quantity, comparison, part/whole, and the constructs space and time themselves -- because none of them can be concretely picked up and found in nature. Rather, they must be inferred -- or as we have been saying here, *constructed*; and thus our minds must be designed in such a way as to do this, or else we couldn't apprehend and deal with our world at all. To Kant, these "categories" and that design were unmediated creations of the divinity. Some decades later Darwin would argue that they could be explained through natural selection: our brain/minds are structured for "categorical thinking" in this sense because that's the structure that is favored by selection and enables us to survive. (Thus the deity could be kept as an even more remote Prime Mover, or else dispensed with altogether, as we discussed in Chapter One). Either way, the brain/mind is *structured for syntax*, for putting the elements of a series into meaningful relationship, so that we can deal with them in a useful (i.e., predictive) way. Our perspective here, the application of the Gestalt model of awareness processes to our understanding of self and human nature, helps us see how this works. Syntax and field-resolution for problem-solving *are fundamentally the same thing*.

It is the need for flexible problem-solving capacity that drives the evolution of language structures and capacity themselves.

But then this in turn is another way of saying that the self we are seeking is syntactic -- since syntactic refers to our faculty for making meaningful relationships among terms that represent aspects and conditions of the field. We are "wired" to make a syntactic resolution of the field, to construct a picture of how one thing relates to another. Adding the dimension of time, we arrive at the same picture of self and self-process that we have been developing here all along: *the nature of the self is to construct an understanding of how one thing leads to another.*

And at this point we have come full circle in this exploration of terms. Once we begin to speak of how one thing leads to another, we are speaking of narrative in its most fundamental structure, the linkage of one thing to another in a contingent way. This gives us the simple process definition of narrative or story that we need for the exploration to follow: by narrative or story we mean *any meaningful series of conditions or events in time* -- where "meaningful," once more, means contingent, one thing depending on or affected by another, the kind of *conditions for predictability* we are evolved to imagine and understand, by the given nature of our self and self-process. The self we are seeking and finding is a *narrative self*, structured by its process nature to construct, understand, store and use *meaningful sequences* of data. These sequences, available and known to us in narrative form, are then what we call *information*, which always has a narrative structure: if this, then that; when this happens, that becomes likely; given such and such conditions, this or that event occurred. Any meaningfully linked sequence like that is a narrative, a piece at least of one or more stories; and such sequences are what we are equipped by evolution to construct, orient to, and use.

All this takes us beyond an older, more linear functionalist view of story growing out of Marxist and other functionalist schools of sociology and anthropology (see for example Malinowski, 1944), which sought to explain the function of narrative by focusing on content. Traditional cultures, according to this view, rest on narrative because of the *content value* of the stories. Useful information -- about nature, about social mores, about tribal values and worldviews -- is conveyed in story form, for easy memory and frequent repetition, often under ceremonial or ritualized conditions that further serve to impress the content on the minds of the listeners.

Of course all this is no doubt true, and not only for oral cultures. In our own tradition, for example, *The Iliad*, which passed from oral to written form some twenty-eight centuries ago, gives us two contrasting value systems and models of manhood, the Greek and the Trojan, with the hero Achilles wavering between the two -- and leaves no doubt as to which reality is privileged, which is the "preferred story" (to use the terminology of narrative therapy; see e.g. White & Epston, 1990). As such it has been taken and explicitly taught to young men as the handbook and the bible of masculine identity in Western individualistic culture ever since, right down into our own century (cf. discussion in Wheeler, in press). Likewise for the Hebrew *Bible* itself, compiled in written form just a couple of centuries later, with its heavy didactic message of how to regulate boundary issues and relations in society -- between one person and another, between the individual and society, among different societies, and between mankind and the deity. In a literate age these two founding texts of our individualist paradigm, both based on ancient tribal narratives, continue to serve as vehicles of the dominant content values of the culture.

At the same time, what that older functionalist view of the uses of narrative in culture leaves unanswered, among other things, is the question of *why* story should be a more impressive or more easily remembered form for conveying information, or a more effective vehicle for the transmission of cultural values. Wouldn't it be more efficient just to tell the moral, and skip the narrative that leads up to it? Why do we *remember* stories so easily, and as such relative wholes? At this writing I can't remember the current President's birthdate, year or day, though they are in the news from time to time, so I am exposed to them -- but I remember every detail of the rich soap opera of his sexual dalliances, which are vastly less important to me than a number of other facts about him, and which I made no particular effort to follow in any such detail. Why? Indeed, when we speak of constructing a "mnemonic device" or trick to aid memory, what we almost always mean is the rendering of isolated data (names and dates, lists, telephone numbers) into story form. We do this because we know instinctively that they will be more memorable that way. I also cannot recite the colors of the rainbow spectrum in order from memory, but I could quickly derive them for you from the meaningless fragmentary narrative sentence, "Roger opens your garage by ventilation," which I committed to memory some forty years ago and now cannot seem to forget. Again, why, and what does this tell us about the inherent self-process we are building a new picture of here?

The strict linear functionalist view also seems less useful when it comes to stories that we seem drawn to for recreation or entertainment. Granted, any mystery novel or television serial may serve to illustrate or reinforce social roles and cultural norms, blatantly or at some deep level; and certainly artists like Dickens, Austen, and Proust, used as examples above, can serve at times to deepen our understanding of motivation and character or social conditions, and thus may in some sense be "good for us," even useful. But is that really why we enjoy them, why we seek out story forms "for recreation?" Why should it *refresh* us to exercise our taste for narrative, and what does that say about self-process and our nature?

Our argument here, by way of answer, is a phenomenological one: *we are drawn to stories because stories have the same form as awareness itself, the same process structure as our problem-solving minds and selves.* We say "once upon a time," by which we mean there were such and such conditions, at such and such a time and place, whereupon this happened, which gave rise to that. But as everything we have developed and discussed down through these pages has shown, this is more than just a learned form: on the contrary, this is precisely the way our aware self-process *works*, this is the particular kind of field-organization we're born and "wired" to do. We are drawn to stories because *narrative by definition has syntactic form,* the holistic organization of contingencies in time -- and we are syntactic selves, born to organize our worlds as contingent wholes of *event in context,* which is to say as stories, linked sequences of conditions and data in narrative form.

In other words, our enjoyment of story is inherent in our very nature, just like the enjoyment of any of our natural faculties: touch, visual imaging, muscular exercise and physical skills training, erotic excitement, or perceptual activity and problem-solving themselves. Given our environmental conditions, these are the characteristics and capacities humans are evolved to have (like all theoretical statements, this sentence itself is a compressed story). The fact that the exercise of those capacities is pleasurable is itself part of our survival equipment, favored by selection for obvious reasons. Indeed, this is what "pleasure" and "enjoyment" *mean*, in both evolutionary and phenomenological terms: our inborn tendency to exercise "for their own sakes" all those faculties and capacities which have been favored by evolutionary selection. An organism which naturally "likes" to exercise those same faculties which serve genetic survival, plainly has a potential genetic advantage over one that doesn't.

To use and extend those capacities without any immediate functional payoff is then what we call "play" or "recreation" -- i.e., it creates us anew, because those integrated capacities are what we are, not just what we "have;" they are the very nature of our human selves. As the philosopher of mind Colin McGinn (1999) observes, there is surely no gene or set of genes for ballet, for example, or for dance in general. Rather, dance represents an elaborated and combined cultural expression of a number of natural faculties which are genetically coded and favored: speed, strength, balance, rhythm, agility -- and, we would add, *complex elaboration and narrative themselves.* And again, the exercise and elaboration of all those faculties is pleasurable, because to take pleasure in that kind of thing is itself an advantageous way to be, in terms of natural selection. This is also why we have science, philosophy, and art, and why we pursue all of them at times "for the sheer pleasure of it." In evolutionary terms all of these are the "overspill," to use McGinn's term, of naturally selected capacities, including play itself, that are integral to our survival.

In an earlier chapter we noted that science and the "scientific method," the classic sequence observe/interpret/ hypothesize/test/evaluate that we traditionally trace back to Bacon, is really not different in form from the natural, holistic activity of scanning/interpreting/evaluating/acting/meaning-making that we have been saying is our very self-nature and self-process *in vivo.* Here we can add that like all systems of knowledge, *science itself is fundamentally narrative in form*: given these particular conditions, when this event happens or this intervention is made, then this will be the result (and therefore reality has such and such a form and process, the wider picture that was tested by the particular experiment or measurement). As a structured sequence of terms, then, an experiment is not different in form from a fable by Aesop: it illustrates and serves to generate a general principle, which is itself understood in generalized narrative form.

As every student knows, as a species we are notoriously bad at storage and recall of "just facts," data outside of context. Apparently that's not the way awareness and memory work, for all the reasons we've been developing in this discussiion. What we call knowledge about the world is necessarily processed and "stored" in our minds in narrative form, *because this is the form our minds are evolved and adapted to construct and hold*, the form that allows us to construct repeatable strategic algorhythms, or sequences of steps, for solving problems and surviving in the real world. Again, our self-process is a narrative process, an organized or meaningfully linked sequence of contingencies that equips us to deal with a challenging field. Memory itself is narrative in form.

The Dynamics of Story in Self-process

If all this is true, and must be true by the exigencies of the field we live in and are part of as a particular kind of being, then how does that play out in our actual lives? How does story operate in us and through us (and *as* us, in a real sense) in the course of that organized negotiation of the field which we are calling self-process itself? To explore what all this means in our lived experience, let us turn back more formally now to our group, with a new exercise in reflection and dialogue. Here are the exercise questions, with space between them for any notes the reader may want to make:

> We've said all through these exercises and this exploration that the self we seek brings an organized ground of expectation, preferences, support and constraint to each new situation, and tries to resolve that situation in the most satisfying way possible, in terms of that ground. Now we're suggesting that that ground and those "possible preferences" *are organized and carried in story form*. The self we know and use is a story. To get a feel for what that means in real life, close your eyes once more, go inside, and go back once again to a time when you had a problem, something you doubted you could solve or get over, something that wouldn't go away. To get to a deeper level, see if you can find something from childhood -- because as we've found over and over, those are the *strong adaptations*, that may still be with us today in some form.

It may be something you've worked with earlier here, or it may be a different issue. Either way, when you've got it, let yourself feel your way into it. Once more, what's it like to live inside that problem? What does it feel like in your body, your feelings, your mind as you look out on the world under those conditions, as the child you were then? Take your notebook or laptop, and write a few sentences or phrases about this, enough to ground yourself in the feel of that experience -- and when we've all had a chance to do that, we'll go on to the next instruction.

Once you've got it, pick a partner, and tell it to him/her -- but tell it in a particular way: *tell it as a children's story*. Since this is an issue from childhood, let it take the form of a story for a child. If you like, begin it with "once upon a time --" and go on from there.. "Once upon a time there was a boy/girl who....." and so on. Tell the child's situation, and then tell what that child was capable of -- and not capable of. Good at and not good at. What was the child's world like -- the family, and then the world beyond the family, as that child imagined it? What was possible in that world? What was likely, and what was unlikely to happen? What *kind of place* was the world, to that child, what kinds of things can he/she do in it? What can that child expect from the people in that world --

what could she or he not expect? How does your story turn out? And then as before, how does the child solve the problem your story poses? What parts of that child get developed, and what parts are left behind?

As you're telling it, notice *whose story it is* -- whose voice is represented, whose eyes and point of view? If there's a secret story only the child knows, that's different from the "outside" story, then tell that too. Partners -- be sure to ask whose eyes the story is seen through, and whether there's any other version, from any other point of view. Take as much time as you need, and then we'll switch the roles around, so that everyone gets a turn.

Now as participants and readers alike will have noticed by this time, these questions recap and integrate all the various steps and stages of self-process that we've explored in exercise and discussion form all through this book. The child's developmental dilemma, the context of that problem in the family and cultural field, and then the creative resolution in the form of a new adaptation in the field, a new development of some capacity for problem-solving and growth -- all this was the subject of Chapter Four, where our concern was to explore and understand the creative/integrative function of self in the context of real life and felt experience. The question of the child's capacities and what was well-received in the outer field was the material of Chapter Five, on reception and support in the whole field of experience. Chapter Six took us into the dynamics of shame, which were all those areas where the needs and longings and dispositions of the particular child were not received and supported, with problematic consequences for self-development and creativity in later life. In Chapter Seven we explored the dynamics of intimacy, defined there in terms of *receptive intersubjectivity*, as the crucial missing support and the key to restoration of a fully energized self-process in the present field of living.

Now in this chapter we are looking at all these same

dimensions, but in their fully integrated form, resolved into those wholes of percpetion, feeling, value, belief, interpretive understanding, and action that we have been saying make up the basic nature and process of the self. We might say that up to now we have been making an extended deconstruction and analysis of "contact" (in the special Gestalt sense of field-resolution, making useful meanings out of the whole experiential field) -- and here we are putting it all back together again. Or rather, the process "puts itself" together spontaneously -- this is the nature of the self, -- and here we are exploring the dynamics and form of that holistic process and product.

And those products, those whole forms themselves are stories. Not just potential or possible stories, but we carry them as actual narratives, or narrative segments, with and often without awareness -- *and then we live our lives according to those stories*, to a considerable degree. We do this, again, because narrative form *is* the basic form and sequence of self-process itself. Our personal "ground," the complex background of expectation, preference, belief, and so on that we bring to each new situation, must itself be organized in order for us to draw on it and use it. And the form of that organization is story form. (The same can be said about our cultural ground, which will be discussed at some length below).

Moreover, these stories themselves then serve as the opening lines, so to speak, of larger wholes (or "holons," to use Wilber's word [1996], organized forms which are then parts of still larger organized wholes, and are themselves made up of smaller, subsidiary wholes). To see how this works, let us turn now to a few of our participants' responses (only a few, because the responses are getting lengthier, the more our exercises come to resemble living, integrated "reality" as we experience it and negotiate it). As in the other exercises, space is left here to accomodate or at least signify the reader's own response and story material:

Jake: Ah me, Jake's story -- you really want this? Okay, I don't have to tell you the situation -- you already know it, it's the same thing, and anyway, the story tells it, really. Once upon a time there was a little boy, who had a curse. His curse was, he wasn't made right for the world. Because you know, the world is not a very sympathetic place. It's hard, it's pretty disappointing, and a lot of times it's just plain mean. Part of him was made right, for living in a world like that, because he was clever, and did well in school -- but that doesn't get you much in the world, really, it doesn't keep them from making fun of you. It doesn't make you, you know, like the other kids. But another part -- well, it was like Jake didn't have as much *skin* as other people. Everything got to him -- he would tear up, it was so embarrassing. They called him crybaby, even his own family called him that -- it so happened he'd been born into a family of emotional morons, who all believed that making things worse would toughen Jake up, so they tortured him for his own good. So the way Jake saw it, the only thing he could do would be to grow another skin, like callouses, all over his body, sort of like Elephant Man. It isn't easy, growing another skin, and it isn't all that attractive -- but after a long long time he managed it. And then things didn't bother him so much anymore, or if they did he could hide it, inside his tough new skin. Luckily he didn't know much about penises at the time, being quite young, so he neglected to grow another skin there. That way, when he grew up, when he couldn't feel much else, he could still feel a lot sexually. Lord, this story is getting *weird*. The end.

Who's telling this story? -- tell the truth, I'm not sure. It's like sometimes it's me then, and sometimes it's them, and sometimes it's me now. I'm not sure I can say, it's all mixed up really --

Eleanor: Okay, here goes. Once there was a little girl who talked too much. She talked morning, noon, and night. Talk talk talk talk talk talk talk. And the thing is, nobody in the world can stand that much talk. They just can't stand it -- it's irritating, it's self-important, and it isn't a bit ladylike. It's also very boring. They told her this all the time -- for her own good (I like that part, I took that from Jake's story). When nothing else worked, they promised her she would never get a husband if she didn't shut her trap. She couldn't shut up all the way -- it would have been like stopping the Mississippi, -- so what she did, she just worked on stopping *every other* thing she wanted to say. And that worked. It did make her sound vaguely stupid, because any intelligent connection there might have been between one thing and the next was missing now. But at least it worked. And so she lived jerkily ever after. The end. And I don't know who's telling it either, exactly. God, I hope it's not me now -- I hope I don't still believe all that crap. Maybe I do --

Kathy: Well, of course you all know the sad sad story about the little girl who wanted to be a boy. Or maybe she thought she *was* a boy -- at least, that's what others told her. Because in this world girls are girls and boys are boys and that's that, and you'd better get that straight young lady, before it's too late. (So I guess they're telling it, that's my mother's voice, this part anyway). And she wasn't one thing or the other. She might have tried to be a lesbian if only she'd ever heard of a lesbian. But in this story lesbians hadn't been invented yet at the time. So anyway, what she did, she decided to fake it. She became a fake girl. If she was really a boy she must have been gay, because when the time came she did like other boys. And they liked her too, once she put on those sexy little white tennis skirts. So then for some years she maybe went a little bit heavy on the boys, just to prove she wasn't one, because they certainly didn't seem to be gay, quite the contrary. (I never thought about it that way before -- so that's why all those guys). And that's it, nothing else happened, This story is about as weird as Jake's. *The end.*

Ricardo: Uh-hmm. This is sort of the same as Kathy's story, and sort of not. Once there was a little boy who wasn't a real boy. And yes, of course he was gay -- at least, from the time he was about three years old, before that I'm not sure, but certainly by then. But that doesn't come into the story, because that's something you have to keep secret, he knows that before he even knows what it is exactly. What's not a secret is, he's not a real little boy. It's there for everybody to see, and he hates them for seeing it, almost as much as he hates himself at times. Not for being gay for heaven's sake, he could be gay as a peacock and his own father wouldn't care, if only he was *manly*, if only he was good at *sports*. And here's something -- you want to know what's the best thing in this boy's life, besides drawing I mean? It's his brother. His brother is a real boy, but still he's not like other real boys, he plays sports all the time, but actually he's *sweet,* he always sticks up for Ricky. His *little* brother mind you.

Even to their dad he sticks up for him. And the dad has to listen, because the brother is good at sports! So that's one good thing. So that's the alternative story -- a little boy who had a *champion*, who had somebody who stuck up for him. That's probably why little Ricky didn't grow up hating himself and other people *all* the time -- because of his brother. I don't think I ever said that before, not to him for sure, I've never even really thanked him. He knows though. And now Ricky has to go because Ricky has to call his brother right now on the cell phone, and thank him for saving Ricky's life. The end.

Who's voice is it? Me now, I guess -- mostly. And Ricky then. Not so much my parents -- they were so outside my world.

At least two things stand out in all this, that are common to all the responses. First, once again, is how easy it generally seems to be for many people to do this, how seamlessly it often seems to flow -- "like a real story," as one participant said. For these participants, of course, the material was already salient and present to mind from all the previous exercises; but still, at least at times it seems as if once started, the story just seems to be *right there,* already whole, fluid and full of feelings both tender and bitter -- and often quite funny as well (barring stories of tragic losses or the horrors of outright abuse). In a good number of cases, it's as if *all we had to do was ask*, and the story was already there. And the second thing is the common difficulty many people have in saying just exactly *whose voice*, whose values and view of reality are represented in the story. In an older model this confusion of point of view would have to be seen as tending toward the pathological, a self that was too poorly bounded, too ill-defined. A rigid individual self-boundary was after all the ideal of the Freudian model, as it has tended to be down through the millennia of the "regime" of individualism (to use Foucault's [1980] term once again). In our model here, we would rather say that this diffusion of voice, this curious shifting of point of view, is indicative of two things: 1) the way the child self -- or any self -- represents and is an integration of the *whole field*, the best we can manage and achieve at a given time; and 2) a particular field which resisted that natural integration.

That is, the child's "inside world" was needing and trying to express one thing, while the "outside world" was receiving and giving voice to something different -- with the result that the self-integration the child achieves is itself incomplete, not "all of a piece." If as a child I sense myself to be one way, with one set of capacities, while you the adult world (or the culture, as represented in the peer world) demand something quite other than what I can give -- then one possible integration I can make is a story of myself as in some way bad, and hiding, and trying as best I can to find some way "to fake it till I make it," if that even seems possible. Or I may cling to other stories, other explanations for why it is that I don't fit in, why the world around me isn't "my world" (I'm adopted, my real parents will come for me someday, or else there's another world faraway, New York or Paris or some other mythic place, where there are people like me). Whatever the story, what we can be sure of is that the child *will make a meaningful whole* out of all this, however imperfectly -- and that that whole will take the form of a self-story: who I am, what the world is like, and how the two terms can or cannot come together.

Not to make any coherent story at all would be a turn into psychosis, a breakdown in the meaning-making process that is the living self in action. Indeed, in phenomenological terms, this would be both diagnostic and definitional of psychotic process: the incapacity to make a coherent self-story, which means the breakdown of self-cohesion as a living process. (To be sure, "coherent" itself is an interpretive evaluation, reflecting the inseparability, ultimately, of the notion of health itself from the idea of dialogic process: a self-story that cannot be brought up for dialogue at all with another person is one that is too cut off from the whole field to be useful for survival and growth. Psychotherapy is then that process of dialogue, about that story and its construction: this is another way of saying the same thing about self-process and psychotherapy alike that we have been building up all through these chapters).

Again, in an older model the presence of these "foreign voices," incompletely integrated into coherent self-process, would be talked about in terms of "identification," "internalization," or perhaps "introjection" -- the idea being that something distinctly "outer" has been transposed more or less intact to a region sharply and distinctly "inner." Developmentally, in the classical Freudian system this was seen as a necessary process, the internalization of the superego, which represents the point of view of the culture as expressed in the voice of the father. Thus the introjection here was basically a good thing, even if it did mean a clear contradiction of the autonomy ideal of the model (superego is of course quite alien and opposite to the self's basic drives and nature, within the terms of that system; to Freud this was the irreducible contradiction of the human condition). Later on, in existentialist and related critiques of classical psychoanalysis, the same introjection of society's standards is a bad thing, and the business of therapy is to get rid of the introjected values, in favor of others more congruent with the self's authentic, autonomous nature (see for example Perls et al, 1951). Either way, the process is basically linear: something from outside is put in, and then can be removed (or else softened, in the case of Freud's view of the overly harsh superego).

Something closer to a more holistic approach to this idea of voice is found in contemporary cognitive therapy's notion of *schema* -- meaning an integrated whole of feeling, action, and belief, which itself organizes other affect, cognition, and behavior (see discussion in Fodor, 1996). A self-story itself, like the ones we have been discussing here, could then be regarded as a schema in this sense, a sort of ground template that will give form to particular figures of action. That is, the story I carry of who I am and what the world is like, and the possibilities for "contact," or integration of those two terms, will tend to determine, or at least constrain, the things I can imagine and thus the things I can then do, the directions that self-story can take from there. To see what we mean by this, we turn back to our group, with instructions for the next stage of the exercise:

> Our next step is simpler: if the story you just told is your story, the story of yourself-in-the-world, then what things are possible for you now, what can happen next? Specifically, think of a time in your life when you operated out of that self-story, when that story was your script, the map and horizons of your world. What happened? What could you do, and what could you not do? How did your story of who you are then change, and how did it stay the same?
>
> And then think of a time when you acted in a way that contradicted that story. How did that happen, what led up to it, where did you find the supports to do things in a different way? What's your story now? Who are you, and

what's possible in your world? If you were to tell a new self-story now, what would it be?

Given below are the same participants' responses, with space afterward for the reader's own story:

Jake: The boy with the scar-tissue skin? The boy who hides so well he loses himself? Easy -- that's my story today, it's my whole life, what do you want me to pick, I do it every waking moment. Probably I do it in my sleep -- *that's how the world is, don't show too much, nobody wants you the way you really are.*

No, really, that part is easy. Now finding a time when I lived out a different script -- that's a little harder. Probably the relationship I'm in now. But it's hard, it's so hard sometimes. Every minute is like an experiment, every time I say what I'm really thinking, I think the whole thing is going to come crashing down. So far she always comes through -- but I don't think I'm through testing her yet, I keep thinking one of these days I'll show her something that'll drive her away. Jesus, what a load to carry in your head --

And work of course, a lot of times I can do it there. I can say what I think, even what I want and feel a lot of the time -- as long as it's not too personal. It has to be for the work. When it's personal, when I really care what the other person thinks about me personally -- then forget it. My story now? -- mostly the old one, I guess. But it's in transition, *I'm* in transition, I will say that --

Eleanor: Well, I do talk, and most of the time I make a lot more sense than I used to, I don't skip the connections so much any more. So I'm a person who makes sense -- that's a new story all right. Where do I still do it the old way? With my mother! I swear my whole family -- my family of origin, I mean, not my family now -- thinks I'm a complete ditz. And when I'm around them, that's probably how I act! It's the self with no place to go, no reception, just like we said. They honestly don't know I'm *smart* -- it drives my husband crazy, which is sweet, you know what I mean. And I still don't write! That's it, I sit down at the computer, and I'm right back in that story, the girl who won't shut up and ought to, because nobody wants to hear it. That's who I am, that's what the world is

-- the whole thing, just like you said.

Otherwise I'm fine, I live a new story -- with my students, my family, my friends. Everywhere just about, except the writing. And my family -- family of origin I mean. But I just avoid them a lot. I avoid writing too, as far as that goes. I don't know, maybe I'm not even in transition!

Kathy: I guess I already told the story of the girl who's still trying to prove she's a girl. That's me in my twenties, sleeping with all those guys. Because they made me feel like a real girl. I know, I know, I should say woman, but the way I feel it is girl. And I wouldn't have needed that if I really felt it myself, right? So there it is, I was living right out of that story. And I can't even tell you whose story it was, it was sort of inside me and sort of just hanging there in front of me, in the air. Like a disembodied voice, you know? -- "you'd better watch out, young lady." That's psychotic, right -- if you hear voices? I mean, of course they were just in my mind, but it wasn't really my voice, it's hard to explain. So great, now I have a new diagnosis.

When is it a different story? Well, with my husband I'm not sure. He's wonderful, he makes me feel like a girl and a woman at the same time, that's why I don't need other guys anymore. But I still need him for *that*, I still have to have that reassurance. So I don't know -- aren't you supposed to get to where you can do it all yourself?

Ricardo: Okay, this is sort of odd, but this is what I came up with. When I was twenty-four, I fell in love -- for the first time I think. Oh, I'd had plenty of crushes before, maybe about twice a day for the past twenty years. But this was different, I was really gone -- he was too, it was perfect. We were perfect. For about two weeks. And then I began to blow it. The thing of it is, I started living it right out of that story. You know, I'm not a real man, I'm not worth anything, he's everything, I'm nothing, I'm desperate. And he was everything, too -- athletic, confident, easy in his body. In a way he was a lot like my brother, because he had a sweet side too. And I just squeezed the life out of it, I was so desperate, I just drove him crazy, you know? I couldn't leave him alone for one minute. And when it started to happen, when he started slipping away, I didn't want to admit it. I was awful, I pretended nothing was wrong, I made scenes, I followed him around -- it was a nightmare. And it was all right out of that child's story, I was living out that script.

And you want to know the funny part? When I try to think, when was I ever any different, when did I ever think I could be, you know, accepted, okay, be a different person with a different story? I mean, there's my work, but I mean personally, like Jake said. It's easier at work.

And it was right in that same period -- that's when I was different. Only with other people, not with him! How to explain it -- it's like, having him, I was okay, I was easy with other people for the first time, because I wasn't obsessing all the time about what *they* thought about *me. I was a person who liked me, and the world liked me back* -- that was my new story. I actually was attractive -- I know, because people were coming on to me all the time. It's like as long as I had him, I had this whole different story. Like I said, that was about two weeks, maybe three tops, out of the past forty years --

Once again, these responses themselves "tell the story" of the points we're trying to illustrate and explore here, as the participants -- and many more like them, in courses and trainings of this kind, -- reach in their own words for a new understanding of story, self-process, and how we construct and hold our own experience. Here we can say again that theory -- any theory -- *is and has to be a story*, in the phenomenological sense of the term that we have been outlining here. That is, given the understanding of narrative structure that we are developing in this discussion, and given the necessary process structure of self as we have explored and articulated it all through this book, our organized attempts to understand the world and render it predictable *necessarily take narrative form* -- because narrative and experience have the same structure, by the terms of our constructive self-process itself. Story is a gestalt, a meaningful whole, in time.

That form, in everyday language, is this: starting with a certain picture of the world, then given some particular circumstances or conditions, then, when such and such a thing happens, you get this or that particular outcome. That's a story: situation - event - outcome. That outcome then becomes integrated, or "fed back," into our meaningful picture of the field, influencing it and modifying it so that the story evolves, in something more than just a linear way. If we only say that A happened, then B, then C, and perhaps some other time D and E, then likely our listener will say, that's not a "good story." It may be a journal, or a travelogue; but the best travelogues and journals are those where we get a sense of development, some learning or change on the part of the traveller/narrator him/herself.

A "good" story, that is, has *development*, some meaningful link in the series -- though notice that just singling those particular things out and labeling them "A, B, C, etc." like that does suggest at least that the linkage is more than random; we never completely separate perception from choice, interpretation, value, and the search for useful meaning -- *because that's the way our attention, our perception, and our self-process are organized.* We are *wired for learning*, which is to say for inferring consequential relations. Like the best theories, the best stories *change* us in some way: the protagonist, or at least the listener, *learns* something, and the story changes. The story at the end is different from what it was at the beginning, and because of what has been learned, the future will in some way be different as well. Again, as Gestaltist Kurt Lewin observed long ago, there is nothing so practical as a good theory. Or, we might add, a good story. (For a related discussion, see also Polster, 1985, 1996).

But then what is the practicality of this insight, that our experience of our very selves-in-the-world is organized in narrative form? The pragmatic value of saying this in this way lies in how it helps us see that our ongoing sense of self, our notions of who we are and can be in the world, *are themselves a story*, what we have been calling here a "self-story," a narrative picture that offers certain possiblities for development, and not others. *We know ourselves as a story, and out of that self-story can come certain next chapters, and not others.* That self-story then forms the opening, the "certain picture of the world" as we said above, which supports us to go on developing that narrative (or perhaps just endlessly repeating it) in certain directions, but not others.

We know that knowledge is power, as the old adage has it. But we also know that not all knowledge, not all ways of looking at things, are equally empowering. Certain stories, certain frames support and empower us to do certain things, while others will support actions and outcomes that are quite different. If my self-story is of a golden child whose every action is blessed by providence, in a world which is my oyster, then I may be supported by that story to live adventurously and carefree, for a time anyway -- but I may not be empowered very well at all by this narrative to protect myself from con artists and unsound ventures which a more prudent person (with a less trusting self-story) would have seen through. Likewise, certain theories -- and for that matter certain paradigms, which are themselves basic, organized stories about what the world is *like* -- will support and empower us to make certain interventions with certain kinds of problems, while leaving us less supported or more exposed in the face of dangers of other kinds. In this sense our self-stories bear much the same relation to our lives as a paradigm does to our theories: i.e., the underlying narrative is the basic frame which can be filled in with a certain range and variety of portrait and landscape canvasses -- but not with just any canvas, any self-portrait, any landscape. It has to fit the frame. To go outside that boundary, we have to deconstruct the frame itself.

Changing our Self-Stories

How can we do that? We know only all too well that self-stories, like paradigms and other strongly-held ideas and adaptations, don't change all that easily, or all that spontaneously. Or more exactly, we find in our own lives, and in the lives of those we live and work with, that in some areas, some aspects of living the story changes and develops, while in others it stays the same, repeating and repeating with maddening constancy, sometimes in spite of our best efforts to make the old story come out in a new way. Indeed, if anything those stories may seem only to stiffen and ossify with the years, self-reinforced as they often can be in that phobic way discussed above. The exercise material of the past four chapters focuses specifically on those stories that *don't* change, and those places within our stories that are painfully stuck. We have seen too what goes into making a stuck self-story: we construct too tight a structure, one that resists outside pressure all too well, and then hold it in *too alone a way*, apart from the dialogic interplay of normal deconstruction and reconstruction in self-process. We do this as we have seen because of a lack of needed support when the story was formed, too desperate a field for self-process back when that particular adaptation, that creative integration was originally conceived and constructed. The problem we were solving was too dire for the supports at hand, the conditions of the field were too constrictive, and the shame and other fears that that adaptation managed were too great, for us to risk "playing around" with it now. In particular, we found over and over that the essential support that was consistently missing, then and now, in those adaptations, those stories we hold too rigidly, despite their clear cost, was *the presence of that intimate witness in whose eye we find the companionship we need*, to bear those feelings and take those risks.

How then do we make a change, at this deep a level? As before, we need two things to deconstruct a basic structure that underlies and pre-organizes a life in much the same fashion that paradigm pre-organizes a culture (and its members, together with the range of their possible self-stories). The first thing, as we said of deconstructing a cultural paradigm in the Preface, is to *find the dissonant places,* those feelings and moments and challenges in life where we did it differently, for a time anyway, where we stepped outside the constraints of our own habitual self-story -- even if only to step back in, oftentimes, in some next moment.

This approach is close to much of the work of the various schools grouped under the general heading of "narrative therapy," most of which have in common the same constructivist/ deconstructivist perspective on self-process and self-organization that we are exploring and articulating here. Michael White, one of the founders of narrative therapy work (White & Epston, 1990), works with the client first to "dis-identify" her/himself from the "dominant story," and then to seek out a time when he/she lived out a different self-narrative, one with more and different creative possiblities and range. Likewise, Freedman and Coombs (1996) speak of the "preferred" story, a term borrowed from deconstructionism, likewise coming out of the assumptions of a non-objectivist, non-authoritarian paradigm, as we do here. That is, the work rests as our exploration here does on the fundamental proposition that we construct our "story" of reality actively, in interaction with the conditions of the physical environment and the social field, as we interpret those conditions. In philosophy and sociology those assumptions derive in part from the "perspectivalism" of Nietzsche (1956), the proposition that views of reality are socially determined and agreed on, and that those agreements "privilege" the covert interests of some particular group. Here we derived similar social constructionist assumptions from the phenomenology of our own awareness and experiential processes.

But then how do we "dis-identify?" One way is to take the narrative approach itself, as we have been doing all through these exercises. That is, our method has generally been to start with a feeling, feel our way back to a time or an issue in life that we can associate with that feeling, and then *tell the story* -- first to ourselves in journal form, but at the same time knowing that we're going to be sharing it with another person in some way. For the most part we've used this approach to "get inside" our own constructive process and take it apart, looking for the ways the field (inner and outer) drives and supports and also constrains our creative solutions, how our assumptions and beliefs (and stories) about the world color what we can imagine and generate, and why it is that some experiential patterns seem so resistant to change.

It is important to note as we do this that the story we tell is of course itself a construction, a creative integration of self-experience. In the individualist perspective, that story (like all behavior) then tends to be regarded as something "internal," something already there "on the inside," now produced and exposed to view. But of course we know -- and the exercise of the last chapter highlights -- that this is far from strictly true. In our actual, lived experience we know that the story we tell at a given moment (even one we have "told before," perhaps many times) is *always somewhat different,* depending on *what the story is in response to, what the conditions of the field are as we feel them, what we're trying to accomplish in the telling,* and *who it is we're telling it to.* (If you doubt this, try writing an important personal letter to one person, as opposed to some entirely different person, or to a number of people at once. In each case you will tell it somewhat differently). In other words, again, the complete relevant unit of behavior, in our field perspective here, is always at least the question (that the story answers), the answer (the story itself), *and* the felt conditions of the whole field (including both purpose and audience). The individualist paradigm always tends toward obscuring the *present relational dynamic,* the present field conditions, from the analysis of motivational or causative factors in any action.

Thus the importance of the question itself (different ways of asking about the story will support attentional focus on different elements, different angles of looking at the "same" material) -- *and of the supportive, receptive conditions of the field.* As we have seen over and over, when intersubjective reception is *there and felt,* new connections become possible in the "same" story, with new configurations of feeling, interpretation, and meaning. Those new configurations are then a new story -- and a new story will support new possibilities, new growth and development in the field.

So telling a story itself is our first intervention for change -- *provided that the felt conditions of the present field are importantly different from the felt conditions of the field at the time that story was first constructed.* If not, we just repeat the "same old thing" over and over, in the telling as in the living. In part, as I tell my "same old story," I may be aware of feelings, connections, and meanings that I am choosing not to expose, because it wouldn't be strategic at the moment, or else just because I feel I would "lose face." But beneath that lies the level of all those connections, all those potential new meanings that I am unaware of myself: like Jake, I may become "so masked I fool myself." In a real sense, I cannot take a new look at that old material by myself -- because the way the story is structured now (as a victim, say, or as a deficient, inadequate person, and so on), which may itself be quite painful, *nevertheless is serving to manage, contain, or at least damp down a level of anxiety, shame, and other difficult feelings that threatens to be unbearable (and is unbearable, we would add, if it has to be borne alone).* Again, any behavior, in our view here, is an integrative act incorporating the whole relevant field as we know and feel it. To change that behavior -- in this case the experienced story, -- we need to change those felt conditions of support, shame, and consequences in the field. An individualist perspective relied on "outer" interventions to bring about change: exhortation, punishment, reward, shame, and so on. A more effective approach, as we've been arguing here, almost always involves *adding a new support in the field.*

Thus our first approach to change in the self-story is to retell that story, in response to a different question with different focal emphases -- but tell it under *different field conditions* from the past. Specifically, those conditions need to be the conditions of intimate, intersubjective receptivity that we explored in Chapter Seven. And note that this is true even -- in a sense especially -- for stories in which the narrator her/himself figures as a perpetrator of destructive, even abusive acts. We say "especially" because those stories are especially unlikely to be told and heard -- and because they are especially important to tell and hear in this receptive way. Unlikely, because of the listener's fear that intersubjective reception of the *experience* of the narrator/perpetrator will be taken for interpersonal *acceptance of the behavior.* This fear is itself supported and magnified by the way the individualist paradigm obscures the dynamic relationship between experience, -- which is a constructive process of meaning and affect management largely hidden from view, -- and visible behavior itself (and the way experience gives rise to behavior, not just the other way around). In fact, it invariably turns out that perpetrators (and all of us in some parts of our lives and selves, at our worst and unkindest moments) have rigid and poorly articulated inner lives, an impoverished capacity for knowing and bearing feelings, and thus little ability to stand off from a given sequence and meaning and deconstruct it in the service of something new. Thus the abuse tends to repeat and repeat. And in almost all cases, that poor articulation goes back to a failure of intersubjective reception in their early field -- just as it does for us all, in those areas of life where we are stuck in old patterns. (And note how often those places are the very places where we end up "acting selfish," letting others down as well as ourselves -- in contrast to the common fear that finding and feeling my true desires will make me "egotistical," another artifact of the distorted lens of individualism itself, which took it for granted that my "real desires" would necessarily be antisocial and destructive). To say this much is not to "make excuses" for perpetrators or other "selfish" acts, much less to turn a blind eye to destructive behavior, which must be contained and stopped, from the outside if necessary. Rather, it is to seek and support *more effective interventions for change*, in an area where change is notoriously hard to come by under the old methods of relying on deterrence through shame, punishment, threat, and more shame.

Thus the person who moves into violence "skips over" a potentially more articulated inner sequence, a fuller self-story, which might go something like this: frustration -- loneliness -- shame -- panic -- helplessness -- more panic -- rage -- violent behavior. For lack of a receptive field for experiencing that full range and sequence, what she/he experiences is frustration-rage-violence, without a sense of supportive conditions for choice. Those who work with spousal abusers, for example, know well how impoverished the inner lives and self-stories of these people are, and how much more change is achieved by working to receive and support their experience and experiential process (see for example Hoffman, 1993) As Gestalt writer Philip Lichtenberg (1994) points out, very much in line with our argument here, supportive reception of the *experience* of the perpetrator is what is required for change. This is not the same as, and does not work against, condemning and placing a limit on the destructive acts themselves.

Narrative and the Body

We can find additional support for a new creative angle by remembering that the creative adaptations which are our behavior and our experience, are themselves integrations of our *whole experiential fields.* And our whole experiential field necessarily includes body experience. Just as our whole self-story is carried and expressed in some way in each behavioral action, so our gestures, posture, stance and bodily carriage will contain and express that story as well. Each emotion, each self-attitude can be expressed in a bodily stance and gesture. But then by the same token, just as we can make an experiment in telling some painful material to another person, or in trying out any other behavior, so we can also experiment with adopting a different bodily stance and gesture -- to see what kind of self-story we might feel from there. To make this more than just a "fake it till you make it" exercise, we might start as we did before, by looking for a time and situation where our story was different, and then trying out the body stance and posture that go with that "exceptional" story (which is not to say that "fake it till you make it" is not itself a useful and at times important strategy and support, as we work to integrate new patterns of self and story.).

This kind of visual, postural exercise is obviously difficult to render in written form, so in lieu of trying to describe participants' responses themselves, we will give the instructions for such an exercise here and then go straight to discussion, leaving the reader the option as always of trying it out for him/herself. The instructions go like this:[1]

> Go back now to the story you were exploring before, of some stuck place, read over what you wrote, and then show your partner with your body, how you felt in your story at that time. You don't need to *act out* the story, just find one body stance or motion that fits with how you felt at that time, and in that situation. You may need to stand up, move around, or take more room to do this. Feel free to sit or lie down or use a chair as a prop, if that's what expresses the feeling. Once you've got it, put words on it for your partner, telling her/him how this stance or gesture fits the feeling you were having at the time. This stance *is* your story, for that time and place. How does it feel? What story is your body telling -- about you, your world, and your possibilities in life?
>
> If the feeling has more than one component, look for a stance that expresses both of them, like hope and fear, longing and anger, or whatever it may be for you. How do you feel about this stance now? What's it like? Is it comfortable or uncomfortable, familiar or unfamiliar? Do you recognize yourself in this stance? Where are you supported physically in this position, and where are you unsupported. Most important, *what kind of things can you do* from here, with this stance as your starting point and your support base? What does this stance empower you to do -- and then what would be difficult or impossible to do from here? What's that like? What is the *story* of a person who meets the world from this physical position?
>
> When you've described your stance to your partner, start again and try out something different, some *other* stance or behavior that feels better in some way. It may be the stance that goes with that "other story," the one about a time you did things differently. Or it may just be a stance you think you might like better, or know less about. And then ask yourself and your partner all those same

1) This exercise was developed in collaboration with Arthur Roberts, who combines extensive theater experience with his teaching, training, writing and clinical work.

> questions from this position: do you feel supported or unsupported? more or less vulnerable than before? is it familiar or unfamiliar? anxious? risky or dangerous in any way? Again, what can you *do* from here, and how is that different from before? What is your story, when you are in this stance? Who are you in this posture, and how do you meet and deal with the world, out of this position?

What people generally find in exercises of this kind is that assuming a different posture physically brings up a different set of feelings along with it. Even a new stance which feels more powerful or less encumbered may also feel risky in various new ways: more exposed perhaps, more likely to attract notice, and with it perhaps negative attention, criticism or even attack. Or the new stance which looks more balanced and powerful to the group, may feel unstable and unintegrated to the person him/herself. In other words, as we keep saying, the old adaptation was itself a creative solution to some problem, and as we move to destructure that solution, then the feelings of the original problem will tend to come back. If I'm anxious, say, about being more exposed and visible in my new, more expansive stance, then clearly the easiest and most familiar thing is just to shrink back into the old stance and story, the one where I showed myself less, at least in this area. If I feel I look too vulnerable in a more open, less masked or combative attitude, and my basic story about myself and the world is that feelings like that will be mocked, or shamed, or used against me, then the urge to mask again, or be combative again (which after all I'm already good at, from long practice) may be overwhelming.

Once again, that's when we need the new support in the field -- generally from the outside as well as the inside, and *especially in the form and person of the intimate witness.* Without it, it may be impossible to avoid the premature closure of just solving that old problem and those old feelings again in the same old way. As with each of the approaches we've used to deconstruct our habitual constructions of experience, here body language and bodily carriage can offer a creative pathway into a new insight and a new connection. *But the support of intersubjective reception will then still be needed, in order for me to move from the momentary excitement of that insight, that possible new story, to the integration of a new self-construction into the ongoing narrative of my life.*

Narrative and Culture

There is yet another dimension to the various ways this focus on narrative and self-story serves to round out our picture of self and human nature, beyond the constraints of the individualist paradigm. This is the way story locates and contextualizes the individual person in the social field, relating the individual person's self-story to the wider narrative frame of *culture*. A culture -- any culture -- is defined by a set of shared meanings, socially agreed constructions about the world which are themselves the products of our active self process: meanings about shared values, shared ways of looking at the world, about what membership in the culture entails, what is supported and unsupported in the group, what behavior is permissible and impermissible, and so on. These meanings, like all the meanings we construct and carry, are themselves narratives: that is, they are constructed and carried in story form -- because story is the structure our natural self-process is evolved and "wired" to hold and use. Making use of this basic structure, cultures always have particular shared narratives, origin myths and legends, remarkable deeds of the founders or other figures, hortatory and cautionary tales that hold and illustrate the shared history and *the values and norms of the group* in a concrete way.

This is true not just for national cultures and states, but for cultures of all types: ethnic minorities, religious groups, political parties, some organizations, affinity groups of various kinds, even some extended families and clans. At each level and in each case, a group is a culture to the extent that they subscribe to shared meanings and shared stories, which carry those meanings and values that make up their boundary of distinction from other groupings in and of the same field.

In a pluralistic culture such as ours in the West today, each of us will participate in many significant cultures, each with its own stories of its shared history, values, expectations and beliefs. Some of these multiple cultural memberships may then conflict -- which is not necessarily a problem for us, as long as two or more conflicting cultural boundaries are not salient for us at the same time. This is what "pluralistic" means: that members of the culture also have salient separate membership in other cultures or sub-cultures on various levels, that may at times conflict with their common participation in the whole. A young person may marry outside her/his birth religion or other group; particular ethnic groups may have conflicting loyalties to a country of ethnic origin, perhaps in wartime (or may be seen to have, as was the case with Japanese-Americans in the US in World War II), and so on. In each case, those loyalties, felt or perceived or both, will be carried as stories about one's own or other groups, at times in a prejudicial or oppressive way: "real Americans" are those (Europeans only!) who were here before, say, 1800; Catholics "take orders from the Pope;" anti-Semitism is "justified becasue Jews are Jews first, Americans second;" this or that group is "unAmerican" (a word which has no parallel in other cultures, and is a sign of the felt fragility of the national identity-boundary, the relative lack of a common story, in US/American culture); and so on.

The relationship of a cultural story to a self-story is a "nested" one, like the relationship of a basic trans-cultural paradigm itself, to the various cultures, ideologies, and worldviews that may spring up within it. That is, the culture you are born into will tend to inform and set boundaries on the kinds of self-stories you can imagine and see yourself as living out. As with basic cultural paradigms, this "transmission" of cultural values and stories is partly or mostly out of awareness, and begins very early in life, in the "coregulation" of mutual activities and space between infant and caretaker (Fogel, 1993). Erik Erikson's classic 1951 study of the replication of certain personality types ("contact" or self-organizational styles, we would say here) through child-rearing practices gives a vivid picture of how this takes place, as such basic "temperamental" values as aggressiveness, sensitivity to distress, playfulness, patience, autonomy/self-reliance, competitiveness, trust, and so on are shaped and "laid down," in broad outline and expectation at least, by the way the caretaker handles and interacts with the infant. As we saw in a previous chapter, this is true as well for subjectivity and intersubjectivity themselves, which must be modeled by the caretaker-as-intimate-witness in a participatory way, for the child to learn how to pay attention to those particular values and processes.

In each case, of course, the broad cultural story of values, beliefs, and expectations is powerfully and variably mediated by the various relevant subcultures of that family, and most directly by the personal style and self-story of the principal caretaker(s) themselves. The degree of variation tolerated by the larger group will itself vary from one culture to another: some cultures, like the US/American, place a positive value on dissidence itself, and carry that value in cultural stories which have echoes and analogues all the way down to the nursery ("permissive" child-rearing standards would be one such case, of a direct echoing between cultural myth and childraising practice: -- even the wide cultural ambivalence and conflict over the value of "discipline" on a political level is echoed on the level of childraising style). A cultural form and norm such as the "nuclear family" will then link one level to another: the "autonomy" of the two- or three-generational vertical family unit, living apart from the wider horizontal family and community, will both express and support a high degree of variability in personal childrearing style, since early childcare will tend to be delivered by only one or two people, mostly out of the sight and immediate influence of other members of the culture.

A bit later on, in the verbal period, these same values are carried and reinforced in the traditions of the family and wider group -- again expressed as story. The US/American value of high individual and nuclear family autonomy, low community interdependence, is carried in mythic cultural and family tales of the lone pioneer family, as codified for example in the immensely popular and emblematic "Little House on the Prairie" series. The tale in that series of the Great Winter, sometime in the 1880's, is gripping and graphic, moving in its themes of resourcefulness and imagination, grace and good humor under pressure, uncomplainingness in the face of suffering and hardship. But what is just taken for granted and never mentioned in the narration is the way the Ingalls family -- who by now live in town -- automatically assumes, in apparent agreement with all the other families nearby, -- that this ordeal is something that must be undergone alone. The idea that acutely short supplies of fuel, food (for body heat), labor and good spirits might all be expanded and maximized by going through this desperate time in the same house with neighboring families just never occurs to anybody. It isn't rejected; it simply never comes up. It is literally invisible as an option because it lies outside the wider cultural story -- the cultural "paradigm" of what is thinkable and thus available for consideration. This is how self-story is nested in family and local community narratives, themselves contextualized in wider cultural values and ultimately the trans-cultural paradigm itself.

Better to sacrifice health and perhaps life itself, in this

cultural story, than to "impose on others" (or worse, "accept charity"). Charity or support may be given -- indeed must be given, to some extent. But they cannot be easily taken, without considerable threat and damage to self-story itself, and to the relationship between self-story and cultural narrative and values -- which is to say, shame. This is a cultural value which we see replicated over and over in personal self-stories in this culture, as for example in the exercise material of Chapter Five, on support and development.

My own family was rooted in the culture and stories of the American Old South, Anglo-European version (with a small admixture of Cherokee, a hidden family story which came to light only when it was no longer a point of shame in relation to the wider culture). More specifically, the primary context for identification was the the tradition known as "Southern Liberal," meaning a self-conscious derivation from a lineage that was politically and racially progressive, back through anti-Ku Klux, trust-busting, anti-Confederate, pro-Abolitionist movements to a grounding in the values of the European Enlightenment. Its heroes were not the conventional ("white") Southern figures of Washington and Lee, but liberal dissenters like Jefferson (ambivalently claimed by both sides because of his own deeply conflicted attitudes about slavery) and Sam Houston, whose signature frontier tales were his adoption into an Indian tribe, and his long opposition to the Confederacy, as President, Senator, and finally Governor of Texas (one colorful narrative has the then elderly hero barricading himself into the Governor's mansion, rather than accept presentation of Articles of Secession from the legislature. The nation would have been spared a great tragedy, I was taught as a child, if Texas had only listened to Houston, because without the Texas Gulf Coast the Confederate cause would have been militarily untenable from the start).

At a family level, these narrative values were expressed in the (male) members' career choices. Only professional careers were imaginable, which is to say shame-free -- teaching, science, medicine, law; -- and if a "liberal" profession like doctor or lawyer, then necessarily in the public service sector. No family tales glorified members who "went out West and struck it rich;" rather, they spoke of public service, donating land for a school, facing down the Klan, or education achieved through personal and family sacrifice, On the level of self-story, this meant values much like those of the Wilder family: autonomy, self-reliance, "never asking anybody for anything," being debt-free, hospitality and a cheerful demeanor no matter the circumstances, and (especially for a boy) being responsible at all times for the whole relevant world, from the body politic to the immediate family to the disadvantaged of society. Film heroes were not the swaggering figures represented by John Wayne, but Gregory Peck (as the lone moral beacon Atticus Finch of "To Kill a Mockingbird") or Gary Cooper (for "High Noon"). The point here is not that these particular values were admirable -- which they often were; nor that they were stressfully autonomous -- which they also were. Rather, the point is that in every case they were *narrative values*, explicated and passed on through stories, given their normative punch in exemplary tales (good and bad), and then incorporated as the contextualizing self-stories of the next generation. It's not hard to see how such values can begin to be transmitted in the cradle, in the way the baby's needs are or are not met and ministered to -- as well as how they are then carried forward and reinforced in emblematic stories later on.

Gender, Culture and Narrative

This brings us to the most fundamental and universal internal cultural boundary of all, one that underlies and interacts with all the other sub-cultural boundaries and intra-cultural differentiations, and is basic to every self-story. This is of course the categorical difference we know as *gender*, a set of socially constructed meanings organized around the boundary of assigned sex (we say "assigned" because some cultures and sub-cultures recognize more than two genders, and in our own culture the real incidence of biological hermaphroditism is largely denied, with infants customarily being definitively assigned, even surgically altered, to fit the two normative categories). Gender, along perhaps with age cohort, is the only cultural category which is found in every culture, and the only one based in biology (again, along with age, and in some societies color).

But to repeat, to say "based in" is by no means to say that gender is biological, or "given" in our biological makeup. Sex is biological, given in our DNA and then expressed phenotypically through embryonic hormonal development. Gender is a cultural construct, a socially-constructed set of beliefs, expectations, and norms which vary according to sex group membership. How much and where biology may set limits on these respective constructions of each gender is a hotly debated question, with a vaguely-defined sociobiological interactive model probably being the dominant view of the moment. Despite decades of intensive formal research, hardly any of the normative and supposedly "inherent" gender characteristics of various societies have been found to hold up under controlled research, other than physical size and muscle mass, speed of language acquisition, and overall motoricity (Money & Ehrhardt, 1972). And even these few show much greater range of variation within each group than there is between the average measures of the groups separately on that variable. To be sure, more or less firmly-held beliefs about the biological determination of this or that particular gender-related characteristic for a particular culture or sub-culture are themselves a deep part of the narrative "truth" of every culture. But these "truths" vary widely from culture to culture, and within our own culture over time -- including within the subculture we know as "science."

Gender and Self-Story

What is important for our discussion here is the way gender enters into and shapes self-story. In a very real sense, as writers on gender have often pointed out, there is no such thing, culturally speaking, as a "human being." There are only *gendered human beings*, men and women, boys and girls. Cases where we do see references to "people" without gender markers are either when gender truly isn't relevant to the information conveyed, as in disaster victims, say, -- or else when it is being obscured, as in phrases like "number of Americans living in poverty" (mostly female), or "number of American casualties in Vietnam" (over ninety-nine per cent male). Even the "transgendered," surgically or otherwise, generally seek assignation to the particular gender they identify with, or possibly to transgender itself, rather than "no gender." That is, in most cases they seek to *change* category, not to erase it.

In other words,, gender is part of our co-constructed self-story from birth -- and indeed, before birth, both from the various folk and scientific methods for determining sex *in utero*, and from the way expectant parents and families plan and project differentially -- i.e., carry or impose different self-stories -- on the yet-unborn child. These projections and expectations -- positive and negative, fulfilled or disappointed -- then color the way the child is welcomed, handled, and bonded with (or not) in the family from the beginning of life, if not from generations before. We saw in the previous chapter in the discussion of intersubjectivity, where culture enters into the earliest handling and parental "projective voicing" for the infant -- gestures and projections that are heavily colored by gendered belief systems on the part of the parents (again, see Fogel, 1993). And the self-stories we then construct, as we have seen here, must incorporate, accomodate, or otherwise adapt to the important stories carried in the caretaking social world, which are part of the child's relevant field (for further discussion and reference, see Wheeler & Jones, 1996).

Once the infant is born, gendered narratives, like all cultural stories and values, then enter into the particular childraising norms and style of the group and family, which will differ according to the sex of the infant. For instance, it is well-established that in this culture infant and toddler boys are played with more, generally given more attention, and also allowed to cry or otherwise show distress longer than infant and toddler girls. The girls correspondingly are given more comfort and less overall attention. Small wonder then if many boys grow up feeling diminished entitlement to relationship and inner life, and more enhanced entitlement (indeed obligation) for outer achievement -- while many girls and women carry self-expectations and entitlements that are exactly the reverse of those for the male case (Wheeler, 1998).

To see how this works in real life, look back at the exercise material produced by participants all through the past four chapters, and consider how many of the challenges and developmental self crises that were reported and discussed were cases of some characteristic or behavior that was *heavily gender-typed.* The acute problem of Jake's being "hypersensitive," Eleanor's acting "too smart for her own good," and Barbara's aggressive energy was that these things contradicted the gender norms of the "preferred stories" of their particular families and culture. Like so many of the individual developmental challenges we all face -- and especially so many of those we face too alone, -- they were "gender-dystonic:" they went against the grain of the available supports in that local field -- *supports that were themselves organized around a gender dimension.*

Even where the particular developmental challenge is not

directly a matter of contradicting a prevailing gender norm, still the problem would be utterly different if the sex of the child in question were different. Kathy's paralyzing shyness might well be even more devastating for a boy, while Sam's physical prowess likely wouldn't have stood him in such good stead as a compensation for his dyslexia, had he been a girl. In each case the child is constructing a self-story, which itself is influenced and constrained by the prevailing family and cultural stories which delimit supports and unsupports in the outer field. And in every case, those limits will themselves be shaped and set in relation to prevailing norms of gender.

The field we are born into is a gendered field; the self-stories we inherit, accomodate, and integrate more or less well, for better and/or for worse, are gendered stories. The particular terms of that gendering will vary enormously from one culture to another. What will not vary is the fact that the culture itself is gendered, and that those gendered values and meanings, like all cultural values and meanings, will be carried in us and as us, in narrative form.

Further Implications of Narrative for Culture and Gender

Our self-organization in and out of the field is ultimately narrative in form: narrative is the basic structure of that "ground" of knowing of self and the world that we bring to each new contact, each new moment of ongoing integration of the experiential field. These things follow from the terms of self-process and human nature themselves, as we have explored, articulated, and built them up in dialogue with our exercise participants all through this book. As we approach the end of this book now, and consider self-process as a whole, we always find that *that whole is a story*, an organized and meaningful gestalt, in the dimension of time. This is true, we have argued, not by chance or by culture alone, but by the nature of our self-process itself, and by evolutionary necessity. Cultures are stories themselves, because narrative is the basic structure of our awareness nature. It is by imagining, retaining, and testing *whole meaningful sequences of condition-plus-event-plus-outcome* that we solve problems so creatively and flexibly, and survive in a difficult field. And those sequences are definitional of what we mean by story or narrative form.

That is, we do this not because this is the "way the world is" (something we can only guess at, ultimately), but *because this is the way our self-process works* (presumably in *some* evolutionary congruence, to be sure, with *some* degree of repeatability of pattern in the outer field). Story is our *basic category of mind*, to use Kant's phrase (1781), for all those relational notions like space, time, quantity, number, comparison, and causation or "outcome" itself which we cannot lay our hands on concretely "out there," but must make use of "in here" so as to organize and deal with our environment at all. The experiential field we are born into and then proceed to interpret and co-construct is a *structured* field, even before our arrival in it and from it -- and that structure, subjectively speaking, is necessarily narrative in form. We are drawn to stories because we are stories: we know ourselves and our world in story form.

Culture is then that narrative made concrete and contextually local. A culture is a story, and a set of stories, which link (in the function of all narrative) value to consequence, present to future and past, and individual to the whole group. Culture is not something "added on" to the separately-existing individual, as the individualist paradigm would have it -- much less something inherently and necessarily opposed to the natural impulses and desires of that individual, as the extreme Freudian/Nietzschean form of individualism maintains. Rather, there are no individuals without particular culture. It is our basic self-nature and process to construct the widest possible meaningful whole in the relevant field -- because the more a given whole of understanding contextualizes smaller wholes, the greater its predictive value. Thus we contextualize ourselves meaningfully and dynamically at the family, group, subcultural, cultural, and ultimately spiritual or cosmological sense, *by the necessities and characteristics of our self-nature and process.*

Conversely, cultural story contextualizes self-story, just as paradigm contextualizes culture and ideology, in a series of relationships that are nested in nature. It is culture that sets the limits on the self-stories we can imagine, construct, and live -- and culture that continues to color and inform those stories, even at times and places where we were sure we had violated or transcended those limits. We are distinct, as individuals, from our social and cultural surround; but it is part of the mythology of individualism to hold that that distinctness makes us *separate* from culture. We are constructed out of a field that is itself culturally structured: thus we are not just "in" culture; rather, culture is in us, as us, carried and passed on in the narratives we live and tell, which organize our lives.

That culture, and those narratives, *are always gendered stories.* Gender is dynamically present in every cultural meaning or story, whether as text, subtext, or both. A phrase like "men don't run from battle," or "you'll never get a husband that way," is a narrative fragment, with the rest of that story implied, and elliptically present. Our basic trans-cultural paradigm of individualism is itself gendered: it translates differently for men and for women, in every culture under its sway (to see for example the transmission of paradigmatic story values from women to boys in our society, viz. e.g. Silverstein & Rashbaum, 1994; also Real, 1997).

Gender is qualitatively different from all the other sub-cultural boundaries. It underlies and interacts with every other internal boundary and differentiation, whether or not those internal boundaries interact with each other (some do, and some don't). For example, to be a poor African-American in US society today has entirely different cultural meanings and consequences from those of being a wealthy or professional-class African-American -- though seventy-five or a hundred years ago it did not. That is, those two boundaries, color and class, did not interact dynamically in the culture back at that time, and today they do. (Which is not to say it was not better to be a prosperous African-American than a poor African-American then as now; it was better, but that didn't change the cultural meaning and effect of the color boundary. Even in my childhood in the South forty years ago, a well-to-do African-American doctor could no more use a department store or hotel rest room in downtown Dallas than a poor African-American could).

By contrast, to be an African-American *man* was a very different thing back at that time from being an African-American *woman*, with entirely different cultural meanings, values, risks and consequences. Not only is the same thing true today, but being, say, a poor African-American man is different again from being a poor African-American woman today as well. *Gender interacts with every other active cultural boundary.*

Gender, again, is a cultural construction, around a difference of biological/anatomical sex. In our phenomenolgical terms here, this means that gender may be defined as a *differential code or map of support and shame in the social field, according to assigned sex.* That is, certain behaviors, attitudes and even experiences are supported for one sex and not for the other, and shamed for the other and not for the one (those behaviors and experiences which are not differentially shamed and supported in this way are not part of gender). The structured field of culture is always a *gendered field*, in every human society: the stories that carry and are carried by culture are *gendered stories*, which inform and constrain our own *gendered self-stories*, in the way that all cultural narratives do. Developmental challenges that involve the violation of a gender norm may then be particularly stressful and difficult for a child (or adult) to integrate, and are likely to be faced and resolved in too alone a way (with the resultant rigidity or self-impoverishment we always find when self-challenge is unsupported).

Summary and Conclusions

The self we are seeking and finding here, out of our own experience as we feel it live it, is an active process of scanning, interpreting, feeling and valuing, estimating and predicting, taking action and making meaning out of the whole field, mapping ourselves into that field as we go. The meanings we make are necessarily useful wholes of understanding, that we then take -- must take -- as the best ground we can find for our next problem-solving integration, our next construction of meaning.

The form of these meanings is narrative form. That is, we organize our worlds, and ourselves in our world, in whole pictures in time, or stories, that have the basic form "when this, then that," "given these conditions at this time and place, when this happened, then that was the result." As modern and post-modern philosophers (and now physicists) have often pointed out, we don't "see" causation in nature; all we "see" is that that followed this (a story which is actually already an organized construction on our part). But we are "wired" to infer cause from sequence where we can -- because that way of organizing the world, into meaningful sequences or stories, has been favored and selected down through our evolutionary history. We survive by solving problems, and we solve problems by creating and remembering and using these meaningful sequences. The aim of the scientific method is then simply to refine this natural interpretive process so as to control for our natural tendency to infer causation from every sequence, by submitting some of those sequences to a more formal test than our ordinary, ongoing data-gathering process usually permits.

Thus narrative is something more than a cultural product -- though it is that as well, of course. Narrative is part and parcel of our self-process, our inherited human nature. We can no more stop making stories than we can stop interpreting our field, *because the basic form of interpretation and meaning is story.* We love stories because we are by our nature the story-telling animal: telling and hearing stories is what we are born to do. Memory itself is narrative in form -- a point like so many others in this argument which we "know" from our own experience, but find unsupported in our dominant models.

We know and organize ourselves in the world by construction of a self-story, a basic organizing narrative that encapsulates who we are and can be, in our available world as we know it. The mutual telling and knowing of our *real stories* -- that is, of the story of our *experience*, not just our behavior -- is then what we call *intimacy*, that necessary window into our inner world. But note that in our constructivist view, there is no such thing as passive perception and knowing. To open up my inner world is to invite participation in that world: the empathic gaze is inherently deconstructive in effect, because of the way it changes the subject's own view and valuation of his/her own story. The self-stories we make under field conditions that include an intimate witness in this sense are qualitatively different, more open-ended and adaptable in the future, than those we make under conditions of experiential isolation -- which is to say, shame. Full self-development, as we have seen is always dependent on instances at least of intimate relationship in this sense. In contrast to the dominant paradigm of the culture, we find that the self is inherently relational by its nature: we are born to share our real stories, and in that sharing lies the path to full growth of self.

Therapy, under any school and method, then acts more

formally to support this kind of deconstruction of fixed and dysfunctional self-narratives, in a variety of ways depending on the method or approach. All therapy is in this sense narrative therapy: that is, it works to open up and heal our self-stories. In narrative approaches to therapy, the organization of the self-story is explicitly taken up for experiment and dialogue -- an organizing process which is fundamentally that of our self-process itself.

Cultures are themselves stories, meaningful systems of belief that are carried, like all beliefs, in narrative form. Our self-stories are contained and contextualized in cultural and group narratives in a nested way: a given culture defines a domain of supported and permissible self-stories, as a basic paradigm defines a range of possible, thinkable theories and ideologies. Like all wholes, cultures contain internal differentiation and boundaries. Of these, the most salient, universal, and structuring boundary is the cultural construct of gender. Gender, like culture, is itself a set of stories, a meaningful map of what self-stories (and their resultant behaviors) are supported and unsupported in the culture, for each sex respectively. The achievement of meaningful change in political and ecological behavior in the world is dependent on a change in our self-stories, our ideology of self at the most basic level. And that change is inseparable from the creation of a new and shared cultural narrative of at least the *whole human community*. And note that this new narrative cannot arise without a radical revision in the social construct and narrative of gender, world-wide.

Today we live in a society and a world of cultural forms in transition and under challenge, and in each important case, the challenge will necessarily involve some destructuring and defiance of prevailing gender norms and narratives. The paradigm of individualism which is sweeping much of the globe, itself gender-typed, is intimately associated with unprecedented, previously unimaginable technological advances -- and at the same time with a level of ecological despoilation and irresponsibility likewise unprecedented and unimaginable in previous epochs. The question now is whether we can arrest the rampant spread of exploitation, competitiveness and alienation that that paradigm has also carried with it, in time to avoid irreversible damage or even the final destruction of a fragile whole-earth ecology, of which humans are a part. To do that we have to have a new world- and self-story, one that restores the interdependent relationships of part and whole, individual and field. And that in turn depends on the deconstruction of the ideology of gender, particularly masculine gender, in the dominant societies of the West -- as part of the creation of new gendered cultural and self-stories, with new understandings of the meaning of health, ethics, and politics for a global community. It is to those final considerations that we turn now, in the concluding section of this book.

Conclusion: Ethics, Ecology, and Spirit -- The Healthy Self in the Healthy Field

We have argued all through these chapters that the individualist self model we often take as an obvious and fixed fact of nature is actually a cultural construct, which only captures and gives form to a part of our self-experience -- and inevitably captures even that part in a distorted way, without the full context of the felt process and phenomenology of real living, in a field of real stakes and relationships. This construct, we have been saying, is deeply rooted in the positivist, objectivist, dualist tradition that we have been terming the *paradigm of individualism*, which came to dominate and define Western culture from at least the time of the early Greeks. We ourselves are steeped in and molded by that paradigm; it informs and also limits the categories of our thinking and experiencing, and thus the language we use to express and give form to that experience -- shaping and coloring not just our thoughts but our desires and feelings, our values and beliefs, and the meanings we construct and assign to ourselves and our world.

At the same time, we have said that the seeds and countercurrents of another tradition, another register of thinking, feeling and self-experience, are actually all around us as well -- in the broad counter-traditions of Romantic poetry and Western mysticism, in some Eastern philosophical and psychological systems, and in much of our own felt experience, ranging from relationship and identification to spirituality and political/ communitarian commitments -- none of which is very well or fully described or expressed by the language and premises of our dominant individualist tradition alone. Together, these two main points and topics -- our individualist heritage and the tools and sources we can use for its deconstruction -- were the material of Part I, Chapters One and Two in this discussion.

Bearing all this in mind, we set out beginning in Part II to seek out and explore the dynamic conditions and parameters of a self that is *actively and necessarily constructive of experience, affective and evaluative, interpretive/predictive, experimental, meaning-making, intersubjective, and narrative by nature* -- all those dynamics and self-dimensions we found to be inherent and essential to our evolved, embodied awareness processes. What we found, in Chapters Three and Four, was a social self-process that is not just interpersonal but *intersubjective*: we orient and deal with our social field by making a picture of the inner worlds and motivations of others. This picture yields a map or topography of that social field. In development -- especially in the long period of childhood where our capacity to change our social self-field is so restricted -- we use that understanding of what is expected and possible to create and integrate new styles and strategies for dealing with the challenges of our world, expressing as much of our felt potential as we can find resonance and room for in that world. This is what development is. The result is that particular kind of over-learned self-story we call character or personality.

Chapters Five, Six, and Seven then explored the dynamic field conditions of that development. First of these is the whole-field dimension of *support*, everything we are able to register as available to us in the creation of new integrations of the field -- which is the ongoing process of living, problem-solving, and growth. Felt ruptures and breaks in that field were explored in the chapter on *shame*, the disorganizing experience of a loss or block in our capacity to find and integrate that whole living field. The enhancement of support and the restoration of self-organizing process we then found in the field conditions we called *intimacy*, the knowing of the inner fields of other people, and the sharing of our own. Selves interpenetrate: without intimate/intersubjective experience, we found, the self never really comes to know its own inner world.

With Part IV we took up the form and dynamics of the integrative self in action, as it makes wholes of meaning and behavior in the field. This form is the basic dynamic structure which we know as *narrative,* a sequence in which one thing meaningfully follows another, under certain conditions of the field. We know ourselves as a story, a meaningful sequence of conditions and events, and organize our lives in terms of the felt possibilities and limitations of that narrative. Inherent to the self-story is the contextualizing narrative of *culture,* which always includes centrally the field-organizing dimension of *gender.* Gender is a differential map of support and shame, by sexual category (itself a somewhat variable construct, from one culture to another). Any important change in field-organization at a world-political level, we have argued, is going to have to involve destructuring and opening up of the prevailing gender norms of the now-dominant Western cultural stream -- and especially the norms and narratives of *masculinity,* which have lagged far behind those of femininity in the deconstructive movements of the past several generations.

In all of these chapters, and in the holistic picture that has emerged progressively from our exploration of self-process out of this new perspective, what we have seen over and over is that *self, self-process, and human nature cannot be meaningfully explored, in any living, experiential terms, as long as we hold to the assumptions and premises of the inherited individualist paradigm of our Western tradition.* That is, as long as we start from the axiomatic assumption that self is prior to and meaningfully separate from the whole field, then we can never work our way back to our felt experience of *relationship, values, developmental creativity, and integrated, intersubjective connectedness in the field of our real lives.* The disjuncture or dichotomy of our original assumptions will plague us right through the theories, methods, and models that derive from that basic assumptive set, separating theory from practice, belief systems from felt experience, and ultimately person from person and group from group.

As we are continually saying here, these are propositions that have implications reaching into every area of living and working with people. As a conclusion to this discussion, we will examine these implications in four thematic areas -- each of which has proven difficult or impossible to approach and deal with in a fully human, fully satisfying way under the terms and restrictions of our inherited paradigm of self. The four thematic headings are *health, ethics, politics and ecology*, and *the evolution of spirit*. Each of these will be taken up in turn, with a view to reunifying a field of inquiry that has long been split, under the fundamental assumptions and consequences of our inherited traditional worldview of self and human nature.

Self, Field, and the Notion of Health

As Erik Erikson observed long ago (1951), every system has its ideal -- a proposition which actually made no sense under the old objectivist/dualistic paradigm, but one which follows directly from the terms and insights of our exploration here. That is, to attempt any description of human nature -- and especially a developmental description, as he was trying to do -- necessarily implies that you have some picture in mind of what qualities and activities you are recognizing as fully human, what you think fully developed human functioning *looks like*. Otherwise (as we have been saying for any act of perception or cognition) you would have no way of discriminating what belongs in your picture from what doesn't, what leads you on or off the path you are mapping. Again, some underlying values precede perception and categorization. To imagine that we can make "purely objective" descriptions at all, much less whole complex theoretical systems, without any such implicit values prestructuring and shaping the inquiry, is the ultimate objectivist fantasy, and a direct consequence of the assumptions of individualism. Our evolved self-process simply doesn't work that way (and recall Nietzsche's warnings, of what gets obscured when we insist on maintaining that it does).

For a model describing human beings and their development, that ideal is the notion of *health*: what capacities, what functions and processes do we regard as definitive of full human functioning? This is in the end a values question, which directs our model in the way described just above, and all through this book. We saw in Chapters One and Two the fundamental error -- in terms of how our own perceptual and cognitive processes work -- of trying to separate the "purely descriptive" or "hard" processes from those that are "merely evaluative" or "soft." As Nietzsche said a century and more ago (and as the various schools of deconstructive criticism have built on ever since), this attempt *will merely serve to cover up whose interests are served by the particular values lying behind our particular description of human nature and the world.*

The organizing value we are representing here, at least for these exploratory purposes, is that of our own process nature *as we experience it, feel it, sense and embody it, and live it in our necessarily relational worlds* (always remembering, as we said at the outset, that we can never suppose that we have arrived at "pure experience," free of all our cultural and paradigmatic assumptions -- any more than we can reach that mythic ideal of the individualist system, "pure description," likewise free of all lingering value biases. Indeed, any critique inevitably partakes of that which it sets out to analyze; and readers of this text in fifty years, if there are any, will no doubt be struck by all the ways we have failed to free ourselves and our language from the very individualism we have set out here to deconstruct).

Still, this value lens, which we have been calling *phenomenological,* differs sharply from other self-lenses of the past that we have considered in some detail down through these chapters, such as Plato's Idealism, Biblical Creationism, Christian original sin, Leibniz's mechanism, Existentialist absurdism, Nietzsche's savage crypto-Darwinism, or Freud's quite similar conviction that our basic human nature is to destroy our own kind (including our own parents and children). All these prior assumptions -- all of them flowing from the same individualist paradigm -- we have rejected here, in favor of an experimental valuing of the phenomenological approach, to the question of how we deal with, develop in, and make necessary meaning of our shared experiential field.

When we take up this stance, what we find again and again is that our experience is *holistic*: we necessarily take account of and incorporate the *whole relevant field*, as best we can -- including the "inner" worlds of others. But this means that it no longer makes sense to speak of *healthy self-process* or *individual health*, without also speaking of *the health or dysfunction of the whole field*. In Part II we saw how the self develops by incorporating, restructuring, and integrating the whole experiential field; and we saw as well what happens when that whole field contains ruptures and blank spaces, where the developing self needs and lacks resonant contact. The result, one way or another, will be the incorporation of those blanks and ruptures into the process structure of the self

To offer that resonance and that contact, the "outer" field must itself be peopled with other coherent selves, other individuals who are integrated enough, and interpenetrated enough with whole-field contact, to serve as that support for other developing selves in this way -- and particularly of course, to serve the infants and children of their own local culture in this way. But this in turn means that those selves, those people must themselves be supported -- and not just by intersubjective others, but also by physical, material, environmental, and socially meaningful conditions in and of that field. *A healthy field breeds healthy selves* -- and *healthy selves by their nature work to create and support a healthy whole field of other healthy selves.*

A healthy field, in turn, is by definition one where the conditions of life, growth, and development are supportive enough to foster and co-create the emergence of these fully healthy selves, full human beings in our sense here. And a healthy self, coming full circle in our discussion, is one where the human processes of perceiving and valuing, feeling and interpreting, experimenting and integrating, and relating to the world intersubjectively and meaningfully are robust, available, and flexible in the service of those integrated wholes of meaning and action that give sense to our lives, and in the process of lifelong growth. Health, that is, is in this sense indivisible: *it can never be located in just one individual person*. By the same token, as we found in Chapters One and Two, the question of human nature and the question of value cannot be separated. And the question of health is the point where those two themes meet and join.

Health and Ethics

But this then has direct implications for the question of ethics, which was left hanging (and declared insoluble) by Bertrand Russell nearly a century ago, as we also discussed in Chapter One. That is, Russell had concluded ruefully, after half a long lifetime of creative contributions to both "analytical" philosophy (i.e., descriptive, the analysis of "how we think," which is a part of the study we call here "human nature") and "practical" (i.e., moral and political philosophy), that the two domains simply could not be brought together, by their nature. Indeed, the acceptance of this split between *science* on the one hand (which is taken to be "value-free') and *meaning, values, and ethics* on the other (which are then taken to have no natural base in our evolved nature) is definitional of what we know as "modern." If anything, a mood of defiant resignation and pride about this disjuncture is the hallmark of many of the movements loosely grouped under the heading "Existentialist" over this past century.

Here we can use everything we have developed in this discussion to take a step, at least, toward reunifying these dichotomized realms. With our persepective here, we are better placed to see what Russell could not see: namely, that the two domains are not only not separate; they are inseparable, like self and values themselves. It is not that no values at all can be inferred from the individualist paradigm, of which Russell was an unreflective exponent. They can and are; but they happen to be values that Russell, with his lifelong commitments to civil liberty, education, social justice, and world peace, did not like and could not accept. That is, the social/political values implicit in individualism *are the values of Nietzsche,* the pseudo-Darwinian ethic of ruthless individual competition and might-makes-right that have been discussed at some length in our exploration here. What was impossible for Russell (or anybody) to do was to derive and justify any *other* system of values, while still adhering strictly to the self-paradigm expressed and laid down by Plato and the Greeks nearly three millennia ago, and dominant in Western culture ever since.

Here, by contrast, we can move toward the derivation and grounding of those other values, out of the perspectives furnished by our radically different conception of *who we are, what self means, and what is basic to our human nature.* If it is our evolved nature to be whole-field-integrative, relational, and intersubjective (as it is), and if our full development of that nature is dependent on a healthy field of other healthy selves in the sense of that term developed above, then it follows that an ethical perspective can be based -- indeed, must be based -- on the criterion of *which actions, which attitudes most foster that healthy development of the whole field.* Such a criterion simultaneously aims toward taking care of both "our own interest" *and* the interest of the whole field. No longer are the two things inherently opposed -- self *versus* other, in the zero-sum way of the old model. And no longer are the ethical systems we are spontaneously and organically drawn to, over and over down through the ages of human culture, seen as sitting unnaturally on the foundation of our evolved, natural human desires, instincts, and selves.

Such a perspective, and such criteria, are of course not a "system," in the way of the lists of concrete injunctions that flowed out of the old perspective (commandments that were often taken to be not in need of any interpretation, as we discussed in Chapter One). Rather, this perspective on ethics tells us how to *approach* an ethical judgment or dilemma -- not what the outcome will be. Rather than denying the need for dialogue and interpretation on ethical matters, this approach insists on that need. Ethics, the application of values systems to practical decisions, is inherently a realm of conflicting claims (if two or more desires or considerations are not felt to be in conflict in some way, then we don't generally even stop to reflect on what the "ethical course" would be; see discussion of this and related points in Wheeler, 1992). In our field perspective here, the idea that an important ethical decision would or should normally be made "individually" makes no more sense than the idea that self can develop and unfold in the absence of resonant contact with other coherent, growing, interpenetrating selves.

Health, Ecology, and Politics

An ethics in turn -- or an approach to an ethics -- implies and contains a *politics*, a stance toward the question of power relationships and dynamics in the whole field. If individual health is dependent on its living context in a healthy field, then the question of healthy self is equally inseparable from the issue of the arrangements of *political power in the real, material world.* Again, these questions have been held as ontologically separate in much Western philosophy and culture since at least the time of Plato. The Biblical dictum, "Render unto Caesar," criticicized as a figleaf over naked power interests by both Marx and Nietzsche, has long and often been taken to mean that there is a private, "spiritual" realm of individual self-cultivation and -development which is inherently apart from, independent of, and even superior to the "outer world." Why, after all, pay attention to the suffering and injustice of "this world" if this world is unreal (Plato), already perfect (Leibniz), or the work of the devil (all the various Manichaean sects and strains in many of the world's religions)?

The politics which grows out of these considerations is by definition an *ecological politics,* or a political ecology in the broadest sense. By this we mean not a political program which *adds on* environmental concerns (as relational concerns are added onto some individualist models), but rather an approach to questions of power over resources that *begins with* the impact of every political/economic policy on the whole human field (including the natural world, which is in us as we are in it). Again, to say this much is neither a policy nor a program. Rather, as with the ethical concerns discussed above, the idea of political ecology is a criterion, a starting point for discourse and dialogue, about which programs and policies most attend to the welfare of the whole human field. Such programs exist, of course. As with so many other considerations in this book, our aim here is to *ground those concerns and those approaches we often "know intuitively" to be right, in a naturalistic picture of self, human nature, and fully human process.*

Self and Spirit

Today we live in a world in which, to build on Nietzche's dictum, individualism has outlived God as an organizing cultural principle. Thus we continue to see people everywhere "cultivating their own gardens" (as that early modern anti-hero, Voltaire's Candide, ruefully advised) -- often centered around private gain, the fostering and protecting of a small family or group, or some other of the many forms of self-aggrandizement in the zero-sum effort to empower the self or some identity group by disempowering others.

Correspondingly, among those many who are dissatisfied or disgusted by the empty materialism or defensive aggressiveness of these concerns, we see a turn toward all those movements we call "spiritual," the quest to find meaning and satisfaction through some form of meditative or religious practice in which we identify with a larger spiritual whole, beyond the "ego," or self in an individualist sense. And yet even here we see the power of the individualist paradigm, in the way enlightenment, or the achievement of states of harmony or union with a larger whole, is so often treated as an individual quest and discipline. As in the old separate-soul model of self, "my" enlightenment, in this approach, has nothing to do with yours -- and nothing to do with the political and material conditions and dynamics of our natural, social world.

As with the questions of health, ethics, and politics, giving up the paradigm of individualism changes our understanding of where the spiritual realm lies, and what "spiritual progress" or attainment consists of. Rather than seeing the quest for spiritual wholeness as opposed to our personal self-nature, as many religious and spiritual traditions East and West have assumed, here we see it as the natural expression of that nature. To cite the Gestalt cognitive scientist Kurt Goldstein again (1940), our only drive is the drive to make integrated wholes of meaning. Each whole picture of understanding that we can resolve and use then naturally becomes available for further integration at a wider level. The concerns we call spiritual, which have to do with where and how we map ourselves in the cosmos at the widest intuitive level, are the natural extension and expression of this drive, which is our evolved self-nature. That is, we are "wired" to be spiritual seekers, just as we are "wired" for relationship, values, intersubjectivity, and meaning-making. We cannot, by our nature, not go on from each whole of understanding to resolve the next wider *meaningful whole picture* -- which by definition will afford a place in the field, as best we can conceive it, for every other whole achieved and used along the way. To maintain that this seeking takes us away from our natural relational and political world is to misunderstand both our own nature and the full implications of a spiritual perspective.

We live in a world, as we said at the outset of this discussion, that is riven with splits and dis-identifications, all those parts of my human field that I hold as utterly *other*, people and events and domains that have "nothing to do with me." As we struggle to burst the painful and obviously destructive confines of our inherited individualist paradigm, we are often tempted to a kind of spiritual retreat we may think of as "Eastern," one which asserts that *only* the whole, only the transpersonal Self exists and is real, while our individual experience is merely deceptive and illusory (the mirror image of our own paradigm). In the face of this experiential/philosophical dichotomy we hold up here a *holistic paradigm*, one in which the unique and distinct nature of each individual experience is validated and honored *as much as* (but no more than) the reality of the whole field, which is coextensive with us, and of which we are born. To paraphrase (and counter) the pop-psychology, individualistic dictum of Fritz Perls (1969), we would rather say here, "'I'm me and you're you' *and* I'm you and you're me (or us)." Both these statements are experientially true, at different times (or at the same time) in different ways. To be fully human is to live fully in the creative tension of and between these inherent poles of human experience, which taken together, make up the whole field of healthy self-experience.

Our world today is plainly set on a spiraling course of self-destructiveness which, as we have said, is only accelerated by the global march of Western individualism, together with all the fanaticisms and tribalisms of various stripes which arise in reaction to the Nietzschean emptiness of our materialist perspective. At any moment, now or over time, that world, and we with it, may literally die of the excesses of these splits and alienations, and the lack of responsibility all of us take for the whole field beyond our own most local concerns. What is desperately needed now is a *new political paradigm*, a different *kind* of organizing principle which envisions a different kind of relationship between and among the parts and the whole of the political world. Rather than a world of warring parts -- or a world unification which is built on the negation and homogenization of its component members, -- the new order, to be healthy in our sense here, must be one in which a *vibrant, meaningful whole is the field condition which nurtures and supports the full development of all its parts, and vice versa*, as we are saying a healthy field of selves must do for and with its individual members. And for that we need a new paradigm of self and human nature.

These insights are not new. At the levels of relationship, ethics, politics, ecology, and spiritual understanding alike, we find them in the wisdom traditions of every culture, in every recorded age. In our own cultural stream we can find this articulated balance of the individual and the whole in the richly integrated formulations of the reform rabbi Hillel, some two thousand years ago. First, says Hillel, "If I am not for myself, who will be?" This is the individual pole of self-experience. And then, "If I am for myself alone, what am I?" This is the whole-field pole. Again, taken together they make up a full picture of self, which as we live it is not just "in here," but is "out there" as well. Our self-experience is inherently bipolar in this way, by virtue of the nature of our awareness and subjectivity, which are constructed around a boundary of distinction *and connection* in a whole field. This same perspective is then echoed in the words of Hillel's contemporary Jesus of Nazareth, who admonished those who would separate their spiritual commitments from their lives as social, political, and economic beings: "Inasmuch as you do it unto the least of these my brethren, you do it unto me."

These sayings and many more express an intuitive truth which is surely as old as human awareness, and as close to us now as the face of someone we love. What we have set out to do in the explorations of this book is to re-anchor psychology, the study of human nature, on a ground of harmony with the deepest truths of that nature and that awareness, and of our own lived and felt experience. Our evolved, human self-process is not something apart from, and opposed to, all of our instincts for relationship, meaning, and a rightly ethical stance in our human world. Rather, in a desperate and suffering world, these instincts and intuitions *are* our nature. Our human world is the arena of the full expression of our spiritual nature *and* of our natural self-process, both of which must ultimately be one and the same. And as Hillel also said, "If not now, when?"

References

Ainsworth, M. (1979). Attachment as related to mother-infant interaction. In J. Rosenblatt et al., eds., *Advances in the Study of Behavior.* NY: Academic Press.

Allport, G. (1968). *The Person in Psychology.* Boston: Beacon Press.

Aristotle (1984). *The Oxford Translation.* Princeton, NJ: Princeton University Press.

Bakhtin, M. (1986). *The Architectonics of Answerability* (M. Holquist, ed). Austin: UTPress.

Borysenko, J. (1988). *Mending the Body, Mending the Mind.* NY: Bantam.

Bowlby, J. (1969). Attachment and Loss. NY: Basic Books.

Bradshaw, J. (1994). *Healing the Shame that Binds Us.* Deerfield Beach, FL: PSI.

Buber, M. (1965). *Between Man and Man.* NY: Macmillan.

Clemmens, M. (1997). *Getting Beyond Sobriety.* San Francisco: Jossey-Bass.

Damasio, A. (1994). *Decartes's Error: Emotion, Reason, and the Human Brain.* NY: Putnam.

Darwin, C. (1873). *The Expression of the Emotions.* London: John Murray.

Dewey, J. (1938). *Experience and Education.* NY: Macmillan.

Drosdowski, F. et al. (1963). *Das Grosse Duden Worterbuch.* NY: French and European Publications, Inc.

Erikson, E. (1951). *Childhood and Society.* NY: Norton.

Fodor, I. (1996). A woman and her body: the cycles of pride and shame. In R. Lee & G. Wheeler, eds., *The Voice of Shame: Silence and Connection in Psychotherapy.* San Francisco: Jossey-Bass, Inc.

Fogel, A. (1993). *Developing Through Relationships.* Chicago: University of Chicago Press.

Foucault, M. (1980), *Power and Knowledge.* NY: Pantheon Books.

Freedman, J. & Combs, G. (1996). *Narrative Therapy: the Social Construction of Preferred Realities.* NY: Norton.

Freud, S. (1999). *The Complete Psychological Works of Sigmund Freud (The Standard Edition).* NY: Norton.

Gay, P. (1988). *Freud: A Life for Our Times.* NY: Norton.

Gibson, J. (1969). *Principles of Perceptual Learning and Development.* NY: Appleton-Century-Crofts.

Gilligan, C. (1982). *In a Different Voice.* Cambridge MA: Harvard University Press.

Goldstein, K. (1939). *The Organism.* Boston: American Book Co.

Goldstein, K. (1940). *Human Nature in the Light of Psychopathology.* Cambridge MA: Harvard University Press.

Goodman, P. (1951). *Novelty, Excitement and Growth* (vol. 2 in Perls, F., Hefferline, R., & Goodman, P., *Gestalt Therapy: Excitement and Growth in the Human Personality*). NY: Julian Press.

Harlow, H. (1971). *Learning to Love.* San Francisco: Albion Press.

Havens, L. (1986). *Contact.* Cambridge MA: Harvard Univeristy Press.

Hegel, G. (1962). *Philosophy of Mind.* Oxford: Oxford University Press.

Heidegger, M. (1962). *Being and Time.* London: SCM Press.

Heider, F. (1983). *The Psychology of Interpersonal Relations.* New Jersey: Lawrence Erlbaum.

Hillman, J. & Ventura, M. (1991). *We've Had a Hundred Years of Psychotherapy and the World is Getting Worse.* San Francisco: Harper.

Hobbes, T. (1974). *Leviathan.* London: Penguin Classics.

Hoffman, L. (1993). *Exchanging Voices: A Collaborative Approach to Family Therapy.* Philadelphia: Brunner-Mazel.

James, W. (1983). *Principles of Psychology.* Cambridge MA: Harvard University Press.

Jung, C. (1964). *Man and His Symbols.* Garden City NY: Doubleday.

Kant, I. (1781/1993), *The Critique of Pure Reason*: North Clarendon VT: C. E. Tuttle.

Kauffman, S. (1995). *At Home in The Universe: The Search for the Laws of Self-Organization and Complexity.* Oxford: Oxford University Press.

Kaufman, G. (1980). *Shame: The Power of Caring.* Rochester VT: Shenckman.

Kenyatta, J. (1938). *Facing Mount Kenya.* London: Secker & Warburg.

Kepner, J. (1996). *Healing Tasks for Adult Survivors of Childhood Abuse.* San Francisco: Jossey-Bass.

Khan, M. (1989). *The Long Wait and Other Psychoanalytic Tales.* NY: Summit Books.

Klein, M. (1932). *The Psychoanalysis of Children.* London: Hogarth Press.

Kohut, H. (1977). The Restoration of Self. Madison CT: International Universities Press.

Kuhn, T. (1962). *The Structure of Scientific Revolutions.* Chicago: University of Chicago Press.

Lee, R. (1995). Gestalt and shame: the foundation for a clearer understanding of field dynamics. *British Gestalt Journal,* 4(1), 14-22.

Lee, R. & Wheeler, G. (eds). (1996). *The Voice of Shame: Silence and Connection in Psychotherapy.* San Francisco: Jossey-Bass.

Leibniz , G. (1965/1714). Monadology. In P. Wiener, ed., *Leibnitz,* NY: Scribners.

Lewin, K. (1917). Kriegslandschaft (War landscape). *Zeitschrift Angewandter Psychologie*, 12, 440-7.

Lewin, K. (1926). Vorsatz, Wille, Bedurfnis (Intention, will, and need). *Psychologische Forschung*, 7, 330-85.

Lewin, K. (1936). *Principles of Topological Psychology*. New York: McGraw-Hill.

Lewin, K. (1951). *Field Theory in Social Science*. NY: Harper.

Lichtenberg, P. (1994). *Community and Confluence: Undoing the Clinch of Oppression*. Cambridge MA: GICPress.

Malinowski, B. (1944). *A Scientific Theory of Culture*. Chapel Hill NC: University of North Carolina Press.

McConville, M. (1995). *Adolescence*. San Francisco: Jossey-Bass.

McConville, M. & Wheeler, G. (eds). (2000). *The Heart of Development: Gestalt Approaches to Children, Adolescents, and Their Worlds; Vol. II, Adolescence*. Cambridge MA: GICPress (The Analytic Press).

McGinn, C. (1999). The Problem of Consciousness. Cambridge MA: Harvard University Press.

Money, J. & Eberhardt, A. (1972). *Man and Woman, Boy and Girl*. Northvale NJ: Jason Aronson

Miller, J. (1986). What do we mean by relationships? Working paper. Wellesley MA: Stone Center.

Nietzsche, F. (1956). *The Birth of Tragedy and the Geneology of Morals*. Garden City NY: Doubleday.

Perls, F. (1969). *In and Out of the Garbage Pail*. Moab UT: Real People Press.

Plato (1993). *Republic*. Oxford: Oxford University Press.

Polster, E. (1985), *Every Person's Life is Worth a Novel*. NY: Brunner-Mazel.

Polster, E. (1996), *A Population of Selves*. San Francisco: Jossey-Bass.

Real, T. (1997). *I Don't Want to Talk About It*. NY: Scribner.

Reich, W. (1970). *Character Analysis*. NY: Farrar, Straus & Giroux.

Russell, B. (1968). *Autobiography, vol. 2.* London: Routledge, Chapman & Hall.

Russell, B. (1972). *The History of Western Philosophy.* NY: Viking.

Sacks, O. (1990). *The Man Who Mistook His Wife for a Hat.* NY: Harper.

Sartre, J. (1956). *Being and Nothingness.* NY: Philosophical Library.

Silverstein, O. & Rashbaum, B. (1994). *The Courage to Raise Good Men.* NY: Viking.

Stern, D. (1985). *The Interpersonal World of the Infant.* NY: Basic Books.

Stolorow, R. & Brandschaft, B. (1987). *Psychoanalytic Treatment: An Intersubjective Approach.* Hillsdale, NJ: The Analytic Press.

Sullivan, H. (1953). *Interpersonal Theory of Psychiatry.* NY: Norton.

Tomkins, S. (1962). *Affect, Imagery, and Consciousness.* NY: Springer.

Voltaire, J. (1968). *Candide.* London: Oxford University Press.

Weiner, H. (1968). *Nine and One Half Mystics: The Kabbala Today.* NY: Collier Books.

Wheeler, G. (1991). *Gestalt Reconsidered: A New Approach to Contact and Resistance.* NY: Gardner Press.

Wheeler, G. (1992). Ethics: a Gestalt perspective. In E. Nevis, ed., *Gestalt Therapy, Perspectives and Applications.* NY: Gardner Press.

Wheeler, G. (1994). Tasks of intimacy: Reflections on a Gestalt approach to working with couples. In G. Wheeler & S. Backman, eds., *On Intimate Ground: a Gestalt Approach to Working with Couples.* San Francisco: Jossey-Bass.

Wheeler, G. (1995). Self and shame. *British Gestalt Journal,* IV, 2, 29-36.

Wheeler, G. (1996a). Self and shame. In R. Lee & G. Wheeler, eds., *The Voice of Shame: Silence and Connection in Psychotherapy*. San Francisco: Jossey-Bass.

Wheeler, G. & Jones, D. (1996b). Finding our sons: a male-male gestalt. In R. Lee & G. Wheeler, eds., *The Voice of Shame: Silence and Connection in Psychotherapy*. San Francisco: Jossey-Bass.

Wheeler, G. (1998). The heart of development. *British Gestalt Journal*, VII, 2, 4-19.

Wheeler, G. & Backman, S. (1994). *On Intimate Ground: Gestalt Approaches to Working with Couples*. San Francisco: Jossey-Bass.

Wheeler, G. & McConville, M. (eds). (2000). *The Heart of Development: Gestalt Approaches to Children, Adolescents, and Their Worlds; Vol. I: Childhood*. Cambridge MA: GICPress (The Analytic Press).

White, M. & Epston, D. (1990). *Narrative Means to Therapeutic Ends*. NY: Norton.

Whitehead, A. (1954). *Dialogues of Alfred North Whitehead*. Boston: Little Brown.

Wilber, K. (1996). *A Brief History of Everything*. Boston: Shambala.

Winnicott, D. (1965). *The Child, the Family, and the Outside World*. Harmondsworth, Eng: Penguin.

Winnicott, D. (1988). *Human Nature*. London: Free Association Books.

Wittgenstein, L. (1972). *Philosophical Interpretations*. Oxford: Blackwell.

Name Index